HARD DRIVING

"It is the harshest — and most titillating — account of DeLorean so far. . . . It is crammed with details that jibe with the growing body of information about DeLorean's business dealings."

— *Business Week*

"Haddad's portrayal of this flamboyant and volatile man is a study in contradictions — a bigot who espoused black people's causes, a touter of business morals who misappropriated funds and was arrested for cocaine trafficking and, finally, a genius who destroyed his own creations."

— *Publishers Weekly*

"Haddad, who toiled as DeLorean's 'company spokesperson' and personal 'sounding board,' builds an impressive case against his former boss: his book could aptly be subtitled 'The Portrait of a Louse.'"

— *Newsweek*

HARD DRIVING

MY YEARS WITH JOHN DELOREAN

William Haddad

PaperJacks LTD.

TORONTO   NEW YORK

PaperJacks

HARD DRIVING

PaperJacks LTD.

330 STEELCASE RD. E., MARKHAM, ONT. L3R 2M1
210 FIFTH AVE., NEW YORK, N.Y. 10010

Published by arrangement with Random House
Random House edition published 1985
PaperJacks edition published August 1986

Cover design: Vincent Priore
Cover photograph: Wide World Photos, Inc.

ISBN 0-7701-0477-0
Printed in Canada

FOR
MEEKS, BEBO, LULIE, STEVIE,
AMANDA AND NOREEN.
LIFE IS FAMILY.

Acknowledgements

Many people assisted and advised me in the writing of this book. At Random House I have editors Rob Cowley, Peter Osnos and Derek Johns to thank for their contributions to the manuscript, and Lesley Oelsner to thank for her legal advice. Howard Squadron, my counsel and friend, not only helped me survive the DeLorean experience but made sure that I put it all behind me. Dee Fensterer, who was with me at DeLorean Motors, reviewed the book at every stage of development. Bill Kennedy, who was an assistant counsel at DeLorean Motor Company, read the final drafts to ensure that my chronologies and financial explanations were accurate. Jim Breuer coordinated the research and made sure we kept tight to our deadlines and to a large extent made this book possible. Bob Kemp ran through a dozen drafts of the manuscript, typing, correcting, editing and rendering valuable counsel. Frank Jennings read the earliest drafts and put his fine learned editorial hand to my work.

Many reporters stood by me during the time that my charges against DeLorean appeared to have been discredited. Among them were Jack Newfield, an editor at the *Village Voice*; Ed Lapham, at *Automotive News*; Hillel Levin, who eventually wrote his own book about DeLorean; Ira Silverman at NBC; and Roger Wood at the New York *Post*. There were also people at the New York *Times*, the *Wall Street Journal*, and the London *Sunday Times*. Their collective persistence helped to unravel the complicated story of John DeLorean.

Contents

Introduction

There have always been men who know no limits and fear no consequences, men of talent and ability whose daring makes them either heroes or villains, while those around them are forgotten. John Z. DeLorean described the type perfectly when he told me about his friend, the late Colin Chapman, a British race driver and industrialist.

"He had ice in his veins and larceny in his heart," John said.

John might easily have been describing himself.

This is the story of that John Z. DeLorean. And it has nothing to do with cocaine.

For most of the fifteen years I knew or worked for John DeLorean, I trusted, respected and admired him. During his rise to prominence I was his friend, associate and adviser.

When I first met John he was ten years into a childless marriage, lived in Bloomfield Hills, an exclusive suburb of Detroit, and relaxed by playing golf on weekends. The core of his life was the automotive industry and his work as a top executive of General Motors, to which he devoted seventeen hours of every day. DeLorean, in 1966, was "Detroit, Detroit": narrow, parochial, dedicated, hardworking and competent.

A few years later, and seemingly within reach of GM's presidency, John suddenly resigned, telling the world he had "fired" GM because the corporation had lost its masculinity. Privately he told me he had rebelled against the corporation's corruption, and clearly that is the story he wanted me to tell my friends in the media. I never doubted his explanation. Earlier he had sent me a copy of a twenty-page confidential memo he had written to GM's new vice chairman, which contained serious allegations about GM and its executives.

I now know that John hadn't fired GM at all. He was bluntly told he had no future there. He had used the confidential memo — and me — to secure a peaceful and profitable separation from the company. That was the first time John deceived me. But it took me fourteen years to realize that John is, above all, a consummate actor. He is protean, changing his nature and his personality as circumstances demand.

I was far from being naïve when I first met John. I had grown up poor in the South. I had traveled the world as a merchant marine officer. I had been a successful investigative reporter, winning a number of awards for exposés of political corruption. I had been an assistant to Senator Estes Kefauver and Robert Kennedy. I was a founder, associate director and Inspector General of the Peace Corps and the poverty program. I was a member of the New York City Board of Education, and vice chairman of the New York Board of Trade. And I ran my own consulting company with four hundred employees.

By 1973 — seven years after I first met with him — John was an authentic American folk hero. In the periods between his two glamorous marriages and divorces he had dated some of the most beautiful women in America, and had forsaken the business uniform of Detroit for shirts that opened to the belly button. He spoke out for the rights of the poor and minorities. He was a critic of business morality, and openly criticized as shortsighted and bullheaded Detroit's decision not to build small cars. Before long he was everything a GM executive should *not* be: visible, controversial and concerned with the world on the other side of Detroit's moat.

When John started his own car company, the DeLorean Motor Company, I joined him as vice president for planning and communications. I was to be his "eyes and ears," he said. As it turned out, he didn't want to discuss with me what I saw or heard. When I began to question a mysterious Swiss bank account, into which over $17 million of company money had been sescretly diverted, he refused to answer. When I reported to him that our engineers were worried about the safety of the DeLorean sports car, I saw no indication that he paid any attention. When I began to question the accuracy of reports we were compiling for the Securities and Exchange Commission in preparation for an underwriting that, if it had gone through, would have made John one of the wealthiest men in America, John transferred me from the head office in New York to the factory in Belfast, Northern Ireland.

My concerns about the company were spelled out in confidential memos I had written to John. Our private struggle became public when John's former secretary took my memos — and a file of John's — to a member of the British Parliament. The British government was our partner; it had invested over $160 million in the DeLorean company. When Prime Minister Margaret Thatcher learned of the memos, she immediately ordered Scotland Yard, the Attorney General and the Public Prosecutor to investigate. Later, she called off the inquiry. Two Scotland Yard chief inspectors, sent to the United States to question me, were called home. A few days later John was cleared. He held press conferences in London and Belfast denouncing my memos as "forgeries." But he and I knew very well that they were not forgeries.

When John returned to New York, he set out to destroy what was left of my credibility in order to ensure that the memos would not trigger another inquiry. It was then that I began to investigate John without the blinders of respect and admiration.

What did I really know about John? He never spoke of his early life except in quotable clichés about his poor beginnings.

What had really happened at General Motors? Had he "fired" GM, or had he been forced out? I had never taken into account John's close friends in my evaluations of him. How did Maur Dubin — a flamboyant interior decorator — come to have the power to influence John's business decisions? Was John's relationship with convicted con man Roy Nesseth more than friendship? Was Nesseth a front for John's questionable business deals? Why had the British exonerated John and discredited my allegations? Why hadn't the various law firms and accountants that handled DeLorean's affairs reported what I had discovered? They were not fly-by-night firms. Indeed, they ranked among the most influential and respected in America. And why had the media missed the darker side of John's past?

This book is the result of my search for the answers to those questions. It is based not only on my long association with John, but on files, records, notes in my possession and conversations with John and others. I have used direct quotations for John and myself throughout the book. While my recollection of some of these conversations may not be word-perfect, I believe they reflect their susbtance and tone. Many are backed by our extensive exchange of memos, which became one of the principal ways in which we communicated.

In one sense, this is the story of my struggle with both John and myself. I was a true believer in DeLorean, and stubborn enough not to allow my doubts about him to influence me. John, I thought, had the potential to lead America in business and, eventually, even in politics. I wasn't basing that judgment on news stories or televsion commercials. I had been there when John thumbed his nose at Detroit's establishment and got away with it by selling more cars than anyone in Detroit's history. I watched as our company transformed an Irish bog into a state-of-the-art automobile factory and became a force in resolving the economic troubles of Northern Ireland. John's book on GM's business ethics, *On A Clear Day You Can See General Motors*, became an international commentary on business morality. He said that with the DeLorean Motor Company we would show the world what talent, imagination and drive could do under honest, concerned leadership. We would build not only an ethical car but an ethical company, one that could serve as a model for others. John's dream attracted people of great talent who almost reached those goals, and who continued to fight for them even after John had abandoned them.

Many of the facts of the DeLorean story are already known. Following his arrest on charges of trafficking cocaine, British and American authors wrote third-party accounts of John's life. Television cameras caught many images of DeLorean: John toasting the success of a narcotics transaction; walking with his head held high, his ankles in chains, hands cuffed behind his back; his dapper appearance, with his stunning third wife, at his trial; his excitement at being cleared by the jury — "Praise the Lord," John now "born again," exclaimed.

What seems to have eluded the writers and the cameras was the man himself. Knowing John as I do, that is easy to understand. He sheds personalities as a snake sheds its skin. I realized that he did not enter a cocaine deal to save his company. He did it to save himself. A bankruptcy would have revealed that his "dream" was empty, just a scam to make him rich.

The jury found John innocent of drug charges. He had been entrapped by the government officers. The jurors, in an unusual meeting with John, his attorneys and the judge, said that their verdict was a message to the government: We don't like the Abscam methods. Go after known criminals. Don't create your own.

Immediately after the verdict, John's lawyers were already preparing to defend him in Detroit, where a grand jury was hearing evidence that DeLorean diverted company funds. This was the charge that I had made three years earlier and that Scotland Yard had considered and dismissed.

In one sense, events overtook this book. When I originally began to write, this was to be an investigative exposé of John's financial affairs, the side the media had missed and the British and American governments had ignored. Without a newspaper to back me, or an institution to believe me, I had no other way to tell this story.

As the latest chapter of the DeLorean story unfolds in Detroit, I believe this book will help to also explain and account for John's complex personality, his charisma and his ability to attract talented men to throw in with him. For there is no doubt that John brought out the idealism that lies beneath the cultivated cynicism of the business and engineering worlds. That this idealism was itself turned toward cynical ends is nothing less than a tragedy.

Chapter One

Something Was Going on Behind Those Eyes

I first met John DeLorean in 1966. We were attending a small dinner party for Detroit's mayor, James Cavanagh. John was one of several automotive executives who came to dinner to pledge their financial support to help wipe out the mayor's campaign debt. I had heard John's name during the campaign and I knew he was general manager of the Pontiac division of General Motors.

John sat across the table from me. He said very little during the evening and what he said was often no more than a perfunctory response to a direct question. He was obviously uncomfortable. His hands were in constant motion, and bringing out a pen, he sketched engineering designs on the white tablecloth. He seldom looked up, but when he did I noticed a nervous twitch below his right eye. Sometimes he jerked his head to the right as if to loosen his collar. While the others relaxed and drank, John nursed his glass of white wine. He ordered a steak, and obviously delighted to have something to do with his hands, ate it with gusto.

Once I set aside the impression of gangliness and nervous-

ness, however, I detected a presence about John, a quiet
strength that involved more than height and looks. His round
face was ruggedly handsome, and even though there was
perhaps a little too much weight on his six-foot-four frame, he
still moved with the grace of an athlete. His hair was cut short,
marine style.

At dinner the conversation turned to politics. The consen-
sus of the guests was that Washington was run by pinko Jews
and Harvard intellectuals. The case in point was Nader (who
was not a pinko, nor a Jew, nor from Harvard). GM's use of
private detectives in an attempt to discredit him had forced a
public apology, but privately they believed no apology had
been necessary. A few lower-echelon heads had rolled, a
settlement had been paid to Nader, and GM's chairman had
made his *mea culpa* before a Senate committee. The GM
executives at dinner were pleased that the hearings had gone
so well. It had been a brilliant move to get Ted Sorensen as
their lawyer and have him sit next to the General Motors
chairman, Jim Roche, one of the GM executives was saying.
The picture of Roche sitting beside Sorensen had made front
pages across the country. GM was smugly convinced that
Sorensen's connection with John F. Kennedy had rubbed off
on the company and made their testimony credible.

I disagreed with them, and with a little too much red wine
and a little too much corporate Detroit under my belt, I
pompously said so.

"That was the dumbest thing I ever saw," I said. "Kennedy
isn't going to rub off on GM just because you hired Sorensen.
That's not how Washington works."

I felt the mayor kicking me under the table and I saw that
DeLorean looked slightly embarrassed. What the hell, I
thought.

"Detroit has a bunker mentality," I continued, ignoring
Cavanagh. "You think the world stretches from GM to Ford
and back again. Chrysler is the third world that you suffer just
to keep the Justice Department happy. Anyone with an Eastern degree is blackballed. You hide in Bloomfield Hills, and if

anyone is caught reading the New York *Times*, he has to pay a fine."

For me, Detroit was a divided world: rich and poor, management and union, white and black. To many auto executives, social justice was an immature concept that you learned in high school and discarded in the real world of business.

There was a moment of embarrassed silence. Someone told a joke. I went to the bathroom. Soon the mayor had the conversation back to the safe high ground of women and football. My outburst was forgotten. Or so I thought.

The next day John DeLorean's friend and attorney, John Noonan, called me at my hotel.

"John wants to have lunch with you today," he said.

"John who?"

"DeLorean."

"Why?"

"He said he didn't understand one damn word you said last night."

"I should have kept my mouth shut. It wasn't my show."

"Will you see him?" he asked.

"Sure."

We met at the exclusive London Chop House in downtown Detroit, and by the time I arrived John was already seated in a circular booth near the entrance, a table reserved for the powerful in Detroit.

At first the conversation went slowly; we had little in common. He talked about Detroit and I answered questions about Washington. He seemed typical of the competent, decent and successful small-town executives you meet in industrial America. The job is their world. Washington and its goverment regulations are, as the clichés of their trade journals maintain, the enemies of free enterprise. But I began to see a side of John that I liked. He didn't pretend to possess great knowledge and he seemed receptive to new ideas. By the time lunch was over, I understood why, at the age of forty, he had become the youngest general manager in Pontiac's history.

A month or so later, John and his wife, Elizabeth, were in

New York, and my wife and I joined them for dinner at a quiet restaurant on New York's East Side. Again we talked only about Detroit and Washington. There was no cultural side to John. But I wanted to know more about his views. As he relaxed, John began to reveal his prejudices. They were not the sort of ideas we later came to associate with him.

He said that the labor unions were destroying Detroit because they protected men who didn't want to work.

"We spend time and money training them, and before you know it, they have a grubstake and are headed back home."

"What's wrong with that?" I asked.

"They have no respect for the automobile industry. They have no pride in their work. We're not a stopping-off place on the way to a farm."

Blacks were all but useless in his view. They filled the dull places on the assembly line where whites wouldn't work and would soon be replaced by more efficient machines. He called them "niggers." "They would rather be on welfare, anyway," he said.

He admitted he had never talked to a black executive or worker and had never been to a black person's home. People in Bloomfield Hills didn't do that.

As for Jews: "They know how to make money without working very hard for it." He confessed he knew few Jews socially. "You know one now," I said. But John didn't react.

My ingrained liberal views would ordinarily have caused me to say something extremely unpleasant or to have abruptly said "goodbye" to the DeLoreans. But I sensed John was repeating clichés to which he was not deeply committed. Other executives I had met in Detroit voiced these same prejudices with real feeling. But John seemed more tentative when challenged. I concluded that he was open to new ideas. As a liberal Southerner, I had watched many of my friends change their views toward blacks and Jews.

Throughout dinner Elizabeth sat bolt upright, obviously made uncomfortable by the discussion and our sharply conflicting views. She hardly said a word.

On the way home from dinner my wife wanted to know what I had seen in DeLorean. In her view he was a bigot.

"I don't really know. But there's something very attractive about him. He's smart as hell and naïve as hell. You don't get to run an automobile company unless you have something special to offer. And he seems to be reaching out."

"Or putting you on," she replied.

A few weeks later John asked me back to Detroit.

"How would you like to work for Pontiac," he asked.

"I already have a business," I replied.

"I mean, work as a consultant."

"What would I do?"

"Whatever I thought you could do. Troubleshoot, report back to me, let me know what's happening?"

A few weeks later my consulting company went to work for Pontiac at $3,000 a month plus expenses.

Chapter Two

From The East Side
To The Fourteenth Floor

When I first went to work with John I knew very little about his early life, and he said nothing to enlighten me. In our talks he seemed to divide his life into "before GM" and "after GM." He could talk for hours about General Motors but would become a sphinx when asked about his childhood. At best, he would recycle a few carefully selected and convincing anecdotes that made him sound like a combination of Huckleberry Finn and Horatio Alger. When you tried to reach beyond the clichés, John would answer questions in one-phrase sentences. He grew up "on the wrong side of the tracks." He worked his way through college playing the clarinet in a band. His mother was a saint, his father an alcoholic. He never spoke about his service in the wartime Army (he never went overseas). It took me almost thirteen years to learn that John had more than one brother. At first I thought it was shyness or embarrassment. Many first-generation Americans run from their back-grounds. John used a space between the De and the Lorean, giving his name a phony French ancestry. Strictly, however, it is one word.

Later, as I probed his background, I came to be impressed. He was all he said he was and more. John grew up in Detroit's East Side, then and now a blue-collar district that mainlines the auto industry when the economy is good and drifts aimlessly when it's bad. Although unions have helped, life is never very secure in the East Side, what with layoffs, shutdowns, retooling and foreign competition.

John's mother, Zachary, was a burly alcoholic from a small town outside Bucharest, Rumania. Zachary's parents were peasant farmers and he never lost his accent. He had been a sheepherder in Montana and a steelworker and policeman in Gary, Indiana. A classic immigrant American who could work miracles with his hands, he could communicate neither with his family nor with those around him. When he worked, it was as a millwright at the Ford plant.

John's mother, Kathryn, was born in Salzburg, Austria, and was apparently better educated and more cultured than her husband. It was not an easy marriage, and in those days divorce was not an acceptable option. She left Zachary three times, moving each time to Southern California, but until 1940 she always returned. They were finally divorced when John was fifteen, and after that he did not see much of his father.

One of the stories John recounted was more revealing than he intended it to be. At thirteen he discovered how people lived when life was not a daily struggle for survival. Playing with friends after school, he was asked to dinner in the exclusive Palmer Woods section of suburban Detroit. John was stunned by the size of the house and the way his friends lived. The family sat around a dinner table and discussed a way of life John couldn't comprehend. They talked about trips and summer vacations and camps for kids. For John, summer in the Depression years meant three months to roam the streets, with an occasional chance to make a few dollars from odd jobs.

There was a calm in this house, an understanding among parents and children — and laughter. John felt uncomfortable throughout dinner, not knowing what utensil to use and worrying about saying the wrong thing. It was a discomfort he would feel all his life.

School was easy for John — knowledge seemed to stick to him. People who knew him at school recall John doing his homework in class as the teacher spoke and using his study hall to help friends. He played clarinet in the school band. When he graduated, he received a music scholarship to Lawrence Tech, one of those small technical colleges that feed engineers into Detroit's industries. In the spring of 1943 he was drafted into the Army. In all the years I knew him, John never once mentioned his military service. It was not mentioned in the official GM biography or in books like *Who's Who* that listed John's accomplishments. Later, when I searched for his Army records, I learned that they had been destroyed in a fire. In all, I found fewer than fifty words written about John's Army career. It seemed John kept that part of his life private — or secret. After his discharge, John went to work for the City of Detroit as a draftsman to earn money for college and to help support his family. He worked from 8 P.M. to 2 A.M., slept five hours, and then went to school at eight in the morning.

John was a big man on campus. He helped to reorganize the band, established a chapter of the Society of Engineers and wrote a popular column in the school newspaper. One of the items he wrote, in 1947, described his poetic view of the life of an engineer:

> Being an engineer is to live in a mean, bare prison cell and regard yourself the sovereign of limitless space; it is to turn failure into success, mice into men, rags into riches, stone into buildings, steel into bridges, for each engineer has a magician in his soul.

In contrast to this kind of rhetoric, however, was an early attempt, when he was twenty-three years old and just out of college, at making some easy money in a very questionable way. This scheme got him into a great deal of trouble, and he narrowly escaped being prosecuted.

John created a new company with a name almost identical to that of a company authorized to sell advertisements for Michigan Bell's Yellow Pages. John's company was called the "Directory Advertising Service"; the Yellow Pages publisher was "The Telephone Directory Advertising Company." He opened a bank account, obtained a mailing address with a secretarial service, clipped advertisments from the Yellow Pages and billed the advertisers on specially printed new stationery. Checks began to arrive, but then, so did the FBI, the county prosecutor and detectives from the phone company and the U.S. Postal Service. John agreed to return the money, but the phone company wanted more information. The rates John charged were identical to the official, confidential rates of the phone company. They suspected that John had a hidden partner. He explained that he got the idea from a stranger he had met at a bar. In the end, John was given the benefit of the doubt, and the matter was dropped.

After this episode, John decided to enroll in the Chrysler Institute, where he received his M.S. in automotive engineering. He went to work for Chrysler and stayed there until 1952. In those days, John still lived with his family in an East Side cottage, sleeping on a cot in a bedroom he shared with his brother Jack. Two other brothers slept in another bedroom.

A few years later, at the age of twenty-seven, DeLorean joined the Packard Motor Company. Two years after this he finally left home, to marry Elizabeth Higgins. He recalls that she was a secretary; she claims she was a telephone company representative. She was tall and attractive, and I'm sure John knew that heads would turn to look at them.

John was quickly promoted to run Packard's Division of Research and Development. In 1956, when Packard and Studebaker were merging, John was recruited to work with Bunkie Knudsen, Pontiac's general manager. Knudsen offered him $14,000 a year. To John, that was a small fortune.

When John joined Pontiac he was on his way to becoming just another faceless engineer, one of the small gears that make Detroit run so smoothly. Knudsen saved him from that. He was not only John's boss but his role model. It was through Bunkie's eyes that he began to explore the world beyond engineering. Knudsen's father had been president of General Motors and Bunkie had a sophistication that John felt he himself lacked. Knudsen made John an integral part of the three-man team whose mission was to change Pontiac's image from a manufacturer of sedate cars for dowagers to a company that, with styling and creative engineering, would reach young people. The third man was the new chief engineer, Pete Estes, who went on to become president of General Motors.

The Pontiac team decided to reach young people on their own level: through music, drag racing, good engineering and fantasy. Jim Wangers, a PR man and stock-car racing enthusiast, created a pop record about Pontiac's new GTO model that sold over a million copies. The music and words of "Little GTO," as sung by Ronnie and the Daytonas, equated the car with the sound of surf and bronzed, blond, teenaged girls on a California beach. It was an image John would not forget. While other executives were listening to the business news or to Frank Sinatra on the way to work, John began to tune in to the rock-and-roll stations, and to understand the language of his new customers, a language that would soon become his own.

Under Knudsen, Pontiac revived, setting new sales records and earning a reputation for engineering and styling. When Knudsen was moved up to become general manager of Chevrolet, Pete Estes replaced him, and DeLorean became Pontiac's chief engineer.

After John hired my company, I traveled to Detroit once or twice a month, but more often talked to John on the phone. These talks with John were often about his growing social awareness. I am not sure what made him change from being a man who called blacks "niggers" to be a man who began to seek opportunities for blacks in industry. But the times were changing and John was tuning in to the sixties. He began making trips out to the West Coast, where he soon developed a circle of Hollywood friends, more sophisticated and liberal than his friends in Detroit. And I think I had something to do with the change. Certainly I was the vehicle for, if not the instigator of, his new social awareness. He had me search out gasoline stations that we could train blacks to manage. He wanted me to see if there were any second men in the Pontiac dealer organization who were black and capable of becoming managers. Sometimes he called from Detroit just to discuss something he had read in the newspaper.

In 1969, John was made the general manager of Chevrolet. He explained to me, using one of his favorite phrases, that this promotion came about because Chevrolet was "in deep shit." Chevy's sales are traditionally the economic bedrock on which General Motors is built. Now its market share had eroded to the point where it threatened to hurt all of General Motors.

There was strong opposition to the move. John had too much visibility, he was not a team player, he had unorthodox ideas. But they needed him. In 1969, Chevrolet, the world's fifth largest industrial corporation, with its $10 billion annual sales equaling those of General Electric, was in trouble. Chevrolet employed 140,000 people in eleven assembly plants. Pontiac, by contrast, had 14,000 employees, managed by 130 people who saw one another almost every day. Even in the best of times, Pontiac's market share was only one sixth of Chevrolet's. Here was the challenge John was seeking.

Once installed, John moved quickly. Before GM's top executives on the fourteenth floor (the seat of the company's power) knew what hit them, John had eliminated 2,400 salaried jobs, reduced duplication and waste, improved quality, and had become the hero of Chevrolet dealers (many of whom would later form the dealer nucleus for DeLorean Motors). In his reorganization he had singled out costly inventories as a target. You don't build cars you can't sell, he said. And he began doing what he had done at Pontiac, designing cars to attract the young and the affluent.

He also began to introduce what could only be regarded as revolutionary concepts. He ordered that Chevy's billboards be pulled down — to the consternation of the fourteenth floor and his advertising agency — because, he said, they were inconsistent with the advertising campaign, which exhorted car buyers to see the American landscape from a Chevrolet. "You don't want billboards blocking the view," John told the critics, a view that won him the praise of environmentalists. His new public reputation was beginning to take shape. (The billboards never came down, however; they were allocated to other GM divisions.) To the cheers of the antiwar lobby, John removed Chevy from the defense business. He maintain that it was more profitable to build cars than tanks. "The next war will be over before they get around to using tanks," he said.

By 1972, Chevy had not only turned the corner and was in the black, but sold over three million cars and trucks, a new annual record in the automotive industry. DeLorean claimed that his salary and bonuses now reached $650,000. He quietly divorced Elizabeth and started to reshape both his personal apppearance and his social life. He secretly had his face lifted and his jaw remodeled, telling other executives he had been injured in a racing accident in Connecticut. (*Fortune* magazine was later to report it could find no trace of the accident, and Elizabeth claimed she found bills for surgery done overseas.)

I noticed the facial changes, but attributed them to John's compulsive new diet. He began to eat lettuce salads, stopped smoking and drinking, lifted weights and lost fifty pounds. His hair color changed; the slight touch of gray was gone. At the office he now wore turtleneck sweaters under his blue blazer, and soft leather Gucci shoes, which most GM executives would not wear even on vacation. (Indeed, in his book about GM, John remembers that an executive was sent home for wearing a brown suit. Gray, blue and black were the uniform colors for GM executives.) Away from the office he wore monogrammed shirts that were open to his navel. Gold began to appear on his wrists and around his neck. Pierre Cossette, a Hollywood producer, who was one of John's new friends, succinctly summed up John's new look: "He looked like a million-dollar picture star . . . like he had been put together by the property department of MGM."

At that time I was editing a book on black economic development for the American Assembly, a project of the Columbia Graduate School of Business. We needed a hard-hitting chapter on racial discrimination in America. When I asked John if he would be a contributor, he quickly agreed. Dave Gelman, then a vice president of my management company, wrote the chapter and John signed his name to it. John was required to submit the manuscript to the public relations department at General Motors, however, and within hours of this, the manuscript was on the desks of GM's president and chairman. They reacted quickly, telling John that he could not under any circumstances publish the chapter under his own name. John refused to budge. It took the intervention of Frederic Donner, a former GM chairman, to get the executives to change their minds.

When the book was reviewed, John's chapter was highlighted; it was often reprinted and quoted in editorials as an example of what businessmen should be doing. John became a hero to many blacks. *Black Economic Development* became a business school textbook; John was deluged with speaking invitations. He was fast becoming the moral man of American business.

John continued his fight for minorities inside General Motors. At the time, the General Motors Institute — the first stepping-stone to the executive suite — recruited few blacks. John announced that the way to make up for past mistakes was to make only blacks, and no whites, eligible for the

Institute for several years. When he made this extraordinary proposal, the fourteenth floor was stunned. It couldn't be done. Refusing to budge, John announced to his fellow executives that, at the very least, all Chevy positions at the Institute would be filled by black students. Again the fourteenth floor balked. Eventually, John was able to assign half his Chevy quota to black students. I made sure that the story leaked to the press.

At Chevrolet, John publicly equated car quality with morality. He insisted that the production people build cars that hold up. He told *Fortune* magazine that "if you do less, it's immoral."

Over dinner in Detroit one evening, John confided to me that he wanted to write a novel. As I listened in amazement, the general manager of the fifth largest industrial entity in the world explained that he wanted to write an antinuclear novel in which the Defense Department would be the villain.

"John," I said, slowly pouring myself a glass of red wine to find time to think, "great idea, but you've forgotten that GM *is* the defense establishment."

But John wasn't listening to me.

"Let me tell you about the plot," he said. "We start with some young people from all over the world attending a conference in Scandinavia, maybe a religious meeting. They become good friends. They're all scared of the bomb and a third world war. They form a secret society and they go back to their countries and help one another move up the ladder. Some go into the clergy, some into the military, some into the nuclear industry. They all keep in touch with one another until there is a world crisis. Then they hiijack some hydrogen bombs and threaten to blow up the major cities of the world unless the big powers disarm. Their friends in high places respond to the threat. They're everywhere. In China, in Russia, here."

I didn't react right away. John came up with an idea a minute and he often made me the sounding board. I was hoping this one would go away. It didn't, however.

"I want you to put it together for me," he continued. "Find a team of writers. I'll pay them whatever they want."

A few days later John called me in New York.

"Did you find those writers?" he asked.

"Are you really serious about this thing, John, or are you smoking something?"

"Dead serious."

I asked a Washington journalist and author, George Clifford, to go to Detroit and interview John. After meeting him and hearing his description of the plot, George refused to work on the book.

"That man is off the wall," he said.

John persisted, and I returned to Detroit with a team of writers, minus Clifford. We spent two days locked in a Detroit hotel suite going over the plot and characters with John. When he left, we ran the ideas through the typewriter. Nothing worked. On the second day one of the writers motioned me into the next room.

"This is insanity," he said. "He wants the National Council of Churches to steal the bomb and threaten to blow up the world unless the world disarms."

"What if we siphon off the insanity?" I asked.

Dave Gelman, who had joined us, looked at me in disgust. "Is he a friend of yours?"

"Sure. He's a friend."

"Then have him committed."

John was willing to make concessions, however.

"You can have any plot you want," he said. "Any characters. We just need to get this idea across to the people."

"Have you thought about the consequences?" Dave asked DeLorean.

"What consequences?"

"They could fire you."

"For what?" John asked in amazement.

Back in New York, Dave said that he, too, would have nothing to do with the project. I would have to look elsewhere for writers, or I could do the novel myself. He was right. It was ridiculous.

I had urged John to keep the project a secret until we had it well launched and could determine how it would develop. He agreed. Yet a month later I got what can only be described as a nearly hysterical call from an account executive at the advertising agency that handled Chevrolet.

"Is John doing a book?" my friend asked. I could tell he was afraid to hear my answer.

"How did you learn about it?"

"John told my boss, who said if we don't sidetrack this, the lid will blow at GM and John will lose any chance he has there."

A few days later the account executive came to New York.

"We've got to stall this," he told me. "John has some problems on the fourteenth floor. This could sink him. I need your help."

I agreed to stall. A writer slowly cranked out four hundred pages, and eventually John lost interest and went on to other things. But he never forgot about the novel. Later, at De-Lorean Motors, he asked me what happened to it, and I had the impression he wanted to revive the idea.

After John took over Chevy he asked me to be the middleman in a real-life drama with a plot that was as bizarre as that of his novel. "I want you to see C. W. Smith," John told me. The Libyans had nationalized some oil fields, and Smith want to do something about it. I asked John what the hell we could do about it.

"C. W. will tell you. He knows what he's doing."

C. W. had been a linebacker for the Chicago Bears and now

was one of John's inner circle of friends. Like some others in that circle, Smith had a volatile temper. According to John, he was "one hell of an engineer." I had no reason to doubt that.

I met C. W. in my New York office and he outlined what he wanted me to do.

"I need to get to Israeli intelligence," he said. He told me that some of his friends were willing to spend $10 million to "destabilize" Libya. He wanted to put together a mercenary team in London to trigger a revolution in Libya. He knew the people. "They're good," he said.

"You don't start a revolution with a team from London," I said.

"We want to start something and make sure the Israelis keep it going. There are two Egyptian tank columns on the Libyan border, and if we can create an incident, they'll move in."

To get Smith out of the office I said I would think about it. I called John in Detroit.

"Is Smith all there?" I asked.

"He's solid," John said.

I explained Smith's plan. John already knew the details.

"What do you have to lose?" John asked. "You're pro-Israeli, aren't you? See what you can do."

"That's not the question. Who the hell is going to believe me?"

"They will. We will give you information that can only come from intelligence sources. That will give you credibility. You just set up the contact. That's all I'm asking you to do."

I arranged a contact and Esther Goldman, the executive vice president of my company, joined me for a meeting with the Israeli ambassador. I had not told the ambassador the reason for my visit, only that it was confidential. Now I hastened to explain that I was just a go-between on what sounded to me like a preposterous idea, but requested that he listen to it for a moment. I opened the meeting by presenting some confidential military information that C. W. Smith had provided me. It was the precise location of certain Libyan and Egyptian units. The ambassador did not react. Then we explained, as quickly and as sincerely as we could, Smith's idea. As I expected, the ambassador said that the concept made no sense and that the Israelis were not in the habit of dealing with third parties in secret plots. I nodded, thanked him, left Smith's phone number on his empty desk and made a hasty exit.

"I'm not sure we should have done that," I said to Esther.

Why, in fact, had I done it? I thought about it then and I think about it now. John was a trusted friend. He ran one of the world's largest companies. He was a client. I liked the intrigue. But I think that in the end I did it because there was a pleasing irony about the right wing putting up $10 million to help the Israelis. Eventually, however, I shrugged it off.

As we got to know each other, John often probed for stories about my relationship with the Kennedys and others. I had been Robert Kennedy's special assistant in the 1960 presidential campaign and had undertaken special assignments for the President while I was in government. I subsequently worked in Robert Kennedy's senatorial and presidential campaigns.

John was intrigued by power and wealth. I sensed he believed the rich and famous were somehow different from himself, that it wasn't just money he lacked. He wanted to know about one of my heroes, my then father-in-law, John Hay Whitney, publisher of the New York *Herald Tribune* and former ambassador to Britain. John marveled that Whitney had houses everywhere and that whenever he stepped into one, the staff would be at the door, the house prepared for his arrival.

"How could you fit into that world?" he asked me.

"I don't fit into it. I live my own life. If I could, I'd like to emulate Whitney, but not necessarily live in that world."

"Bunkie is like that to me," John said, in one of his rare reflective moments. I wondered if Knudsen was not a substitute for the rich, successful, understanding father John never had.

While John was putting Chevy back on track and making it one of the most successful companies in the world, living a fantasy life in California and developing a reputation as the man who could lead the poor, he fell in love with Kelly Harmon. Of John's three wives, I liked her the most. Kelly was the creature of the GTO song, the twenty-year-old girl-woman, innocent yet seductive. The GM wags said she was the ticket back to John's lost youth. A model with a college degree in music, Kelly was the daughter of Tommy Harmon (the University of Michigan football hero of the late 1930's, and war hero of the 1940's) and Elyse Knox, the actress. She had a soft grace, a cultured voice and the ease of someone raised in wealth who had gone to the right schools. For John, she had "background."

After their honeymoon in Europe, the DeLoreans returned to Detroit. But Kelly was never accepted there. John was aware of her unhappiness. He told me that when they entered a room full of GM executives and their wives, the men would all turn and look at Kelly while most of the women would seek the corners as far away from her as possible. John asked me to help Kelly find something socially useful to do with her time so that she would not brood. Then the DeLoreans decided to adopt a child. John was apparently convinced he could not have children. The baby, Zachary, became part of the house-hold, but he wasn't enough to keep the marriage alive.

There were several stories about the divorce. Kelly couldn't cope with Bloomfield Hills and kept retreating to the security of her relaxed California lifestyle, first for weekends, then weeks, later months at a time. There were locker-room stories about John's manhood and his inability to keep pace with a twenty-year-old child-woman. At the time, I saw John as a man married to a career with little time for a wife. If Kelly had had a profession, something of her own, it might have worked.

When they decided to divorce, John demanded sole custody of Zachary, something almost unheard of at the time. I was convinced from my talks with John that Kelly wanted to flee Detroit, to resume her life on the Coast, and that a baby would be a hindrance to her. In researching this book, and going back over the marriage, I learned for the first time that in fact Kelly had also wanted Zachary and that the resulting arguments were bitter. I now believe that once divorce was inevitable John decided to play business hardball with his GTO princess, grinding and intimidating Kelly until he had all he wanted. I was to learn that was the way John worked.

It wasn't long after this that John met Cristina Ferrare, the Virginia Slims model and *Harper's Bazaar* cover girl, who, at twenty-three, was very much at home in a world John was just discovering. Cristina had been making her living as a model and starlet in Hollywood since she was seventeen. She met John in his lawyer's office, where he was completing his divorce from Kelly.

In New York in early 1973, my wife and I joined John on his second date with Cristina. Her leg was still in a cast from a skiing accident. The contrast between her and Kelly and Elizabeth was striking. Cristina did not seem to be intimidated by John or discomfited by his habit of losing touch with the conversation. When John dropped his eyes and retreated inside himself, Cristina would confront him. "Where are you going, John?" she would ask, a smile on her face. Cristina was a strong woman, I thought. Strong enough and smart enough to hold John's interest. As a successful model and budding film star, she was secure enough not to be dependent on John. Before long, the two were living together. They were married in May 1973.

Meanwhile, there were rumblings inside General Motors. Although DeLorean was making and selling more cars than anyone else in Chevrolet's history, he nevertheless believed that a cabal on the fourteenth floor had decided that John had strayed too far from the fold and had too many outside interests. Some believed that John was riding high on the achievements of others, that he was spending too much time on the Coast, that his name, picture and views were too often in the media, and that it was time to rein him in. John could have his choice: he could be a Member of the Team and continue to enjoy the rewards and perquisites that go with that membership, or he could stay on the outside and take his chances.

The first shot across the bow had come from Richard Gerstenberg, GM's new chairman. An item in the *Gallagher Report* of April 11, 1972, was headlined: DICK GERSTENBERG TAKES HARD LOOK AT CHEVROLET. It said:

> New General Motors Chairman unhappy with perform-
> ance of Chevrolet General Manager John Z. De-
> Lorean. Too many outside interests. DeLorean part
> owner of San Diego Chargers football team, Bowie
> Racetrack in Maryland, still under cloud from internal
> investigations of kickbacks from Chevrolet suppliers...

There was more — although it would take ten years before I learned the real story. Inside General Motors a four-man investigation team had been created to look into charges that John was using his official position for personal profit. One inquiry focused on a company that sold audiovisual presentation equipment to Chevrolet dealers and on the suggestion that DeLorean and a used-car salesman from California named Roy Nesseth were partners in the company. Later court actions disclosed that John and the company's chief executive were business partners and that Nesseth had been employed by the audiovisual company. GM never publicly accused John of any misdeeds, however.

If John worried about the internal investigations, he never let on. It seemed that the more he was criticized internally, the more he spoke out in public. It was at this point that he turned to me for help. He wanted his story told. It was not a difficult task for me. I was impressed with his apparent courage in challenging Detroit's values at the risk of his own career. He told me that he was opposed to GM's plan to request a one-year delay in implementing the 1975 exhaust emissions standards. GM, he told me, could not only meet them, but beat the deadline. I let reporters know that John was fighting GM on the issue.

John told me that he had argued, inside the corporation, for using air bags in GM cars. GM was convinced that it was impractical and expensive. When John told me the air bag was "on the shelf, ready to go," I was surprised.

"Why don't they use it?"

"They're convinced safety doesn't sell cars," he explained, asking me to let the Nader people know where he stood on the issue.

He continued to argue that GM should move into the smaller-car market, both for reasons of self-interest and national responsibility. The Germans and Japanese were selling small cars very successfully in the American and other markets.

While this behind-the-scenes struggle was taking place, General Motors announced on October 1, 1972, that it had promoted John to the fourteenth floor. He became group executive for the domestic Car and Truck Group, an operation that posted $40 billion in yearly sales and was responsible for 87 percent of GM's profits. For tactical reasons, John at first fought the move. He threatened to quit and take a Cadillac dealership in Florida. Later he said he wanted to be assured that Chevrolet was passed on to someone inside the divison. What he actually feared was losing his base of power. As long as he kept Chevrolet profitable and progressive, no one would dare to touch him. On the fourteenth floor he could not directly influence profits and might quickly become a cog in the committee wheel. A group executive had a large, wood-paneled office, but only a secretary for staff. His time would be spent in committee meetings reviewing the work of others.

On the fourteenth floor John immediately showed his independence. He refused to eat lunch every day in the executive dining room with the other men who ran GM. He preferred to drive into town and meet with friends who were not in the automobile business. He wrote some very critical reports. In one, he claimed he could save GM $1 billion a year by eliminating duplication and waste and tightening up on decision-making procedures — a version of what he had done so well at Chevrolet. No one seemed to care. John had not been promoted to the fourteenth floor to change the system.

John soon had his first major confrontation. A few weeks after he arrived in his new job, Richard L. Terrell, his immediate superior on the fourteenth floor, called him in for a discussion of his new role. John dropped into the seat in front of the desk and Terrell reached behind to push a hidden button, closing the heavy wooden doors to his office.

Without preamble, Terrell bluntly told John that he didn't want to read John's name in the newspapers and see his face on television. The fourteenth floor worked through teamwork and cooperation. The fourteenth floor established the policies that others were required to follow. John recalls that "Terrell's message was as obvious to me as the dark suit and white shirt he wore: 'DeLorean, disappear into the boondocks.' "

The crisis climaxed a month later at the Greenbrier Hotel in White Sulphur Springs, West Virginia. There, every three years or so, several hundred of GM's top executives gathered to discuss confidential plans for the future. Fourteenth-floor executives were each assigned a topic. John's topic, Product Quality, was a sensitive issue at GM. DeLorean prepared a speech that among other things criticized the corporation's quality controls. Why, he asked, had warranty repairs reached the half-billion dollar mark? This figure had hitherto been a closely guarded corporate secret.

DeLorean revealed a second secret. Studies indicated, he said, that a new, efficient rotary engine, the Wankel, would be in "eighty to one hundred percent of automobiles within the next ten years." He revealed the GM could manufacture the

Wankel for less money than the conventional piston engine, even though the Wankels then on the market were more expensive. The Wankel was something GM wanted to keep from its competitors.

It was a powerful and candid speech. The only trouble was that an early draft had been leaked to Robert Irvin, the automotive editor of the Detroit *News*; excerpts appeared in the *News* the night before John delivered his speech. John later wrote that "the leak destroyed the Greenbrier conference for me and was probably the single thing that hurt me most in the Corporation."

John claimed that his enemies on the fourteenth floor — most likely those in GM public relations — had leaked the speech to get him in trouble. He believed that they had in fact done so once before, when a negative story about John appeared in the papers on the day he was to make an important presentation to the GM board of directors. He went so far as to hire private detective, C. J. Pickrel, to investigate the leak. Then, in a curious twist, GM took over the investigation, and Pickrel was ordered to report his findings direct to GM's security office.

On December 8, 1972, John was called to meet with Tom Murphy, the new GM vice chairman, and Ed Cole, John's friend and the new GM president. The doors were closed and John was told he had no future at GM. I doubt that GM was prepared for what happened next.

A few days later, after his meeting with Murphy and Cole, John called me at my office in New York City. "I'm sending you a memo by courier," he said. "I want your opinion. Let me know as soon as you read it. It's important."

It was a twenty-page memo written to Tom Murphy by John after the December 8 meeting, and it was explosive. In it, John leveled damning charges against General Motors and its corporate officers, alleging that safety had been disregarded and innovation stifled. After reading it for a third time, I looked out from my office across Central Park to the General

Motors Building, which dominated the skyline on the eastern edge of the park. I remember thinking that the foundations of that building are sunk so deeply into Manhattan's bedrock that even an earthquake could not shake it. I felt the same way about General Motors itself. That building, and the Corporation, had seen DeLoreans come and go. I had no doubt now how a confrontation between GM and DeLorean would end. John would lose.

I called John in Detroit.

"I just finished reading your memo to Murphy," I said. "You should not — repeat, *not* — send it to Murphy. I'll come to Detroit in the morning and we'll discuss it then."

"I've already sent it. And I told them I sent you a copy."

"John, what the hell are you trying to achieve? They'll have to defend themselves. They'll find some loophole, they'll find you in bed with a woman, or with your hand in the till . . . they'll be forced to blow you out of the water."

"No," John said, "Murphy's a good man. I've known him a long time. He's the only hope of changing GM. He's not locked into the system like the others . . . he came up a different way."

"But you cut off your options when you sent the memo. Murphy can either change things or get rid of you. That memo is a ticking time bomb."

"That's not my objective," John said. "I just want to change things around here."

"Why not wait a few years until you're running the show?"

"I had no other choice. It's now or never. This is my hole in time."

"You're crazy, John," I said with admiration. "What do you want me to do?"

"Wait. Let's see what happens."

I never thought to ask why John had no other choice. It was not until ten years later that I learned the reason.

I never had any doubt about the authenticity of the Murphy memo. It used a kind of shorthand to refer to incidents and named the people — many of them still at GM — who purportedly could verify what John was reporting. It was an investigative memo, describing what John regarded as the corruption within GM. The memo was John's counter-attack. If I go down, I'll take GM with me, he was saying. John thought in those grandiose terms. It was both his strength and his weakness.

John was later to show me how he played high stakes poker with his adversaries. He had a phrase for it. He called it "getting a little shit on their shoes." You collect and validate derogatory information. Then, when the time comes, you close the door with your adversary and lay your information on the table. This was the DeLorean technique, one that he was to use many times.

I do not know whether Murphy actually read the memo, or what happened thereafter. John describes it in these terms in his book, *On A Clear Day You Can See General Motors:*

"In January [1972]," he relates, "I wrote a stinging and critical analysis of GM's management and system. The criticisms were aimed directly at a lot of corporate people and their actions. I felt many of the people around and above me would be shocked by this report.

"I had two objectives in sending the memo. If it was at all possible, in a last-ditch effort, I wanted to jar management into a realization of the deep-rooted problems upstairs. Since I was pretty sure this would not be effective — because my previous efforts at reform were not well received — I figured this memo would demonstrate to management that we could no longer exist together and it was in their best interests to let me resign on my own terms, which were to leave and receive my accrued bonus . . . I figured I had to leave quickly, because if I stayed on the job much longer, the attempts to discredit my business reputation would hurt me."

One of the subjects John vividly describes in the memo — the flaws in the Corvair model (which Ralph Nader had earlier reported) — was made public in his book. It went beyond what Nader had learned and, as was later reported, confirmed what he had written.

The Murphy memo began:

For almost a week now I have contemplated how to reply constructively to the views expressed by Mr. Cole and yourself during our hour-long conversation on December 8. I have concluded that the best way to respond is by being absolutely candid in the honest belief that what I have seen from within GM will be of help to you as you move into control of the corporation . . .

In reviewing our conversation, one point kept returning to my mind . . . both you and Mr. Cole said my managerial performance in turning Chevrolet around was outstanding, and you both agreed that I was certainly a prime candidate for the GM presidency in a few years . . .

The one hindrance to my advancement, Mr. Cole warned, and you concurred (and later reiterated the next day) was my expressed social conscience and my active concern for the well-being of our country and its people, particularly the disadvantaged; this, you believed, constituted a handicap to my progress in General Motors. You both agreed that if I continued to take my concerns for the poor, the minorities and the disadvantaged seriously, you would have to disqualify me from present and future consideration for promotion within GM, regardless of my performance.

With his protective cotton in place, John relates one damning incident after another, each with far-reaching consequences in the world outside GM. Then, with his charges firmly in place, John returned to the high ground, citing his sponsorship of "minority or black capitalism" ventures and his "insist-ence on a substantially higher negro enrollment at GMI [which] was met by you, Mr. Roche and Mr. Terrell with considerable criticism."

America has been good to me and, as I said, I feel strongly an obligation to devote a portion of my life to the betterment of our country. I cannot believe that, as you and Mr. Cole say, this conflicts with General Motors' interests. If it does, then I'm afraid I must agree with you that I have no place in GM's future.

John ended his memo on this note:

I am too much of a manager to be idealistic. But these same managerial values tell me that we must and can change. That is why I am willing to write you this personal memo in full understanding that it might be misinterpreted or misunderstood. Please regard this as my effort to continue to work with GM's system and to provide you with my views on what I have seen inside this corporation and to place my value judgments on them.

In your new post as Vice Chairman and, hopefully, someday as Chairman of General Motors, you will have an opportunity to correct these things. I assume you will tell me to destroy this memo as you have so many others — but I hope you will keep your copy at least as a thought starter. It is in General Motors' best interests to build a better world.

I later talked to Pat Wright, who had written DeLorean's book for him. He told me had often asked John for a copy of the Murphy memo, but that it was not forthcoming.

GM will not comment on John's departure — at least they

refuse to go beyond the public statements. Nevertheless, it is a fact that John left General Motors on his own terms; with his deferred compensation, accrued bonus, and with his reputation intact.

Chapter Three

Not A Bad Investment
For A Skinny Engineer

John left General Motors with a formal handshake and a bland press release on April 1, 1973. GM Chairman Richard Gerstenberg announced that John was leaving to help his country:

"[John] has been active and articulate in a number of areas of social concern, especially the problems of minorities, of youth groups and the disadvantaged and unemployed," Gerstenberg said. "We are gratified that he will still be associated with the Corporation and at the same time will be able to more actively involve himself in personal interests which are so important to him and indeed to all of us."

John echoed the theme. "I really feel I want to spend a lot more time getting involved with my fellow man," he told the Detroit *News*.

As part of the termination agreement, John received a Cadillac dealership; it was worth $1 million in gross income a year. He also kept $800,000 in deferred salary, which would be paid out over the years if he stayed out of the automotive industry.

Under the published protocols of his departure, DeLorean was to be named the president of the National Alliance of Businessmen, an organization chartered and financed by the government to train minorities for jobs in industry. (The blueprint for the NAB had come out of my typewriter. Under the direction of Under Secretary of Commerce Howard Samuels and his assistant Ken Auletta, now a writer and columnist, the concept was developed into an organization that is still operating in 1985.) The board included the nation's top CEO's; Gerstenberg was about to become the 1973 chairman. The presidency was a nonpaying job, but traditionally the chairman loaned a top executive for the job, keeping him on the corporate payroll. John was to receive $200,000 from GM for his year at the NAB. It was a neat fit.

John and Cristina continued to live behind the white fences of his three-and-a-half acre estate in Bloomfield Hills. In Washington they rented a town house and made the social rounds. They were invited to countless dinner parties and receptions. But John never felt comfortable in social situations he didn't control, and he lacked the polish and sophistication that can make a lasting impression in Washington. Over the next few years, whenever I saw John, I would ask him what he planned to do next. He didn't have an answer. He was drifting. During those years John and I talked on the phone every few weeks and met for dinner once a month, usually when he came through New York. I tracked his career from the sidelines, helping him occasionally, until the spring of 1979, when I joined his company.

During those years I, too, was drifting. My marriage broke up and I wrote a painful book about joint custody. Later I settled into an exciting job that enabled me to use the subpoena in conducting inquiries, the dream of every newspaperman. The New York State Assembly created an investigative office that I headed. We functioned as a committee, but we had no members and no chairman, a unique situation. Instead, we serviced all the committees, which allowed me to conduct a wide range of investigations. We looked into the penetration of organized crime into the sports industry, the uranium cartel, the high cost of prescription drugs, the New York fiscal crisis, and the withholding of gasoline and home-heating oils from the market by the major oil companies.

In those years John was no longer center stage as he had been at GM; nevertheless, the DeLorean story slowly turned into a legend. In its September 1973 issue, *Fortune* magazine established the myth that was to last for almost a decade.

"DeLorean," *Fortune* wrote, "had created the hottest cars to come out of Detroit since World War II. He holds over 100 patents*, and was responsible for dozens of design innovations." And as a manager, the article went on to say, he had rescued Chevrolet from a downturn that bordered on catastrophe, a crisis GM has successfully kept secret. "In view of his achievements and seemingly brilliant future, DeLorean's departure was not only a surprise, but a mystery . . . There is not the slightest hint at corporate headquarters that De-Lorean was fired or even that he left under a cloud. But that still leaves the question of why he chose to interrupt his career at such a momentous point."

And John was learning to give the right answers to the media.

"The automotive industry has lost its masculinity," he told the magazine, a comment that triggered front-page news stories around the country. *Fortune* concluded that the substance of John's complaint seemed to be that "encroaching government regulations have taken the fun out of the business, reducing it to the status of a utility," and that GM's sheer size "has led to mind-dulling bureaucratization which left no room for an individualist like John DeLorean."

Fortune said the John had walked away from a $550,000 compensation package. When Gerstenberg announced John's resignation, the New York *Times* estimated his compensation

---

* Actually GM owns all patents.

package at $300,000. Later, John was to say it totaled $650,000, the estimate accepted by the media between 1974 and 1983.

Whatever the figure, John's greatest residual benefit from GM was not his compensation but his reputation.

Before he left the NAB in mid-1974, John had established the John Z. DeLorean Corporation in Detroit and for a time worked out of Bunkie Knudsen's office. He soon had consulting contracts that he later claimed were worth over $3 million a year in fees. Among his early clients were the Allstate Insurance Company, Ryder Systems (a truck-leasing concern), W. R. Grace (a shipping line that had become a conglomerate) and Renault. I went along with John on some of his consulting assignments; if GM had been boring, these jobs must have seemed deadly. At GM — and even at NAB —John had support systems to help him, but now he worked without backup, a difficult task for someone accustomed to ringing for a private jet. Later, at DeLorean Motors, even when money was tight, John insisted on living and traveling as if he were still at GM.

John had also invested in the San Diego Chargers football franchise, but, needing money to maintain his increasingly lavish lifestyle, he sold his 8 percent share to Barron Hilton just before the NFL signed a lucrative television contract that would have made him a small fortune. When asked why he sold out, John cited allegations that team members had been using drugs, a story that made news and hid his real motivation. I later came to realize that this kind of cover story represented a standard DeLorean technique.

When we talked during those years, John always seemed distracted. It was clear he was searching for something to do, and his name was often mentioned when top corporation jobs opened up. None of those opportunities worked out. Down deep, John didn't want to work for anyone. He wanted to run his own company. He had learned his lesson at General Motors.

"You did the right thing," he once told me. "You ran your own shop. No one can tell you what to do." John's desire for a business he controlled grew into an obsession in the years that followed.

In 1975, John asked me if I had any contacts in the Soviet Union. "They have a car I think I can sell here," John said. The car was the Zhiguli (based on the Fiat 124 and called the Lada in the United States). As it turned out, I did have a contact with the Russians, a close friend, David Karr. We met when Vice President Johnson sent him to see me at the Peace Corps in 1961. David was a partner in the Lazard Frères bank in Paris and chairman of the hotel chain that owned the Pierre in New York and the George V and the Plaza Athénée in Paris, three of the world's most exclusive hotels. He had homes on both continents and a hundred-foot fully staffed yacht in the Mediterranean on which he quietly entertained important people. David was a secret envoy between the White House and the Soviet leadership. He had easy access to both, and not only carried private messages but was a sounding board on delicate issues. I once watched David arrange the release of some Jewish dissidents from Russia.

I called David, and several weeks later John and I went to Paris to meet with Dzhermen M. Gvishiani, who ran the Soviet Union's State Committee on Science and Technology. His real power, however, came from his marriage, for he was Soviet Premier Alexei Kosygin's son-in-law. David made a point of giving Gvishiani the Athénée's most luxurious suite. When we had breakfast the next morning with Gvishiani, the Soviet official was quite at ease in these surroundings. He wore a well-tailored suit and soft leather loafers. He was polite, attentive and impressed by John's credentials. But nevertheless he was not interested in John's request for the exclusive right to market Russian-made cars in the United States.

"That agreement is about to be signed with someone else," he said. He did have an assignment he wanted John to consider, however. The Togliatti truck factory on the Kama River in Central Russia was in trouble. There were problems that DeLorean might be able to resolve. If that worked well, maybe they could consider other prospects. John said he would think it over. Karr advised us to consider the offer.

"The Russians are very slow in making decisions," he said, "but if they trust you, you could write your own ticket."

(Karr died in Paris a few years later. At first his death was attributed to heart attack, but his wife refused to believe it. The Paris press hinted that Karr had been murdered by the KGB. The police exhumed his body for an autopsy, which revealed that he had not in fact died of a heart attack. The New York *Times* later assigned investigative reporter Jeff Gerth to the mystery. In a front-page story Gerth revealed Karr's influence but was unable to discover the cause of Karr's death.)

John decided against going to Russia. It was then that he told me he wanted to build his own automotive company, and that consulting was only a means to that end.

One of his consulting accounts was W. R. Grace, which paid him $25,000 a month for his advice. In analyzing the U.S. automotive market for them, John saw the need for a luxurious, lightweight, fuel-efficient recreational vehicle (RV). Grace had a RV division, Shasta, and John was convinced he could make the company the leader in the field. J. Peter Grace, the head of the company, agreed.

Grace was reported to have spent $1 million on the project. But John's RV never made it. A mock-up was built, but was destroyed in a fire. I was later to learn that John took liberties with the Grace money. Although Grace had authorized only two office salaries in addition to John's $25,000-a-month consulting fee, John instructed Robert McLean, the first of the GM executives to join his new company, to charge the entire cost of John's Detroit office to Grace. Eventually, Grace sold the RV division. By the time John settled in New York, Peter Grace had dropped from John's social circle.

Grace doesn't talk about the relationship, but others have. Early DeLorean executives say that John blew a great opportunity by not giving his full attention to the development of the RV. Once John had secured a contract and collected his money, he lost interest and went on to other things.

It was another automotive consulting contract that helped to launch John's car company. Archie Boe, Allstate Insurance Company's chief executive, was convinced that highway deaths could be dramatically reduced if cars were built with air bags. He asked John to put his name behind the project and to write an air-bag safety report. John agreed. His consulting fee for this was $250,000.

John's Allstate report — prepared by Robert McLean — attracted national and congressional attention. John was not an academic or a liberal politician, but an experienced Detroit executive who had managed most of General Motors. In arguing for the air bags, John made no mention of the charges against GM he had outlined in his confidential memo to Murphy.

Allstate was ecstatic. Now they turned to John for another "impossible task." For several years the federal government had tried but failed to interest the major car companies in building — with government financing — a prototype of a safety car. Several small companies had tried to fill the vacuum, but they lacked the experience to design a salable mass-production model. Their cars were safe, but they lacked style: they looked like tanks and weighed almost as much. Allstate offered him $600,000 to build two prototypes. It was exactly the challenge John was seeking.

Allstate said that the car should match or exceed the then current safety and emission standards, survive a 40 to 50 mile-per-hour barrier crash, have no front-end damage in an accident at 10 miles an hour, be easily repairable, have no protruding parts or ornaments that could injure pedestrians, have extraordinarily good brakes, weigh no more than 2,500 pounds, and get 25 miles per gallon at a sustained speed of 50 miles per hour. The car was to be commercially attractive, sell for under $7,000 (in 1974 dollars), and be capable of mass production at 50,000 cars a year. The project would start on November 1, 1974, and the prototypes were to be available for crash-testing at the end of 1975. When the project was completed, John would own all rights to the car.

What Allstate asked John to do for $600,000 was to revolutionize the automobile industry. I believe that no other top automotive executive would have been capable or willing to undertake this challenge with the meager financial resources available. But once again John was in the right place at the right time. The Allstate car was code-named the DSV — the DeLorean Safety Vehicle. Allstate had not only financed the project but created for DeLorean the standards he later used in describing the DeLorean sports car that the DSV eventually became. With them, John said, he was introducing "ethics" into the auto industry.

To turn the concept into a car, John hired Bill Collins, an engineer who was right behind John at Pontiac and was now on his way up the GM ladder. Collins had been assigned one of GM's most important engineering projects: to scale down the full-sized "B" models in an attempt to catch up with the Germans and the Japanese. It was a signal to the outside world that Collins was a comer.

John told me that Collins had worked with him on the XP833, a prototype for a powerful, two-seat fiberglass sports car that John had been prevented from building at Pontiac. Zora Arkus-Duntov, a Russian-born engineer who was Chevy's resident genius and the designer of the Corvette, had liked the XP833 but had argued against it, since it represented competition for the incredibly profitable Corvette. GM subsequently killed further development. The XP833, which originated as Collin's idea, was to become the basis for John's belief that he could find a corner of the market — what he called "the cracks between the piano keys" — where he could compete against the automotive giants. "GM doesn't believe in tinkering with success," John told me. "It's a price you pay for size and organization."

For Collins, leaving GM was a major step. He would give up the accumulated security of twenty years. But, as Collins told me later, he was excited about having restraints on his initiative removed, and for that reason alone he was willing to take the risk of joining DeLorean. Collins later regretted his enthusiasm, for it almost ruined his career.

John had an impressionistic image of the car he wanted to build, a romantic conception of a gull-winged sports car, modeled along the lines of the XP833; Collins had the engineering talent and persistence to convert John's concept into a workable prototype.

In November, Bill and John went to Turin, Italy, with a new member of the team, Raymond Prussing, a former GM executive with extensive friendships overseas. At the Turin auto show they met thirty-six-year-old Giorgetto Giugiaro, whose company, Ital Design, had already designed many of Europe's famous cars, including the Lotus Esprit, the Fiat 850 Spider, the VW Dasher, Rabbit and Scirocco, and Maserati's Bora and Merak. (Giugiaro's newly designed shape for pasta is currently the rage in Italy's kitchens. The design, which permits the sauce to be retained inside the pasta, is derived from an automotive door-seal gasket.)

"Giugiaro was the man we wanted," Collins told me. Bill traveled to Turin every three weeks to coordinate the design and the engineering. By the fall of 1975 he had the first working model. The XP833/ DSV had become, in Collins' hand, the DMC-12, the new code name created to conform with the name of the recently formed DeLorean Motor Company.

The DMC-12 was also designed to incorporate a revolutionary new process to reduce weight and increase mileage, Elastic Reservoir Molding. The ERM process, which produces a material that "is stronger than steel and lighter than aluminum," was a major selling point in financing the company. It was McLean who first brought it to DeLorean's attention. He had heard of the process while he was a safety expert at GM's styling center. Until the advent of these new materials, the lightweight fiberglass used in some cars fragmented in accidents. To compensate for its use, a heavier and stronger chassis was required, increasing weight and reducing fuel efficiency. John realized that ERM would be in the forefront of the next generation of materials, and quickly obtained the rights to ERM patents from the Dow Chemical Company and the Shell Oil Company. He later transferred the patents to the Composite Technology Corporation, a wholly owned subsidiary of the John Z. DeLorean Corporation.*

For reasons that were never clearly explained, Allstate dropped out of the DeLorean project. They never received their prototypes for testing. They continued to maintain that their relationship with DeLorean was harmonious, however. One DMC executive told me that John complained to Allstate that his air-bag study had cost him $600,000 in deferred compensation from GM and that giving John the project was a way for Allstate "to pay him back" for that loss.

With the engineers at work turning John's raw ideas into an ethical sports car, John was putting his reputation to work raising the money to build it. He estimated it would cost $77 million to bring the DMC-12 to market; later that estimate jumped to $90 million, then to $160 million, and finally to $250 million. Outside automotive experts estimated it would take $340 million to start a company like John's, and they were about right: when the now bankrupt DeLorean Motor

---

*When DMC declared Chapter 11 (the first stage of bankruptcy) in late 1982, W. R. Grace acquired the Composite Technology Corporation. John was correct about the next generation of lightweight materials. They are now being used in Detroit, and also to build lightweight jet airplanes. Their Defense Department applications are potentially worth hundreds of millions of dollars in contracts. CTC executives once complained to me that John had lost interest in their R and D work.

Company's outstanding debt is added to the $250 million John raised, the total approximates the experts' estimate.

To raise the money, DeLorean decided to downplay his financial acumen and become a simple engineer.

"As an operating engineer at GM," he would say, "all I knew about financing was that if you needed $500 million to build a foundry somewhere, you'd fill out a form and send it off, and four months later it would come back with a hundred signatures, saying 'go ahead and spend $500 million.' Of course, that's not the way it works when you're a skinny little engineer trying to finance a car."

John was right about the challenge of building a new car company. No one had suceeded since Walter P. Chrysler in 1923. Kaiser/Frazer failed (losing $100 million); Tucker failed; Studebaker and Packard were gone. The Bricklin, a gull-winged car built in a Canadian pocket of poverty and launched with great fanfare, had failed the year before. America had not recovered from the shock of the first oil embargo, and the major automobile companies were rethinking their ideas.

The man who made the difference for John was Tom Kimmerly, a shrewd, careful lawyer. The two met when John rented space at One Hundred West Long Road, a two-story building in Bloomfield Hills. Tom was his landlord. In the years that followed at DeLorean Motors, he guided John through incredibly complicated financial dealings.

Tom was in his early sixties when he met John. He had moved his three-man law firm from downtown Detroit to Bloomfield Hills in anticipation of retirement. A CPA as well as an attorney, Tom had worked closely with the automobile industry and was tax counsel to some of its top executives. His specialty was corporate law, trusts, estates and taxes. He had subleased part of his floor to John, and when John's tax attorney died, Tom took over his work.

Tom was as unassuming as John was flamboyant. He was shy socially. He wore glasses and dressed in clothes off the rack. Even when Tom was talking at the top of his voice, he was unobtrusive. Tom had a narrowly focused mind. He knew the tax shelters where rich men liked to hide their money and he knew how to structure low-risk deals where slightly taxed profits flowed to the investors and the losses to the government. Tom created for John the tangled corporate structure within which he operated.

Tom's first financial plan established the standard and style for what was to follow. In order to raise $3.5 million from thirty-four investors, Tom created the DeLorean Sports Car Partnership (DSCP). It was a classic research and development tax shelter from which investors could almost immediately reap a tax advantage at several multiples of their investment. American tax law is full of such opportunities. What was unusual, however, was Tom's use of the shelter to launch a car company. The investment money was needed for research and development, and the expenditure under the tax laws created enormous tax losses.

On December 31, 1975 — the last day on which the 1975 tax benefit was available — John assigned the design rights of the car (developed with Allstate and Grace monies) to the partnership. In the new arrangement, the partners would own 50 percent of the DSCP. John's new company, the DeLorean Motor Company (which had replaced the John Z. DeLorean Corporation) would own 49.9 percent, with .1 percent going to a DeLorean executive. For his share, according to a 1979 *Automotive News* report, repeated in 1981, John's "only investment documented by public records, was $20,000." This figure was reported by Ed Lapham of *Automotive News*, who said he could never find a trace of any other investment. When, later, reporters asked me to trace John's investment, I asked him for details, but I found it difficult to get him to answer me directly. Finally, he told me it was $4 million, and that this figure was based on the money he would have earned at GM if he had not quit. I was puzzled by his answer and advised him not to use this estimate again. He did not; he simply created even higher ones. In the fall of 1981 he told the British press he had invested $25 million; meanwhile, in New York, Cristina said he had invested $4 million. The media accepted these contradictory statements almost without question.

John was afraid of losing control of the company to outside investors, but Tom showed him how to raise the money without losing that control. The 50 percent share owned by the thirty-five DSCP investors could be converted by John into nonvoting preferred stock in DMC, a company of which John had complete control through the John Z. DeLorean Corporation. Eventually John raised almost $250 million for DMC; he continued to control over 80 percent of the voting stock.

With his first money raised, John turned his attention to creating a network of dealers to sell his car. For this task, he hired C. R. (Dick) Brown, who had built Mazda USA into a company with dealerships throughout the country. Almost from the first day, John and Dick's egos and business philosophies clashed. Like John, Dick was a product of Detroit, a graduate of the Chrysler Institute. But Dick had preferred marketing and entrepreneurship to moving slowly up the corporate ladder. When he met John, he was already a rich man. Brown, a straight-arrow conservative, disliked what he considered to be John's grandiose pretensions. He resented John's taste for publicity and his willingness to claim credit for what others had accomplished. At first it was merely a clash of personalities; later it came to involve the very integrity of the company. Dick was committed to the concept of an ethical company building a new car, but not necessarily committed to John, a distinction John could not understand. "It's my name on the door," John argued. "But that's not where the money came from," Dick answered.

It was Dick who first suggested that our dealers should also become investors in the company, a revolutionary concept of financing and franchising. Under Dick's plan, the dealers would get a franchise in return for investing $25,000 in the company and agreeing to purchase between 50 and 150 cars in the first two years of production. With 400 dealers, we would have orders for more than 20,000 cars a year. Since 10,000 cars a year was our break-even estimate (we later learned that our break-even point would be 6,000 cars), dealership orders would make the company extraordinarily attractive to investors. As is standard in the industry, dealers were also required to provide a letter of credit (a "flooring plan") to finance an inventory of cars.

Everyone realized that in a pinch the dealers could not be held to the prepurchase plan — there were too many contingencies that would allow them an out. But at the very least it was a vivid demonstration of dealer commitment.

John accepted the idea immediately. With dealers as investors, sales ought to be higher, and an adversarial relationship between the company and the dealers would be eliminated. And with an estimated $4,000 profit per car, the dealers would recover their investment with the sale of the first six or seven cars sold. They had little to lose.

The prototype was an attractive car, low and sleek, a "gentleman's sports car." Better yet, it had a story, the DeLoran story of an attempt to build a durable, safe, ethical car that was "conservative of resources" and offered quality and the latest technology. The DMC-12 was designed both for people who drove racy Corvettes and those who rode in status-symbol Cadillacs.

To raise money from dealers, the company was required to submit its plans to the Securities and Exchange Commission, which carefully regulated what John and his team could say about the car. To avoid violating the stipulations, Jerry Williamson, a brilliant California public relations and sales executive, created an inexpensive twelve-minute film that showed the DeLorean car moving across the landscape to a background of music. The car began its journey in the suburbs, the colors of dawn reflecting in the stainless steel, climbed into the steep mountains, sped across the desert, cruised along the ocean, and in the colors of twilight, slid back into the city. It was a spectacular and effective film. It told dealers what they needed to know and satisfied the SEC because nothing was claimed for the car.

The car was demonstrated to dealers by a kind of traveling road show. DeLorean, Brown and Williamson would arrive in a town to meet the local dealers in a hotel conference room. Brown would give the SEC-regulated pitch and introduce John, who would say a few words. Williamson would dim the lights and show the film. As the lights came on again, Brown would dramatically unveil the DMC-12 prototype, which had remained covered during the film and the pitch. The dealers would get the feel of the car, ask questions, and then the meeting would be over. Williamson would load the car and the presentation equipment into a truck and move to the next stop, sometimes 700 miles away. Brown and DeLorean would meanwhile return to the hotel room and, using the Yellow Pages, call car dealers farther down the itinerary. This method was effective: one out of three dealers who were called came to the meetings, and 5 percent of those who came signed up, some right on the spot (despite warnings, required by the SEC, that this was, to say the least, a high-risk venture).

Earlier, in conversations with the SEC, Brown had said he would need 150 dealerships to make the company viable, and the SEC gave him four months to prove it; unless all 150 dealers were signed by then, the underwriting would be canceled and John would have to begin all over again. With eight weeks to go, Brown had signed 112 dealers. Although Brown insisted that he would meet his target, John was skeptical, then uneasy, and finally, frightened. And when John was frightened, he turned to his friend Roy Nesseth.

Nesseth, I later learned, was a former used-car salesman who had once been convicted of forgery and grand theft in California. He liked to cultivate the appearance of a small-town farmer, pulling down on his lapels with his thumbs and chewing grass while carefully formulating his words. When he was crossed, however, Roy's six-foot-six frame would shake, his face would change color, he would raise his voice until it could be heard throughout an office, and then, for emphasis, he would smash something.

Roy recruited a team of used-car salesmen and created a "boiler room," where high-pressured phone calls were made to Brown's leads. "If you don't sign up today," the pitch would run, "you won't be able to get into this deal." This would be followed by a string of promises and claims that were in fact prohibited by the SEC. A $1,500 commission was paid to the salesmen for each completed sale. Brown claimed that not only were the boiler-room operation and the sales pitch illegal, but only registered brokers could earn a commission. "We've got to get the job done," John told Brown. "And Roy is the man to do it. You can't cut the mustard." Brown almost quit over this incident. "I had sold my friends as well as John's on the company," he later told me. "It was my reputation as well as his that was on the line. And I thought maybe John had panicked. He didn't have the structure of GM to protect him. He was on his own."

In the years that followed, John used Nesseth to intimidate and humiliate Brown. "If we left it to Brown," John told me, "we would have failed. He couldn't get the job done. Roy could." John regularly threatened to replace Brown with Nesseth, and he purposely heightened the tension between the two men. The technique was not new to me. I had seen politicians and editors manipulate the ambitions of people around them, causing what some would justify as "creative tension." I have always found the process distasteful and destructive.

Roy's team signed 46 more dealers. When underwriting was closed, 158 dealers had paid almost $4 million for the right to market the non-existent DMC-12. DeLorean had doubled his working capital.

John raised another $1 million from two private investors, entertainer Johnny Carson and Canadian banker Edmund

King. Carson, John's California neighbor, selected the "bombastic" Henry Buskin (as Carson describes him on television) to join the DMC board of directors, enhancing the company's credibility and adding to the glamour of the operation. Buskin was Carson's attorney and financial adviser. King, the managing partner of Wood Gundy S.A., a Swiss-owned Canadian investment bank, had previously invested in the failed gull-winged Bricklin. He also became a director.

Five million dollars was a far cry from the hundred million plus that John would need. But shortly afterward Alfred Bloomingdale offered John a shortcut to finance his company and to make an immediate multi-million-dollar profit. Bloomingdale, who had founded Diners Club, now held stock options in the ailing American Motors Corporation. The AMC chairman was retiring, and the company was looking for a new president. Bloomingdale's Wall Street partners agreed with him that John would be the perfect choice. His name alone would send the stock soaring. Bloomingdale and Wall Street could exercise their options, make a multi-million-dollar profit, and give American Motors the shot in the arm it needed. John was interested. They agreed to finance the sports car, make him AMC's president, underwrite the new company's growth and give John enough stock options to make him an instant multi-millionaire.

While John agreed to this arrangement, he quietly developed a scheme that would give him the upper hand in last-minute negotiations. It was a technique he used time and again at DMC. John told reporters he was "seriously interested" in joining AMC. He knew that would please Bloomingdale and the partners because it would increase the price of AMC stock. John knew also that if, at the last minute, he decided not to join AMC, the reporters would return to him for a reason why. What he said then could determine the value of the stock already held by Bloomingdale and the others. On the day the agreement was to be formalized, John called one of the Wall Street partners and demanded a larger share of the spoils. But this time John had miscalculated. They refused. When John tried to back down, they wouldn't listen. They considered the deal off. They were privately delighted that DeLorean had shown his stripes before they committed themselves. John had not only lost a chance for a multi-million-dollar windfall profit, but alienated Wall Street investors who would have financed the DMC-12 as an American Motors project. When John's "flirtation" with AMC became public, John told me he hadn't wanted to join a company on the verge of bankruptcy. It sounded credible enough then. But it would be years before I learned the true story.*

John had to move fast now. He had his prototype, but in the automobile business styles change with the seasons. He had to go after the big money.

In late 1976 John called me in New York to ask about the possibility of building his factory in Puerto Rico. By then, I was conducting my investigations for the New York State Assembly. John knew I had served as the campaign consultant to the former governor of Puerto Rico in a come-from-behind election, and that my company had worked closely with the Chamber of Commerce and the Puerto Rican Manufacturers Association.

I was enthusiatic about John's plan. I knew from the surveys my company had conducted for the Commonwealth that the productivity of Puerto Rican factories was sometimes higher than that of sister plants in the States, a fact overlooked by businessmen who had an image of Puerto Rico as a sleepy "manana" island. Puerto Rico also offered a seventeen-year exemption from federal taxes and provided generous grants and low-cost loans.

John wanted a written report, which I prepared within a week; my conclusion was that Puerto Rico was made to order for-his plans. Both major political parties there recognized

---

*Reporter Hillel Levin tracked down the Bloomingdale incident and reported on it in *Grand Delusions*, his book about John.

that their best hope for the future as to link social progress and business profits. John wanted me to open doors for him, particularly with the banks. A friend of mine ran the largest bank on the island. I went to Puerto Rico on vacation and used the opportunity to tell everyone I knew that John was a man they could trust; he had the experience and talent to make his dream work.

John asked me to come to work with him again as a consultant, but I told him my work with the state prevented this. I suggested we talk again when my investigations were completed. Whenever we chatted afterward on the phone, John would say the Puerto Rican deal was "still in the works." It was not until several years later that I pieced together the true story.

John's negotiations with Puerto Rico began in March 1977, but the final verbal agreement was not reached until the week of July 28, 1978. Fifty lawyers gathered in the law offices of Stroock & Stroock & Lavan in New York to complete the details of the agreements John and the Puerto Rican government were about to sign. At the head of the table was John's representative, Bob Dewey, one of the founders of DMC and then its chief financial officer. Like Collins and McLean, Dewey had left a secure job at General Motors to join John because the new job offered challenge and excitement, an opportunity to do what few others in the automobile industry had done before. At Chevrolet, Bob was a highly respected "numbers man" and a "skinflint" — exactly what John needed alongside him in business. John could create the grand design, but he needed men like Collins and Dewey to work out the details.

As far as the Puerto Ricans in the room were concerned, they had a final deal; all that remained was routine paperwork. The United States Department of Commerce and the Farmers Home Loan Administration had agreed to guarantee $40 million of private loans to DeLorean, and Puerto Rico had agreed to another $20 million in grants and loans. The plant would be located at the former Ramay Air Force Base at Aquidilla in northwest Puerto Rico, a hundred miles from San Juan. Its buildings could be converted into a factory, and its runways made an excellent test track. John was to raise $25 million through a research and development tax shelter developed by Oppenheimer and Company, the investment bankers. The investors would share in the large estimated tax losses, but would have very little control of the company. Under the Puerto Rico arrangement, John was to spend the $25 million before the other loans and grants were released. It was Puerto Rico's way of insuring that John would remain committed to the program.

The agreements were ready to be signed, but John had not appeared, and the attorneys were asking where he was. In fact, after the negotiations had begun, John had called Dewey and told him, "Stall them as long as you can." Dewey had done so, but now time was running out.

What the Puerto Ricans did not know was that John was also secretly negotiating with the British to build his factory in Belfast, Northern Ireland. Walter Strycker, a West Coast businessman and a DeLorean consultant, and Alan Cohen, a lawyer with Paul, Weiss, Rifkind, Wharton & Garrison in New York, were nearing final agreement in Belfast. That arrangement would provide John twice as much money as the deal Dewey was about to conclude. The Puerto Ricans and the U.S. government were unsuspecting, believing they had a commitment from John not to shop around for another site until these negotiations were over.

Earlier, John had also secretly negotiated with the Republic of Ireland for a plant in Limerick. When it came time to sign that agreement, John changed the deal and asked for more money and previously denied concessions. He was confident his last-minute tactic would be successful. Limerick was in the constituency of the Minister for Industry, Desmond O'Malley. It wasn't the minister's money, so why would he refuse to go along with a deal that would bring jobs to his district? It didn't work out that way, however. Confused by these sudden demands, the negotiators consulted the minister, who ordered that negotiations cease immediately. On June 14, 1978, the Irish formally withdrew their offer. Like Bloomingdale, the Irish didn't want to do business with John. O'Malley's decision haunted his government for a while later on, when De-Lorean seemed headed toward success across the border.

John later told the press he had rejected the Irish proposal. The facility the Irish had offered was antiquated, he said, and the manager of the last company to use it had been shot by terrorists. Hearing of the aborted transaction, the Puerto Rican government had demanded John discontinue looking for a new site. He ostensibly had agreed.

But John had no intention of giving up his search for a better deal, if for no other reason than to use the threat of ending negotiations to pressure Puerto Rico into providing more money for his company. It was John's way of doing business.

On June 8, 1978, when the DeLorean team knew that the Irish government would reject their offer, someone suggested a last-minute phone call to the Northern Ireland Development Agency in Belfast, which was desperately seeking investment for the British-ruled six counties of Northern Ireland. The call brought an instant response. Yes, the British were very interested. A high-visibility factory in Belfast was just what they needed to advertise the fact that Belfast was a safe location for international investment and that the British were prepared to be generous in providing grants and low-interest loans. John knew he had the British hooked. They had shown their hand, and he could use this to his advantage. He told the British that they must move quickly, for he was about to sign an agreement with Puerto Rico. And he also mentioned the offer from Dublin. When the Irish formally withdrew, John did not inform the British of this.

For the British government, the timing was perfect. The U.K. was growing weary of the never-ending sectarian violence, which had now spread from Northern Ireland to mainland Britain. Terrorist bombs were exploding in London restaurants, and British diplomats on the Continent were being assassinated. Over 12,000 British troops were stationed in Northern Ireland to maintain order. Roy Mason, the Labour Party's Secretary of State for Northern Ireland, was taken with both DeLorean and the idea of a car plant in Belfast. Mason was enforcing a hard-line policy against the Irish Republican Army, winning the praise of the opposition Conservative Party. But the fight against the IRA seemed hopeless in the face of staggering Catholic unemployment in Belfast. Many unemployed Catholics had moved from downtown Belfast to Dunmurry in West Belfast, an IRA stronghold and a fertile ground for new recruits. Several thousand jobs might all but end the chronic unemployment there. They might also help to stifle arguments that when new companies came to Belfast they were located in the less violent Protestant neighborhoods. A GM seat belt factory, which had recently been located in the Protestant eastern section of the city, was a current political irritation. Catholics would seldom cross town to apply for jobs in Protestant areas. Belfast, in the working-class neighborhoods, is a segregated city, with Catholics frightened to traverse Protestant controlled areas and vice versa.

Mason wanted the DeLorean factory at almost any cost. John understood that need and constantly raised his ante, until eventually Mason's deputies balked. They adjourned the negotiations and sought out Mason, who was hosting an official dinner at his residence. In a hurried conversation in his library, Mason gave in to John. It was to prove a fatal mistake.

"We fought long and hard for the establishment of new industry in Northern Ireland," Mason later wrote.* "At the

---

*Mason was a hard-liner on the IRA, but frequently articulated his belief that improving the quality of life and providing employment for Northern Ireland's Catholic minority was the only solution to terrorism. This statement was published as a defense of the loans to DeLorean when the British auditors were considering moving the company into bankruptcy. It accurately reflects the bias of those who saw DeLorean's project as a major step in forging a new British policy in the North. I agreed with Mason.

time the DeLorean project was launched, social conditions in the province were awful. Housing was disgraceful, and in West Belfast, the Bogside and Londonderry unemployment was appalling . . . As Secretary of State I decided that the remedying of these ills was a priority . . . One had to recognize that when talking about money, orthodox Treasury economies never recognizes the part it might play in undermining the terrorists' recruiting drive by providing jobs. Politically, we must win in Northern Ireland, and if another 4,000 jobs are provided, with a spillover of many hundreds more in other plants, the young Catholics *will* look towards the Government as the real authority that has given them hope for a decent standard of living and a future."

Mason's decision coincided with the arrival of the Puerto Rico team in New York. But John could not afford to lost the Puerto Rico deal — yet. He had to keep the negotiations going until he had actually signed with the British.

Back in New York, Dewey called John at his suite at the Waldorf to warn him that he could not stall the lawyers much longer. "Disappear," John told him. "We're close to signing in Belfast. Just go to your hotel room and don't answer the phone. Or take a walk around town." Dewey found the instructions distasteful, but as a corporate soldier he obeyed and disappeared while the lawyers grew increasingly restless.

On August 3, 1978, less than a week after the Puerto Ricans had arrived in New York and forty-five days after the British began their negotiations, Walter Strycker signed for DMC in Belfast. John agreed to build a state-of-the-art factory over a bog adjacent to the Twinbrook Estate, a Catholic Community in Dunmurry just across from Seymour Hills, a Protestant community. John would recruit, hire and train 2,500 workers. He would complete the factory in less than two years, insuring a quick political reward. By unwritten agreement, the work force, from foreman on down, would be half Catholic and half Protestant. In return, the British guaranteed an investment of $120 million, almost twice as much as Puerto Rico was offering. It was the deal John had dreamed of making.

That afternoon John told Dewey to call the lawyers for the

Puerto Rico government and tell them that the deal was off. "It was one of the hardest things for me to do," Dewey later told me. "We led them into believing we were serious when we were only using them to up the ante in Belfast." The espisode was so distasteful to him that he quit DeLorean. For Dewey, who had given up his career at General Motors, it wasn't an easy decision. "Where I come from," he said, "when you give your word, you give your word." Like so many others who rallied to John's crusade to build an ethical company, Dewey was a man of integrity. In the end, he was forced to conclude that John DeLorean was not.

The small print of the British deal was very favorable to DMC, resulting in an investment of almost $50,000 a job. The British would pay for John's factory, his tooling, the start-up costs and 50 percent of his labor costs for the first six months. The British company in Belfast would build the car and contribute $160,000 a month toward DeLorean Motors' stateside operations until cars began arriving for sale. This was in sharp contrast to Puerto Rico's stipulation that John spend his money first. DMC in New York would contribute $1 million, compared to the $25 million Puerto Rico had required.

A complex corporate structure was created, but from the outset John maintained complete control. In New York there was the DeLorean Motor Company. Approximately 83 percent of DMC's shares were owned by a holding company in which John controlled all the shares. In Belfast, a subsidiary, the DeLorean Motor Cars, Ltd., was created, and John had overwhelming voting control of that company as well.

Two British nominee directors sat on the DMC board in New York, but over the years they proved to be no more than rubber stamps for John's decisions, limited in large part by the less-than-truthful information provided them. The board of directors in Belfast included the key working directors of DeLorean Motor Cars, Ltd., or DMCL; the two outside British directors; and DeLorean, Brown, Strycker (when he replaced Dewey as chief financial officer) and Kimmerly. The administrative structure of both boards was controlled by Kimmerly. When I joined the company in the spring of 1979, I was the only outsider who attended and participated in board meetings in both Belfast and New York.

The British, for their $120 million investment - which later grew to over $160 million — acquired a $45 million equity in DeLorean Motor Cars, Ltd., and were to receive a $370 royalty on each of the first 90,000 cars built; thereafter, they would receive $90 per car. John could buy out the British equity at the investment cost plus interest; in effect, if the company was successful, the British would problably not share in the rewards. The monies came in outright grants, low-interest loans, loans that became grants after achieving certain performance levels, and training awards.

Key to the complex arrangements was John's authority to set the "transfer price" of the car shipped from Belfast to New York. In other words, John could determine exactly what the New York company, DMC, would pay the Belfast company, DMCL, for the car. Earlier, the Republic of Ireland, in the Limerick deal, had balked at this arrangement because it gave John the opportunity to disproportionately charge expenses to the Irish company, creating an unrealistic profit for the United States company, in which John owned 83 percent of the stock. Under the arrangement with the British government, the entire loan was a debt owed by the Belfast corporation. With large profits and no debt, the DeLorean Motor Company in New York would be an attractive company in which to invest.

The British, however, attached some strings to the deal . . . or so they thought. DMC in New York would be required to provide all the monies required for research and development of the prototype until it was ready for mass production. The company could not dilute its shares, restructure itself or raise funds without permission of the British. John could not use British monies for investment or projects that they did not approve. The company's chief financial officer was subject to British approval, and quarterly financial reports were required. And John could not sell off his personal stock until the British were repaid.

The *sine qua non,* however, was that John was to devote his *total* energies to the car company. They were, after all, buying his experience — there were few other assets. In fact, John personally promised to spend six months in Belfast when the car moved into production.

What the binding "Master Agreement" overlooked was the reality of controlling an ongoing project with high visibility in a sensitive and potentially violent entertainment. John was a master at confrontation, and as the British realized in retrospect, no agreement could control John unless they were willing to play the same game and to back up their words with actions. As it turned out, they weren't, and John knew it.

Later that August, in a symbolic ceremony in Belfast marking the signing of the agreement, British government ministers and DeLorean planted three trees, a trinity, marking the joint efforts of the Catholics, the Protestants and the British. Outside the gate, an IRA demonstration heckled the British, protesting the imprisonment of Catholics in the "H Block," a wing of Belfast's Maze Prison in Long Kesh. With civil liberties suspended and trials without juries, the H Block was filled with suspected and, in the estimation of the British, potential terrorists as well as those actually convicted of crimes. Trial by jury was not possible, the British said, because no matter who served on the juries, the retaliation of the IRA would be swift and sure. The men in H Block were romanticized as the "boys on the blanket." They refused to wear anything but a blanket, and rubbed the walls with their excrement. They pledged to remain unclothed until the British gave in to their demands. As "prisoners of war, not criminals," they demanded the right to wear their own clothes and to manage their own affairs inside the compound. Their protests climaxed with the hunger-strike death of Bobby Sands on May 5, 1981. His wake took place less than a hundred yards from where John and the ministers had planted their trees of peace in 1978.

Cristina was at the signing with John. Her looks attracted as much comment as the ceremony itself. It was the first and last time she came to Belfast. The noisy, though peaceful, demonstration frightened her. A Catholic, she was torn between support for the militant Catholics, who claimed that the many injustices of Northern Irish life were due to the British "occupation," and her fears that the IRA would destroy the factory and would someday kill John.

After the ceremonies, John took Dick Brown aside. "Do you know anyone who can build a factory?" John asked.

Brown later told me he was stunned. John had assured the British that at least two members of his team had previously built factories for GM. Brown, who was to become the Acting Managing Director in Belfast, told me that John had told the British "it was no trouble at all" to build the plant.

"Dixon Hollinshead built my Mazda headquarters, and he might be available," Brown told John. John's luck held. Hollinshead was free, and agreed to supervise the construction of the DeLorean plant. Within two weeks he was in Belfast.

A week later, back in New York, John was faced with another critical problem. Although he had locked up $120 million, it would take time to convert the agreement into cash to run the company. Until then, he needed $250,000 for payroll and operating expenses, but, he told Brown, "we only have $150,000 in the bank." He couldn't expose that weakness to the British, who were looking for a $1 million contribution in capital from John. "It wouldn't look good," John explained.

Brown loaned DeLorean the $100,000. "You know," Brown was to recall, "he never said 'thanks.' I never understood why he didn't reach into his own pocket." Brown was slowly learning what we all later came to understand, that John was determined to build DMC on other people's money.

Brown, who had relatives in Ulster, was sent to Belfast to

recruit management for the new company. He learned that in the Twinbrook Estate — a community of row houses and sloping green lawns — half the men were unemployed and on welfare. Many fathers and their sons had never worked, and without the jobs the DeLorean plant offered, it was unlikely they ever would.

Most of Belfast's Catholics who did work were employed in unskilled jobs. The biggest employer in town, the Harland and Wolff shipyards, drew its Catholic workers from Short Strand, a walled enclave of Catholics in Protestant East Belfast. Even when its employees numbered 20,000, there was not a single Catholic foreman.

When Hollinshead began construction, there were cows grazing on the seventy-two-acre bog that was to be the plant site. In the middle of the bog stood the "faerie tree." We soon learned that superstition is a powerful force in Belfast, where fact and fancy tend to merge. It was just a scraggly bush, but to the trained eye it had mystical qualities. According to the legend, if a person cut down a faerie tree, he would soon lose a limb in retaliation. No workman at DeLorean would touch it. Bulldozers skirted it, trucks avoided it. Workmen refused direct orders to cut it down even after Hollinshead spread the word that $100 was buried under the tree. Then one morning it was gone. The workmen suspected that a frustrated Hollinshead had done the deed himself.

"It's a bad sign," the workmen agreed. "It's a dark day. You have wrecked everything we're building. The faerie tree will see to that."

While Brown was recruiting executives and Hollinshead was building the factory, John and Tom Kimmerly were busy in New York cleaning up loose ends and, I was later to learn, preparing to transfer over $17 million* of the financing for the project to a mysterious Swiss company, General Products Development (GPD).

Earlier, Tom had neatly rolled the DeLorean Sports Car

*The exact figure is in dispute. It is somewhere between $17 million and $18 million. I will refer to it henceforth as $17 million.

Partnership — the financial vehicle that John used to raise the first $3.5 million for the company — into the DeLorean Motor Company. In return, the original investors received preferred stock in DMC. As part of the deal, the investors also transferred the rights to the car, which they owned, to DMC. John had owned only 50 percent of DSCP. He now owned 87 percent of DMC. The DSCP stockholders had no complaints, however. The tax laws are such that they had recovered a multiple of their original investment in tax decuctions, and they now held preferred shares in a new company that would spin off interest payments to them each year. What they did not know was that this transaction enabled John to enter into another complicated tax deal, using the rights to the sports car as bait.

As part of the Puerto Rican arrangement, John had been required to raise $25 million, which Puerto Ricans demanded he spend on the project before their grants and loans were used. John had returned to Oppenheimer and Company, the prominent New York investment bankers and stockbrokers, for help. They devised a creative tax shelter that, once again, provided investors with a mutltiple of their investment in tax deductions. Legally, the partnership was known as the DeLorean Research Limited Partnership (DRLP), but at the company we called it the OPCO Partnership, for Oppenheimer and Company.

No one with less than $500,000 in annual income could participate in OPCO. Each investor invested $150,000, but only $75,000 of it was their own money. The remaining $75,000 was borrowed for them, using their collateral, from Chemical Bank, with DMC agreeing to pay the interest charges from dividends. Under the terms of the agreement, DMC would become the "general," or managing partner, and the 130 others would become "limited" partners. The limited partners would share 99 percent of the losses, which were expected to be extensive during the first years. For some, their entire investment would be amortized during the first year. After that, all monies would be sheltered profits.

In addition to the tax advantage, the investors were to

receive a royalty of $375 per car on the first 90,000 cars produced, or 23.4 percent of DMC's gross profits, whichever was greater. The British, for six times the investment, received only a royalty of $370 per car, and had no profit-sharing option.

To guarantee the investors, John transferred the rights to the car to the partnership, which, in turn, would lease them to the Belfast company actually manufacturing the DeLorean car. These rights could only be repurchased after $36.5 million had been paid in royalties to the limited partners. The repurchase price would be $28 million before December 13, 1981, and $56 million thereafter.

Earlier, Oppenheimer had balked at moving its investment, which had been raised for Puerto Rico, to Belfast. John turned to the British to replace it, and after some negotiations, they agreed. For the British, it was a major step. John had previously been required to provide all research and development monies needed to bring the car up to production standards, and the OPCO monies were to be used for that purpose. Now the British would be paying these costs as well. When Oppenheimer reversed its decision and agreed to raise the money for research and development (for a $2 million fee), John turned down the offer from the British that he had solicited.

John's refusal to accept the British deal confused Brown and Strycker. It made no sense to give up the rights to the car, which would now be leased to Belfast, and to create a heavy debt.

"We didn't need the money," Strycker told me eighteen months later, when I began to examine the transaction. "And we certainly didn't need it at that price."

Trouble was also brewing in San Juan. Romero Barcelo, Puerto Rico's governor, was stunned by what he considered to be John's double-dealing. He publicly accused DeLorean of duplicity and bad faith and threatened to take legal action. But John wasn't fazed. He hinted to reporters that the real reason for abandoning the Puerto Rican deal was that certain unnamed officials wanted "money under the table."

A Puerto Rican banker sent me clips from the San Juan *Star* outlining the conflict. I had missed the small business-page item in the New York *Times* announcing John had decided on Belfast. I was convinced from my earlier talks with John that he would locate in Puerto Rico. When I called John at the time to find out what was happening, he told me the controversy was a "tempest in a teapot," explaining that the British had given him twice as much money as Puerto Rico was offering and that as a businessman he couldn't turn it down.

"It's also more of a challenge," he said. "If we're successful, we'll be part of history. We're going to solve the Irish problem for the British."

When I asked him about the alleged kickbacks, he said that Dewey and others had been approached.

"John," I said, "if there is one place I know, it's Puerto Rico. There are problems there, but government corruption is not one of them. Would you mind if I talked to Dewey?"

"Dewey is out of the company," John said. "He's had a nervous breakdown and he's back in Detroit." (I later learned that this was totally untrue.)

A few days later I received a copy of the letter John had written to the governor of Puerto Rico. Like the GM memo it began softly, then picked up steam.

"I think you should also be aware," John wrote, "of a number of special requests that arose that troubled me as an American business man and which certainly encouraged me to consider alternative locations. Since DeLorean Motor Company is my whole life, I will admit to being frightened by the request for fees that at a minimun approached the 'sensitive payments' area that is so carefully scrutinized now in the United States."

John cited three examples and concluded: "I have called these most significant instances to your attention, since I assume you may not be aware of them. Believe me, they are troubling to an American businessman."

The message was clear. John, the man who quit General Motors on principal, would make his integrity the issue. Barcelo wrote John a letter (which I did not see until two years later) in which he angrily denied the charges; but he let the matter drop. John's tactics had succeeded.

When I called John to talk about the letter to Barcelo, he changed the subject. "We've got our financing," John said, "and we're going to start building the factory in Belfast. When are you going to come to work for us?"

I hadn't lost my interest in working with him, so I kept the door open. "When I finish up my investigations," I replied.

"Don't miss the bandwagon," John said.

Chapter Four

Beginnings

In 1978 I left New York State to accept an offer from publisher Rupert Murdoch to become an investigative editor and columnist for the New York *Post*. Newspapering is in my blood, and as exciting as John's venture seemed, I was not sure I wanted to trade a newsman's independence for the constraints of a businessman's life.

DeLorean and Murdoch, a conservative Australian businessman who was expanding his newspaper empire to the United States and the United Kingdom, lived in the same luxurious Fifth Avenue building overlooking Central Park. (John's apartment was valued at $4-$5 million in 1983.) I introduced the two men, explaining to Murdoch that coming to work with him instead of DeLorean was a close decision. Six months later, when my columns were proving a little too liberal for the *Post*, I told Murdoch I would like to join John's company.

"Can I influence you to change your mind?" he asked.

"No," I said. "This is not a negotiating posture. If I want to join John, this is the moment to do it. He's financed and ready to start operations."

John had already raised almost $150 million from the British, the Oppenheimer partnership and private investments. Now, in his tastefully decorated penthouse office atop the Bankers Trust Building at Forty-ninth Street and Park Avenue, he explained, that DMC had other hurdles to jump.

"We need to find engineers who will work in Belfast, we need to build a factory in half the time it takes to build a factory in Detroit, and we need to train a work force."

"Is that all?" I asked.

"No, we have to reengineer the car, purchase seven thousand components, contract for the tooling, and sell cars before we run out of money."

It was John at his best. Problems became challenges. He called them opportunities.

"What do you want me to do?"

"Planning. Corporate development. Work with me."

"Okay," I answered, and John said, "Make up a title."

I became vice president for planning.

My contract with DMC generously provided for salary increases, perks, bonuses and stock options. My share of DMC options was worth, if we were successful, over $1 million. I felt very secure with the arrangements. I was facing a new challenge with idealistic goals, and if we were successful, I would have all the income I needed for the rest of my life.

My first action was to terminate the contract with DMC's public relations agency, Rogers and Cowan. They were paid a $10,000-a-month retainer. It was a difficult decision for John to accept.

"It's wasted money," I explained. "If we need press, I'll handle it."

John looked at me for a moment before answering. "It's your show," he said. "You do what you think is right." I was impressed.

I became the company spokesperson, and "communications" was added to my title.

It wasn't long before I learned that there were tensions

beneath the excitement of working for DMC. On my first trip to Belfast in the spring of 1979, Dick Brown pulled me aside at the Ritz Hotel in London, where we were spending the night.

"You know," he said. "I was against your coming with the company."

Before I could react, he continued.

"You're not an automobile executive. You don't know the business, and you'll keep John in the papers."

"What's wrong with that?"

"We must build the car before we talk about it. We need people to control John, not encourage him."

Then Brown went on to talk about the dark side of DeLorean.

"John doesn't understand we are a public company, and he can't spend corporate money as if it were his own. We're not General Motors. He can't push a button and have an army of people move. And he's more interested in making new deals than getting the car built."

"That's a strong indictment. If it's true, what are you doing here?"

"I helped put this together," Dick explained. "All my friends are involved."

I suspected there was more to the story than Dick was willing to tell, but I held back. It wasn't the time. There were only half a dozen executives running the company and Dick and I would have to work closely.

"Now that you're aboard — part of the team — I'll help you any way I can," he said, holding out his hand. I took it. I had no choice.

As time went on, Brown and I were frequently at odds over policy and turf, but he was true to his word. He helped me to learn about the automobile business, and by the time I left the company I realized that Brown had been a lot wiser about John than most of us.

Getting to Belfast gave me my first taste of what it would be like living under strict military scrutiny. At London airport we emptied our pockets into a plastic bag, which, with our hand luggage, was taken from us. We were allowed a paper or a magazine, nothing more. We passed through a metal detector and were then hand-searched.

Some British journalists have written that the IRA was never interested in us. But as the person responsible for DMC security in Belfast and New York, I knew that the British security forces didn't share that view. We were a highly visible project that the British were using as an example of how economic growth and jobs could help turn the tide against the IRA. As such, we were closely monitored by the IRA. British security forces instructed us to book one hotel and stay at another in both London and Belfast; to make several plane reservations; and not to develop predictable routines.

As a journalist, I had written about terrorism around the world and had some understanding (and a CIA briefing) on how the IRA operated and where it got its arms and money. It was only after the British returned to Northern Ireland in force in 1969 that the IRA was revived. By then the IRA had dwindled to a few men and a dozen hidden rifles. In 1970 the IRA was a movement led by hardened Marxist revolutionaries who not only wanted the unification of the six Protestant counties of the North with the Catholic South, but dreamed of a "people's republic." Next to the United States, Libya was their major source of arms and money. Revolutionaries were trained in PLO camps and had links to the violent underground movements in Japan, Germany and Italy. Despite all this, however, for many militant Catholics angered over centuries of discrimination, the IRA was the only hope of obtaining the religious independence they had lost eight hundred years earlier.

By the time we arrived in Belfast, the center city was a walled fortress; entry was on foot after a body-search. But at least the downtown bombings had stopped. Although Twinbrook, at our rear gate, was regarded as an IRA stronghold and was monitored by armed British helicopters, violence seldom interfered with our operations or directly touched our lives. During my time at DeLorean, aside from the hunger strike riots in 1981, there was only one shoot-out with security forces in Twinbrook. In my West Side Manhattan neighborhood there are more shoot-outs in a week than in all of Belfast in a month.

John never conquered his fear of Belfast. He never stayed overnight in the city, preferring to catch the 8 A.M. shuttle up from London and return the same day. I tried to convince him that if we ever got on the IRA hit list, it was doubtful that these precautions would stop them. The trick was to make sure the IRA understood that killing a prominent American could dry up their access to U.S. money and arms. That, and living up to our promises to the unemployed Catholics in Twinbrook, was our best protection.

Personally, I came to love Belfast. I miss it now. I looked forward to my trips there every two or three weeks. There was genuine excitement at the plant. The executives and engineers became close friends of mine and used me as an intermediary with John. I knew almost all of our foremen and many of the early workers. I was often invited for "a homecooked meal."

I came to understand that most people in Belfast were war weary. They avoided politics, trying to live out their lives between the two extremes, praying that peace would descend on them. Those who could do so left for America or Australia to join other generations of Irishmen, Catholic and Protestant, who had sought saner places in which to raise their families.

Dick Brown, who had roots in the North, brought his family to live in Belfast while he recruited the management team. Chrysler was closing down its European operations, and many of our first recruits came from Chrysler. By mid-1979, Brown's task was completed. The auditors the British had hired to monitor our operations paid us the finest compliment. They said the DeLorean men reminded them of the RAF in 1940: a combination of talent, black humor and suicidal determination.

The city of Belfast monitored our progress closely from the day Hollinshead began work on the seventy-two acres of swamp. As the buildings began to take form, people stood in line to be interviewed for jobs. The people of Belfast knew when the first Catholic foreman was selected to supervise Protestant workers.

The plant was completed in eighteen months — less than half the time it would have taken in the United States. We had used Belfast construction firms, and the achievement became a matter of local pride. It was a factory of the future. There were no pits under the production line — everyone worked at eye level. There were no paint sheds to fill workers' lungs with poisons. Robots silently moved the car from station to station. On the line, each worker had several responsibilities, and decisions were often made collectively at the working stations. The assembly plant was as neat as an IBM computer installation.

Most significant of the spirit then was the fact that sectarianism stopped at the factory gate. When John said, "I'm starting to recognize that God stuck me here to be part of the solution to the crisis in Northern Ireland," no one laughed. John was changing people's lives.

In New York, John and I settled into a daily routine. I arrived before eight in the morning, put on the coffee, and then disappeared into my office to clean up the paperwork and read the papers before the phone began to ring. John would arrive around eight, stop by for his coffee, walk across the marble floor to my office and drop into the chair alongside my desk. For half an hour we would talk about everything from politics to personnel.

John said he had a dream about the company. He wanted to build on the success of the sports car and turn DeLorean Motors into a multibillion-dollar conglomerate involved in everything from energy to communications. And he wanted to use government and tax shelter money to do it. He summed up his thoughts in a memo dated June 19, 1979, to Gene Cafiero (the former vice chairman of Chrysler who had just come aboard as our new president), Strycker (who had replaced Dewey as our chief financial officer), Kimmerly, Brown and me. I remember calling the memo "And Tomorrow the World."

At the heart of the congolmerate, John wrote, would be a car company, modeled after BMW, with gross annual sales of $2.5 to $3 billion. Under that umbrella we would market a complete line of automobiles designed and built to our specifications. We would then add lower-priced cars from Japan and Korea as well as trucks and farm equipment. These distribution activities would add another $3 to $5 billion to our sales ... "if proper financial arrangements can be made." John defined these as requiring "no direct DMC investment ... in each instance the government of the host country ... would be expected to provide the bulk of our financing."

Next we would make acquistions in related industries and enter the energy market by building power plants on Indian reservations where there were coal reserves, and transmitting the electricity produced there to the national grid.

In addition to using someone else's money, John's plan called for minimizing "the management required by leaving most of the manufacturing to others."

It was an exciting formula; but John's corporate strategy memos unnerved his executives; they represented exactly what Dick Brown had feared. We faced major problems just getting the DMC-12 launched, and then planning for a second car, a four-door sedan. I reacted to most of John's memos with equanimity, but, unlike some of the others, I was not frightened by his dreams. What he talked about seemed possible.

One such idea, an idea that fired my own imagination and led to a great deal of initiative and work on my part, was to design and build an advanced new bus. General Motors and Grumman Flxible, the nations's two bus manufacturers, had not responded to the challenge of building a new generation of buses, and an opportunity was clearly there. John asked me to develop the idea, and over the next several months I took the project almost to the stage of contracting to build a factory in a depressed part of Miami. Ultimately, however, John would not commit to the project. The bus was just another business deal, the professed social commitment a means to an end. It was after the failure of this project that I too began to have doubts about John's real motives and intentions.

Chapter Five

"Getting A Little Shit On His Shoes"

John had negotiated his contract with the Labor government, but in May 1979 Margaret Thatcher's Conservative Party took power. One of my many assignments was to open up political communication with the new government. I knew several Members of Parliament from previous family and political associations, and had access to others through them. Some friends in the media also opened up doors for me with the new government. I did not share John's concern that Thatcher would change our contract. We had one important thing in our favor, which was that British politicians tended to regard Northern Ireland as the exception to all the rules. And we were in Belfast to reduce Catholic unemployment, the highest in the United Kingdom.

Although it was British money that had put John in business, he never trusted them as a partner. When I tried to explain that it was not easy for the British to justify our program, he was outraged. "We're solving their number-one problem," he said.

A Conservative sub-Cabinet committee came to Belfast to

review our project, and while I knew they were impressed, they were noncommittal. Theirs would be not a business decision but a political one. A few months later the government announced its continued support of the DeLorean project, noting that it was legally bound by the contract. When we were criticized in Parliament — often by Conservative backbenchers — it was the Thatcher government that rose to our defense, basing its arguments in large measure on the reports of civil servants in Belfast.

One MP, Jock Bruce-Gardyne, wouldn't let up, however. He denounced John as a fraud and a spendthrift and the project as a colossal boondoggle. Although he was a backbencher, and not a Cabinet member, he was a personal friend of the Prime Minister, was often present at her dinner table, and wrote some of her speeches. He was also an influential columnist for the Sunday *Telegraph*, one of England's leading newspapers.

I didn't know it then, but Bruce-Gardyne would play a major role in the DeLorean affair. In those early days I regarded him as "the enemy," but later, when my own outlook had changed, I would look to him as the one person in government who really saw through John and understood what he was trying to do.

Two events occurred at the end of 1979 that, had I been more suspicious, should have alerted me to the possibility that I had seen only one of John's several personalities. One incident involved Walter Strycker; the other involved the publication of John's explosive best seller, *On A Clear Day You Can See General Motors.*

Walt Strycker was tall, soft-spoken, understated and sophisticated. He effectively presented our case to bankers and potential investors, where looks and manner, I am convinced, are 50 percent of the game. He was also the buffer between John and British civil servants who, while admiring John's entrepreneurial qualities, were worried from the outset about press accounts of his personal lifestyle and his apparent disregard for orderly procedures. His image as a jet-set play-boy provided hostile Members of Parliament with constant ammunition, which they used in questions to the Prime Minister. Was John's extravagant taste (buying expensive homes and fine art, traveling on the Concorde, and staying in the world's finest hotels) being financed by British taxpayers' money? Jock Bruce-Gardyne was often joined in his attacks by Robert Cryer, a Labour MP. They were cheered from both sides of Parliament, and the government's responses were often received with derisive jeers.

John knew that Dewey's sudden resignation would raise questions unless the job of chief financial officer was filled quickly. Only one person could do it — Walt Strycker, who had worked with the British in shaping the Master Agreement. Walt lived in the San Francisco Bay area and had no intention of moving anywhere else. He had been a successful business executive who now consulted and also managed his own investments. John said he could continue to live in San Francisco, manage his business investments and serve only until we found another CFO. Walt agreed. His contract provided for $200,000 in salary and $1 million in stock options.

In Belfast we were growing so rapidly that our financial reporting systems were overtaxed. The British civil servants, already worried about John, wanted to monitor how we spent our money. Walt and I respected their balance, between authority and nonintervention in business decisions. They walked that tightrope with judgment and courtesy.

Walt and I became good friends. His interests were broad: he was a patron of the San Francisco opera, and had quietly helped to finance black businesses. In all of our conversations, he had never revealed any hostility toward John, so it came as a surprise when one day my assistant, Ellen Kugler, closed the door to my office and handed me a confidential memo from Walt.

"Trouble?" I asked.

"Yes," she said.

Ellen had been my assistant — with the exception of my time at the New York *Post* — for eight years. She was my eyes and ears at DeLorean, and frequently she knew more about what was happening inside the company than I did.

The memo *was* trouble. It was dated December 7, 1979, and addressed to me. In the memo, Strycker formally notified me that two employees — Jonathan Mazzone and Edward Chasty — were on DMC's payroll, but were not working for us. Mazzone was supposed to be a driver and supply clerk in the New York office, but, Walt wrote, "he spends 90 percent of his time on non-DMC work," including among other things working as a personal chauffeur for Cristina. Chasty, he said, "is a personal servant of the DeLoreans as well as a driver for the family."

He reminded me that CEO's of other companies had had serious problems with the Securities and Exchange Commission for personal use of corporate staff. He also accused Maur Dubin of using the company van for himself and one of his employees. The van, Walt said, had been in an accident the night before and the driver was "a non-DMC employee."

Dubin, an interior decorator, was one of the strange characters who floated between John's personal and business lives. The first time I saw Maur he was wearing a full-length mink coat. There was a breathless, impatient air about him. He was disdainful and intolerant of many people, and dismissed them with a wave of his hand or a bitchy remark. When life became too difficult for Maur, or the pressures mounted, he would announce he was going to Florida "to mellow out." Then he would depart — often for weeks at a time — leaving behind a series of half-finished jobs. He had no official title at DeLorean, but undertook a number of special tasks for John. He was also John's "cultural adviser," helping John and Cristina furnish their homes and buy their art. It is easy to caricature and ridicule Maur, but none of us underestimated his influence on John. He could, as I was to find out, have someone fired if he had a mind to.

I asked Ellen to check with accounting to see if these men were really on the DeLorean payroll. In a few minutes she reported back. "They're not only on the DeLorean payroll," she said, "but they're charged to this office." I dictated a polite, but firm, memo to accounting. I wanted the men off my payroll. Then I called in my deputy, Dee Fensterer. Dee and I began working together when she walked into Robert Kennedy's Senate campaign headquarters and volunteered to work with us. She was a solid executive with sound judgment. I asked her to check all the expenditures charged to our office. In an hour she was back. In addition to the salaries of the two men, we were being charged $25,000 a month for "Replica Cars," a project I had not heard about.

"What's behind the memo?" Dee asked.

"I don't know. I had dinner with Walt last night before he left for San Francisco and he never said a word about this."

We tried to find Walt, but he was traveling. That night I went to see John. I handed him the note.

"Just an accounting error," he said, in an attempt to dismiss the matter.

"It's more than that," I said. "And the issue is not two servants in your house. Walt has put this on record and put me on the spot. I told accounting to take the men off my payroll and I removed Replica Cars from our department. But that's not going to solve the problem. What's going on between you and Walt?"

John mumbled something about the British being unhappy with Walt and this being Walt's counterattack to confuse the issue. That was the first time I learned that John and Walt were feuding.

"We can't afford to lose another CFO now," I said. "The British were upset over Dewey. And that memo would make good reading on Fleet Street. I don't know what was permissible at GM, but we're using public money. Walt's memo would confirm what Bruce-Gardyne and Cryer are saying in Parliament."

John refused to confront the issue. When Walt returned, his

explanations were equally vague. Eventually, Walt explained his concerns.

"John can't distinguish between his own money and company funds," he said, "and he's going to wind up in trouble. I hope you don't find out too late."

I respected Walt and I knew John. I decided the two men must have had a confrontation that had gotten out of control. I thought about it for a week and went to see John again.

"Walt's a friend of mine, and you're a friend of mine," I said. "Maybe I can be a middleman and see if I can work out a solution."

John agreed, and I began to serve as a messenger between their two offices — which were adjacent to each other. As a result of the memo, John had stopped Walt's salary on trumped-up charges that he owed the company $24,000 for disallowed expenses.

During these discussions I returned to Belfast for two weeks. When I returned, Ellen said to me, "When you were away, they broke into Walt's desk."

"Who broke into Walt's desk?"

"Walt's secretary and Marian Gibson [John's executive secretary]. They opened the desk with a crowbar and removed his files. They did it in the middle of the afternoon when everyone was around."

Walt's secretary had been transferred to work with Gene Cafiero, our new president. She said John told her he needed the papers in Walt's desk. I went to see John.

"John, this is hurting the entire company. Let's have it done with." John agreed to remove his claim against Walt's expenses; he would pay the $20,000 Walt claimed was owed to him. Walt would continue as a financial advisor for $10,000 a month, but he would not earn stock options. The three of us had a good-natured meeting in John's office and the deal was consummated. Walt and I had dinner that night. He believed he had made the best out of a bad deal. I felt I had averted a corporate crisis. Walt left for San Francisco.

On my desk the next morning was a memo to Walt from

John, evidently dictated after I left the office. It ignored our agreement and accused Walt of improperly using the company van to pick up his wife at the airport, and Walt's wife of charging gasoline for the van to the company. The memo was ridiculous. Walt had been earning well over $200,000 a year, the van was a stripped, uncomfortable vehicle, and, in any event, the gas bill might have totaled $10.

I confronted John with the memo. "What the hell is this?" I asked.

"Cristina and I took Walt and his wife into our home when he came here," John yelled. "We treated him like one of the family. Now all this disloyalty."

"I don't give a shit about what happened last year. When I left the office we had an agreement. Walt accepted it."

"There's no agreement. Walt's a crook. He's going to jail. He's going to be indicted by a federal grand jury in Kentucky."

I was stunned. "A federal grand jury? For what?"

"It has to do with coal mines he owns in Kentucky."

I knew that Walt owned coal mines in several states. "I don't believe it."

"It's true."

When I asked John for his source, he balked. I knew he wanted me to pass on the charge to Walt to let him know how dirty the fight was going to get, but I wouldn't do it without checking it out personally. Finally John relented. His source was C. W. Smith, who was now on our payroll in Detroit. I remembered Smith. He was the one who had wanted the mercenaries to invade Libya.

I called C. W. in Detroit and asked him to see me in New York. We met at the Waldorf bar, across from the office. I pressed him for his source of information. At last, he told me.

"I saw a list of cases on Bunker Hunt's desk," he said. "Walt's company was one of them."

Bunker Hunt was one of the richest men in the world. John had told me that Smith had worked with Hunt. "What would a grand jury action be doing on Hunt's desk?" I said.

"I don't know."

"Which one of Walt's companies was named?"

"I couldn't read the names."

"What jurisdiction?"

"Louisville."

I tracked down the names of Walt's coal mines and had Smith's charges investigated and checked with federal and local authorities. I quickly established there was not a shred of truth in them. I reported back to John.

"C. W. is off the wall," I said. "He gave you a bum steer."

I later wondered whether the allegations began with Smith or whether John had originated them and used Smith to give them an independent aura.

When I talked to Walt later, I learned that when John couldn't get the story back to Walt through me, he had used others to communicate it. Strycker told me it was John's way of letting him know that the stakes had been raised and the confrontation could get nasty. "You don't get into a pissing match with a skunk," he said.

When I went back to John he handed me a letter dated January 17, 1980, from Dennis Faulkner, Director of the Northern Ireland Development Agency (NIDA), which monitored our operations and was our partner. They had the authority to approve our chief financial officer. The British, John said, wanted him to fire Strycker for what John said was "incompetence."

I read the letter. It did not in fact accuse Walt of incompetence. It urged John to improve his financial controls and to report to NIDA as required. I called Shaun Harte in Belfast. He had left NIDA to join our staff. I asked him if he knew of any charges against Walt. He didn't. The complaints were about the company. The British wanted to know how we were spending our money. I later learned that Walt had also called Harte and had received the same message.

There was another paragraph in the letter that disturbed me.

"I would welcome assurance from you," Faulkner wrote,

"that other projects will not be undertaken without prior discussion with us and that in no case will other projects be considered if they cannot clearly be shown to be complementary to the DMC-12 project." I regarded this as a complaint about the bus.

"Do we have a go-ahead on the bus or not?" I asked.

"Yes," John said, "but be careful. They're looking at you."

At the time I was too naïve to understand that John was warning me not to be too supportive of Walt's cause.

I called Walt. "What's going on?" I asked.

"Money is flowing out of the company and the British want to know where it is going. John won't tell them."

A few days later I received my first indication of how John played hardball. He sent me three memos he had written "to file." They had a dual purpose. One was to prejudice my view of Strycker; the other was to rewrite recent history.

The memos accused Walt of incompetence, of using corporate funds for private purposes and of attempting to convert a company business deal into a private transaction. None of the accusations was true, but John had put them on paper and later sent a synopsis of the charges to an outside attorney for an "evaluation."

Most revealing for me was that Walt had taken his charges regarding Mazzone and Chasty to our auditors, Arthur Andersen & Company, several months before he had written his memo to me.

"This action was very disturbing to Arthur Andersen," John wrote.

I asked Walt what had happened to the Arthur Andersen investigation.

"John had an explanation for everything," he said. "They accepted his word."

The second incident that disturbed me involved the publication of John's autobiography, *On A Clear Day You Can See General Motors*, written for John by J. Patrick Wright, a former Detroit editor for *Business Week*. The book was a devastating attack on GM's management. It portrayed John as the voice of integrity with an imcompetent bureaucracy, a place, as John wrote, where "moral men make immoral decisions."

Back in the fall of 1974, John had decided to tell his GM story and had hired Wright to ghostwrite it for him. Wright was an excellent choice. He knew the automotive industry and had a jaundiced view of it. He had watched John close-up, and admired him. He believed that through this book he could let the outside world see how the world's largest corporation functioned. Wright quit his job, and using a $35,000 advance to DeLorean from Playboy Press, began reviewing John's papers and interviewing DeLorean.

As the book neared completion, John began to withdraw his support, but without telling Wright why. Instead, he insisted upon change after change. Finally, however, Wright sent John a manuscript ready for publication. John, who had by then raised the first monies for DMC, said he was worried that the book would anger GM and that they would "destroy him."

Wright argued that John had nothing to fear. John refused to listen. Then, in September 1979, *On A Clear Day You Can See General Motors* appeared in bookstores throughout Detroit. Wright had raised $50,000, mortgaging his home in the process, in order to publish the book himself.* Its sensational nature, and the unique manner of publication, combined to make the publication front-page news and the book an instant best seller. John wanted to disown the book, however, an action I thought was inconceivable.

"That book is the best thing that ever happened to you and the company," I said. "It reminds everyone of what you did at GM and although it is your book and your view, everyone is treating it as a news story written by an independent journalist."

---

*The Playboy commitment was later resolved.

"I'm worried about GM," he said.

"What the hell can they do? You fought like hell to stop publication. Wright secretly released it over your objections. Everyone will know you're building the car GM wouldn't let you build. Your dream is a national story. Everyone will be watching us."

John didn't see it that way. He wanted to denounce the book, saying that it was inaccurate and did not reflect his views. I left John's office and returned with a yellow marker and a box of paperclips. "Mark the book where it doesn't represent your view," I said. "That's exactly what the press is going to ask you to do. Wright is no fool. Lawyers have read it. Every word has a backup document."

That afternoon Colleen O'Neil, John's longtime personal secretary, turned over three cartons of documents to me. "John wants you to check these documents against the book," she said.

John was asking me to do his work for him. Dee Fensterer and I spent the next forty-eight hours comparing the information in the documents with that in the book. Wright had written what John had told him. But this time the press was clamoring for John's comments on the book. Reporters from Europe and Asia had joined the American press is seeking confirmation that what Wright had printed was true. John stalled.

What I did not know at the time was that Tom Kimmerly was in secret contact with Otis Smith, the general counsel of GM, to explain John's desire to disown parts of the book. He told Smith that John "did not trust Wright" because of the "double-cross he pulled on JZD" and that John feared the consequences of a lawsuit.

Finally John agreed to confirm the accuracy of the book, but said its tone was a little more strident than he would have liked. "I wanted this to be a positive book," he told the media at a crowded press conference in his office that drew reporters from around the world. "I wanted to help General Motors, not hurt her."

John was his usual masterful public self. He "confessed" that he had left GM for ethical reasons. For him it had been the right decision. Now he was doing what he could not do at GM. His ethical car was just over the horizon. He invited reporters and television crews to see for themselves. The book was only half the DeLorean story. The other half — his answer — was the DeLorean car.

On A Clear Day was reprinted in several languages, including German and Japanese, and major newspapers throughout the world ran synopses, including an update on John and his ethical car company. In Northern Ireland and the U.K. John became a hero.

Then one day John called me into his office to tell me that he was forced to sue Wright. "What the hell are you talking about?" I asked in disbelief.

"We have to do it for our own protection."

"No one is going to see it that way."

"Tom says we have to do it."

"Fuck Tom," I said. "You sue Wright and you'll blow yourself out of the water."

A week later John came into my office to say, "We have the lawsuit drawn up. But we want to sue him in New York. If we do it in Detroit, the newspapers would be all over us."

"There's no difference between New York and Detroit. They'll still eat you alive."

"I want to know when Wright is going to be in New York so we can serve him."

"So?"

"I want you to find out when he will be here."

John subsequently wrote me several notes suggesting names of New York reporters who might lure Wright to New York for an interview. Soon John's secretaries, pretending to be researchers for radio and TV shows, called Wright's publicist to inquire when he might be in New York. Finally I wrote John a memo asking him to get off my back. I could not and would not be a party to suing Wright or to using newsmen to lure him into the city to be subpoenaed. John thought I was being "tight-assed." What was wrong in using a journalist to lure Wright to New York, he asked. Well, if you don't know, it can't be explained.

I realized that I did not know the details of the lawsuit, and I obtained a copy from one of Kimmerly's secretaries. John was planning to sue Wright for $10 million, charging that he was being "unjustly enriched by the earning of substantial royalties based on his willful and intentional appropriation for his own use and benefit of all materials pertaining to the life and experiences of DeLorean . . . Defendant Wright has willfully, maliciously and intentionally embarked upon a scheme to cause damage to the good name and reputation of DeLorean in the automobile industry and has caused DeLorean personal embarrassment, mental strain and has damaged DeLorean's personal reputation in the community . . ."

I couldn't believe what I read. Wright had made John an international hero and helped us distinguish our car company from all the others. Wright had told the press that John would receive half the writer's royalties as outlined in the contract, and John had said that he would donate the money to charity, perhaps in Northern Ireland.

DeLorean was out of town. When he returned I was waiting for him. I had the lawsuit in my hand. I wielded it like a club.

"You're suing Wright for money," I said. "That's going to make one hell of a headline."

"Where did you get that?" he asked.

"From Tom's office."

"That's the only way we can protect ourselves against lawsuits," he said. Then he paused a moment. "You know Wright's a liar. He never mortgaged his house." John said that this fact entitled him to half the publisher's profits as well as half the author's.

"Is that what the lawsuit is all about?" I asked.

"Partly. He lied about the mortgage."

"John, I told you before and I'll tell you again, they'll drag you through the mud if you raise a finger against Wright. We've already endorsed the book. He's made you a hero."

Back in my office I called Ed Lapham of *Automotive News*.

"How well do you know Wright?" I asked.

"Very good friend. Why?"

"What kind of a guy is he?"

"Decent, honest, well-respected. Fun to be around."

"Did he really mortgage his house?" I asked. "I mean, literally."

"He put every last nickel he had into the book, including the mortgage on his house — and I know that firsthand."

It was what I expected to hear. I was damned angry, and let John know it in a memo. John never sued.

These two events, concerning Strycker and the book, served to warn that there was more to John than I had learned during our long friendship. He was a professed humanitarian, but also a hard-nosed businessman willing to take advantage of an adversary's weakness. But I was not as yet convinced that he was anything worse than this.

John lived in fear that GM would one day find a way to destroy both him and the company. I found that fear irrational. I once asked him why GM would risk an antitrust action against a "nickel-shit company" like ours. "You just don't understand GM," he had said. When I pressed him for examples he described how he had arranged for the first DeLorean financing through the Chase Manhattan Bank. All that had been needed to complete the deal was a courtesy call from the bank to General Motors, a prime customer of Chase.

"After that call," John said, "the bank stopped returning my calls. They dropped me like a hot potato. That's how GM works. In the dark, around the corners, behind the scenes, under the bed, everywhere at once. One day you'll look down and your balls will be gone."

John had devised a strategy for dealing with GM "when" (not "if") GM came after us. The first step was a "black book"

John wanted me to compile on GM. He planned to request a conference with GM's chairman, should it become necessary, and close the door and lay out the "black book" for him to read. GM would know in advance the price it would pay for a fight with DeLorean. I remember thinking: "So that's how the big guys play the game."

Our discussions about GM continued throughout my time at DeLorean Motors. Sometimes John would tell me an anecdote over our cup of coffee in the morning; other times he would send me a more formal memo. Sometimes he gave me details, and other times he just passed along hints or rumors. My assignment was to produce third-party validation for the information. It could not be John's word alone against GM's. I personally had no great respect for GM, and I went along with John on this.

For starters, I had John's memo to Tom Murphy, the memo he had written when he left GM. If I could substantiate it, there would be enough dynamite to blow some GM executives right out of the water. But the memo was by now dated. Within a few years, most of the top-level people involved would be retired and the statute of limitations would prevent federal actions. But, nevertheless, the insight into GM would prove enlightening to the media and the public. I now urged John to let me leak the memo.

"Let me give it to Ben Bradlee on the [Washington] *Post* or Abe Rosenthal on the [New York] *Times*," I said. Both were editors I knew and could trust.

"This is not the time," he said, closing out the discussion.

Given our work on the GM black book, I was not surprised when one day in late 1979 John called me into his office to discuss another black book. When I walked in, John was standing behind his desk, his half-glasses twirling in his hand.

"Bill," he said, "you don't like Roy Cohn."

"That's the understatement of the year."

Roy Cohn had worked alongside the late Senator Joseph McCarthy at the anti-Communist hearings in the 1950s. Now, thirty years later, he was a powerful force in New York and national politics and his views were once again being sought by the media.

"And you like Henry Ford."

I had worked with Ford in setting up the National Alliance of Businessmen, and my company had represented the Ford Motor Company. I found Ford to be a tough-minded person with a genuine compassion for the poor and the unemployed.

"He's a first-rate human being," I said. "Why?"

"How would you like to get Cohn and help Ford?" John asked.

There was a strange lilt in John's voice, a tone he uses when he is very pleased with himself and can't quite disguise it. I called it his "pig-in-shit" voice. (It was the tone of voice he used when he toasted the cocaine deal in a Los Angeles hotel room before his arrest.)

"Henry is being killed by all those stories about payoffs overseas," John began, "and they're all coming from one place." (In recent months the newspapers had carried allegations that the Ford Motor Company had made covert payoffs to gain business in Indonesia.) "They're not just news stories," John explained. "They are planted as part of a plan to put pressure on Ford to settle his fight with Edsel."

Edsel Ford, Henry's nephew, was conducting a well-publicized struggle to regain a seat on the Ford board of directors. He had been passed over and dropped from the board. There had been confrontations between the two men in public stockholder's meetings. Henry Ford held most of the cards in that contest, but his mother still controlled a sizable share of Ford stock, and she wanted a reconciliation. Edsel and Roy Cohn had teamed up. And the fight had turned ugly.

It was also rumored that Cohn was advising Christina, Henry's wife, in their divorce action. That situation, too, was turning nasty, with newspaper reports that the divorce trial would reveal everything from sexual escapades by famous people to allegations of business improprieties. It promised to be a sensational trial, a look behind the scenes at how the rich and famous lived their private lives.

"What's your interest?" I asked John.

"I think Lee Iacocca is feeding Cohn."

Iacocca, then and now chairman of Chrysler, had previously been chief executive of Ford, and had been unceremoniously dumped.

"We need a friend in Detroit when GM comes after us," John continued. "If we help Henry now, he'll help us later."

The logic of this explanation seemed flawed, but I was intrigued. My own logic was doubtless flawed by my dislike for Cohn and my desire to help Henry Ford. My interest was also fueled by my newspaperman's instinct for a good story. I never uncovered an iota of proof of an Iacocca-Cohn link, and I have no reason to believe it exists, but what unfolded tells as much about DeLorean as any episode in our relationship.

John had a simple plan. A friend of his, Tom Corbolloy, had access to certain information about Chrysler executives who were visiting Rockwell International's retreat at Bimini Island, in the Bahamas, for private parties. Women were transported to the island on Rockwell planes to entertain these executives.

I was puzzled because I knew that Robert Anderson, Rockwell's chairman and a former GM executive, was John's friend. I said as much. "He is," John said, "but he's not involved. I'm sure he doesn't know anything about this. We'll be doing him a favor."

"What do you want me to do?"

"Confirm the story."

"If I confirm it, then what?" I asked.

"I turn it over to Ford's lawyers and they use it to stop Cohn from leaking those stories about Ford. We have an ally in Detroit and we have another story for our file."

Later, Corbolloy himself came to my office and without prompting began to relate the same story John had told.

"How do you know?" I asked.

"I went along on the trips," he said.

"How do we prove it?"

"Easy. I know the women."

Soon Corbolloy introduced me to two women who had made trips to Bimini. They were not prostitutes but, rather, attractive companions taking a break from their regular jobs. I called George Clifford, who had earlier helped me with John's novel, to help me verify the story. I enlisted the help of a private detective in the Bahamas who had once helped me on a newspaper story. Before long I had some information, and a roll of film to back it up. I wrote a report to John, detailing our findings.

I wrote that during the period from 1972 to 1975 or 1976 a group of business executives, including Chrysler executives, would retreat to Rockwell's corporate vacation house in North Bimini, where women were flown in for their entertainment. The entertaining was done by some Rockwell executives, presumably to boost business. The women, I wrote, were interested in a good time in luxurious surroundings. They were shuttled in and out by Rockwell aircraft. Once, I reported, a former state governor nearly spoiled the show by bringing in a planeload of prostitutes. The women who did go along maintained their independence. Sex was a "personal matter," not part of the deal.

I attached the names and phone numbers of people who could confirm the story, and gave John some (nonsexual) photographs taken at the resort to confirm that the people named had in fact been there. I had one long interview on tape confirming what the report and photographs revealed.

John was delighted with the report. "This is great," he said. "Just what we need."

"What the hell are you going to do with it?" I asked.

"Take it right over to Ford's lawyers."

"Let me do that, John. It's safer that way. If anything goes wrong, they can blame me, not you."

"No, no," he insisted. "I know them. They won't tell anyone where this came from."

I persisted, but John was determined to do it himself. So I dropped the argument and went back to building cars. I was later to suspect that John might have had a quite different use in mind for the information in my report than the one he professed.

Chapter Six

Building The Impossible Bus

"How would you like to build a bus?" John asked me one Saturday morning as he settled in for a cup of coffee in my office.

On the last Friday in May 1979, I had sent John a note to tell him that General Motors and Grumman's Flxible Corporation had refused to respond to a $125 million bid by a consortium of cities to build the futuristic Transbus that Congress and the Department of Transportation had mandated for American streets. The government pays 80 percent of the cost of every new bus and Secretary of Transportation Brock Adams had announced that after September 30 he would subsidize only Transbus. GM and Grumman were evidently confident no one could fill the vacuum if they both failed. That, I wrote John, was our opening. We could combine social need and business opportunity. John agreed.

It was a rare opportunity, I thought, to show America what DMC was all about. It also suited my own view of what business could do to end poverty by providing jobs and training the so-called unemployables to fill them. It was the reason I had joined DeLorean, and now I could shape my own program.

GM held a virtual monopoly on the American bus business and had stubbornly refused to meet mounting pressures for change. American buses used too much fuel, broke down frequently (especially the heating and air conditioning systems), cost too much money, were uncomfortable and the mountain of stairs at the entrance made the bus inaccessible to millions of passengers, especially the elderly and the handicapped. It was, I thought, what happens in America when competition is stifled by business pressure on government.

Earlier, a Congressional report noted that "although GM technically accounts for 75 percent of current bus production, its only remaining competitor, the Flxible Company, relies on GM for diesel propulsion systems, major engine components, technical assistance and financing." It was, the report concluded, "a classic monopoly."

I quickly learned that the real problem was the GM bus engine, which was "excess capacity" for the mass production line for GM truck engines. The engine was designed for trucks, not buses. In Germany, they had neatly tucked their fuel-efficient bus engines under the bus and were able to create a modern vehicle used in the rest of the world. That bus could not be imported into the United States. Nor could an American bus company copy the German design. The GM bus specifications had become, through politics and pressure, the DOT standards for subsidy.

DOT had provided $30 million to build nine prototypes of Transbus. AM General, a subsidiary of American Motors, built three, as did Flxible and GM. But GM decided that in the interim they would introduce a new bus, the Advanced Design Bus (the ADB), and convinced DOT to provide subsidies for it. Flxible quickly designed its own ADB, using GM parts. AM General said the companies would retool for Transbus, but the ADB approval undercut the government's commitment to Transbus and left AM General out on a limb. They could not afford to design an ADB and they had committed their resources to Transbus. They sued, lost and went out of the bus business.

What followed next is the DeLorean story in a nutshell. The Transbus challenge created great excitement. Using De-Lorean's name and reputation, doors suddenly opened and talented people helped us. When we had achieved what the media, bus specialists and even government thought was impossible, John destroyed it all by overreaching, by attempting to turn to his personal advantage all of the idealism that had enabled him to build what the media had labeled "the impossible bus."

After our cup of coffee on Saturday morning, events moved quickly. John knew the former manager of the GM bus division, and we called him that morning.

"Can Transbus be built?" John asked Bob Manning, as I listened in on the extension.

"Hell, yes," he said. "That was my project. I built the GM prototypes."

"Why wouldn't GM build the Transbus?" I asked.

"Why should they? They have the ADB and we sell Grumman the parts to build their buses."

On Monday morning Gene Cafiero, the respected former Chrysler vice chairman who was now DMC's president, said his next-door neighbor in Bloomfield Hills, Tom Poirer, had run AM General. Yes, Poirer told me on the phone, he'd love to help, but he warned me that GM could be rough.

"They put us out of business and we were doing what the government asked us to do."

In Washington that afternoon I sought out the director of the Transbus program and asked him for the name of "the best bus engineer in the world."

"Otto Schultz," he answered without hesitation.

Otto had designed and built the prototypes of Germany's current bus, the VOV I — the best in the world — and was now building the prototypes of the VOV II, the next generation of low-floor buses.

I flew to Hamburg that weekend and discovered the VOV II

was Transbus and more. But we needed to pull the bus through unique U.S. regulations. Otto introduced me to his talented son, Rainer, who had been an engineer in the States for a dozen years, and the two of us spent a week at their family place on Lake Constance in Switzerland and redesigned the VOV II to U.S. standards. Otto reviewed our work and sent us back to the drawing board, but by the time I returned home I knew we could do it. The engineers agreed.

Buck Penrose, who had been at Booz Allen before DeLorean and had helped to develop the business plan for Northern Ireland, joined our team and quickly put together a business plan that proved we could build the bus and make a profit. The Transbus team was managed by Buck, Dee and myself (in addition to everything else we were doing for DeLorean).

By the end of June I was able to call Brock Adams and tell him DeLorean was ready to build Transbus. Two weeks later our team of DeLorean, Cafiero, Schultz (father and son), Poirer, Penrose, Fensterer and Haddad met with fifty DOT executives, explained our plan and won their support. They would keep the Transbus option open for us.

In Hamburg I had made arrangements to lease a VOV I, had it painted a fire-engine red and renamed it the "DMC 80" (for 1980). I had the bus photographed and Dee and Buck prepared a brochure that indicated the DMC 80 was Transbus and more. We said it could be purchased at half the $250,000 that GM and Grumman had told Congress the Transbus would cost. The elderly and the handicapped tested the bus and quickly gave their approval. It was the political support we needed.

We chose the annual meeting of the American Public Transit Association (APTA) to unveil our bus. We were not on good terms with the association: at first they had refused to allow us to join, arguing that we were a brochure and not a company, but we pushed our way in with the help of transit operators interested in a new bus. Then we had challenged their "scientific" studies that indicated Transbus could not be built with the current generation of technology (in this they were supported by the American Academy of Science). They were also unalterably opposed to providing accommodations for the elderly and the handicapped in public transportation: it was too costly. I soon discovered that APTA was another name for GM.

The convention was held at the New York Hilton and the bus show was in the parking lot behind the hotel. Our bus had arrived a few days before, and on Sunday afternoon Rainer drove it from the dock to the parking lot, moving it into the space we had leased between the Grumman and GM ADBs. The contrast was startling. Our bus was shorter, lower and built along powerful classic lines, giving it a handsome, rugged look. And it was red. Their buses were a dull white with blue lines. When we hung out our sign, the APTA executives exploded.

"Welcome aboard the bus they said could not be built."

When we arrived the next morning for the show, our bus was gone. APTA had moved it during the night into an alley between two buildings. We learned GM had threatened to leave the show unless APTA took some action against us.

"Why should you have equal accommodations?" the APTA manager told us. "General Motors pays our bills. Your dues don't." He was right; dues were paid on sales volume. But they had leased us the space.

While I fumed, Dee Fensterer and Walt Strycker disappeared, and when they returned I learned they had rented half of the lot that had been reserved for commercial cars. Rainer moved the bus into that open area (you had to pass by it to get to the bus exhibition), and we added a second sign:

"This is the bus they didn't want you to see."

In the lobby of the hotel some of New York's loveliest models handed out fliers to the delegates as they moved into the convention hall to hear the keynote address.

"Come visit the bus they said couldn't be built," they said.

Inside, the keynote speaker, a Congressman, taken by our ingenuity (and a tour of the bus that Cristina had given him), interrupted his speech to tell the audience that the transit industry needed more innovators like John DeLorean, men willing to challenge established concepts, and he invited them down to see our bus. The other companies, locked into their plush entertainment suites, fumed while the delegates followed our models to the bus after the speech. Cristina welcomed them aboard. We had stolen their show.

After the convention we took our bus on a tour of the country and the headlines were incredible. "The little red bus that could" had taken on a character of her own: people waved to us as we rode down the street and cars beeped to us on the highway. Ed Lapham, in an article for *Detroit Monthly,* "Building The Impossible Bus" (in which he called me "the country's most unlikely auto executive"), catalogued GM's frustrations.

"GM," he wrote, "was none too pleased by the presumption DeLorean had shown in building the bus at all. . . . [They were] also piqued by the endorsements of DeLorean's bus from the elderly and handicapped groups before the [APTA] convention which lent DeLorean, Haddad and the project the look of innovation, social concern and good-old-fashioned Yankee ingenuity."

A Congressional committee held a hearing on the bus and we drove it to the door of the American Academy of Science and invited the executives down to see the bus they said could not be built.

George Clifford and a team of ex-reporters tracked the ADB failures in major cities and compiled a report which we sent to all cities. Passengers in Houston, angered about the failure of the air conditioning system, had kicked out the sealed windows; the frames of the hastily designed Grumman ADB had begun to show cracks; transit operators were complaining about the cost of maintaining the bus; and politicians were asking why the bus was in the yard as often as it was on the streets. Now local reporters could relate local events to a national story, undermining arguments that the troubles were caused by potholes, bus drivers, union mechanics or careless passengers.

We had one major hurdle to cross. The specifications for American buses were developed by U.S. companies, including GM, and for the DMC 80 to be tested on American streets a waiver was needed. We needed help from Congress and we turned to Congressman Robert Duncan, an Oregon Democrat, who was against developing a bus for the handicapped because of the cost. As chairman of the DOT appropriations subcommittee Duncan was "the eye of the dragon." I knew Duncan, and when I asked him to see John he agreed, but warned me that he was against the idea.

"Hear us out," I said.

John was impressive. He made our case, explaining that the DMC 80 would cost less than the ADB and had the support of the elderly and the handicapped.

"You can really do all that?" he asked John.

"Yes. And more."

Duncan thought a few minutes.

"Okay," he said, "you deserve a chance to prove what you claim. I won't stand in your way. What can I do to help?"

The so-called DeLorean amendment was created to allow new buses to be tested head to head with existing buses. It was the opening we needed.

Now we had a bus, but no money to build it. The British urged John to devote all his resources to the car, but at my prodding, John got their permission to build the bus. In all, excluding our time, we had spent $165,000 on developing the DMC 80.

Buck, Dee and I developed a business plan with a social mission. We would locate the factory in a depressed area and train 2500 people, many of them hard-core unemployed on welfare, for the jobs. In one shot they would be in a union with a job and out of poverty.

Since most of the poor were single mothers, we provided for a five-hour shift (to build seats), which enabled them to come to work after the older children had left for school and to be at home when they returned. On site we planned a child development center modeled after Bank Street, one of the best child educational systems in the country.

I got the union to agree that if we hired high-school dropouts a condition of employment would be enrollment in an educational program. We planned a high-school degree program on site. We also planned to take title, in the South Bronx (one of the nation's worst poverty areas), to 200 homes which we would have repaired. If the worker stayed on the job for a fixed period of time, the down payment we advanced would become a bonus.

Sam Meyer, the United Auto Workers leader in New York, said he realized suddenly what we were doing.

"You're building a company town," he said.

"What do you care," I said, "as long as they're in the union?"

UAW tentatively committed to a lower hourly wage during training, which helped make the program feasible.

We had one serious problem. We needed federal grants, and the White House, I quickly learned, would have nothing to do with John. A letter from a friend (on White House stationery) warned that the bureaucrats had not forgotten how John had "sold them out" in Puerto Rico.

I was in the middle of these negotiations when the riots in Miami erupted. A White House team was formed to help rebuild the city and the Mayor of Miami, Maurice Ferre, asked me to work with them. I had monitored the urban riots in the sixties for the White House, and it was Mayor Ferre who had asked me to go to Puerto Rico to help his uncle who was running for governor.

When he heard about our bus factory, he urged me to consider Miami. The on-site White House team was enthusiastic. That was just what we needed to fight back against John's enemies in government. Under the leadership of Congressman Claude Pepper, the local mayors formed a committee and assigned one person to work with me. It was Belfast revisited. Within 45 days we had a $90 million package developed — more than enough to build and operate the plant. Miami and Florida agreed to order enough buses to carry our overhead for four years. We located a factory site and approached key personnel, some still working in Detroit. We told them they could live in their retirement homes while they were still young. Their down payments would be the bonus for coming with us. We soon assembled a team of the best engineers and managers in the country.

All we needed now was $5 million, our cash share of the $90 million. One day John finally told me we didn't have it.

"Let's borrow it," I said.

"We can't."

"Why?"

"The British won't let me."

Once again John's luck held. George Clifford called to tell me that Marilyn Malkonian, the counsel for George Lucas, who had created *Star Wars,* was scouting for businesses with social utility. DeLorean looked like a perfect match. He had talked to her and she was excited. Could we see her? Could we!

John and I flew to Los Angeles to make our presentation to the Lucas Films President, Charles Weber, and Mrs. Malkonian. They liked the idea, and we soon had a hand-shake understanding to proceed. The final meeting would take place at a dinner in New York. I could see the headline: "*Star Wars* to build bus GM couldn't build." Lucas and DeLorean were both modern American heros.

We arranged dinner at the Board Room, an exclusive dining club on the 41st floor of our office building at 280 Park Avenue.

Marilyn came with Weber, and George joined us. It was too good to be true. We were on the verge of doing in America what John was doing in Belfast and it wouldn't cost us a penny. When the dinner was over, we could pay the British back the $165,000 we had spent on the project and we could begin to hire full-time staff to manage the bus program. If it worked, DeLorean would have created a model for other businessmen to follow.

The dinner began well, but as we were discussing the final details, John suddenly changed the subject.

"You know," he said, "you might be better off investing in the Motor Company. We're raising $20 million, but if we got that from you, Lucas Films could be a partner in the holding company when we go public. You would have both the bus company and a good investment."

Marilyn, George and I could not believe what we were hearing. We knew Lucas was in this deal because we would provide the elderly and handicapped with a bus that could open up their lives. He wasn't interested in building a sports car in Belfast.

Weber, however, was intrigued. John had read him correctly. He finally agreed.

Star Wars went home with its $5 million check, and the next week a team of experts arrived to evaluate DMC to decide if we were worth a $20 million investment. We had moved back from social excitement to car company reality. The car company was still a high-risk venture until we sold some cars. Five weeks later the team decided it was too risky and Lucas backed out. John did not get his $20 million and the bus company did not get its $5 million.

Without the seed money, John began to drag his feet on the bus. One excuse followed another.

"We need $125 million from Miami to make this work," he said.

"Buck has stretched the $90 million to cover every contingency. We can't justify $125 million."

"Unless we get the money, there won't be a factory down there. How do you think they will like those apples?"

"John, they're my friends. I gave them your word. The governor is willing to sponsor special legislation so we can sell more buses there. We can't leave them holding the bag. We're already on good time from the White House because of Puerto Rico."

"I didn't go to Puerto Rico because they tried to shake me down," John insisted.

"What's that got to do with anything?"

When it came time to sign with the Germans, John delayed again.

"I have some problems with the contract," he said.

I finally flew to Hamburg with our associate counsel, George Haywood, and we systematically isolated and resolved every problem John had raised. The Germans couldn't understand the delay. Otto had used every credential at Daimler Benz to encourage them to supply us components, including the pancake engine. Earlier, Cafiero and I had gone to Stuttgart to meet with Daimler's board and had received a cold reception. Rainer told me that someone high up in Daimler thought John was dishonest.

"It must have been something with General Motors," John said. "We were head to head on trucks."

While John was stalling, Ronald Reagan was elected President.

"That kills the bus," John said. "We missed our window in time."

"Maybe not," I said. "Let me give it a try."

I met with the Reagan transportation task force. They approved the demonstration on straight conservative grounds: it was free enterprise at work. Reagan's new Secretary of Transportation, Drew Lewis, agreed to allow the project to continue. Preliminary meetings were held with transit operators in Washington, and 24 cities selected the DeLorean bus for the government-financed demonstration. Even without a factory, we had the money for the remodeled German buses. All we needed now was the signed contract. When I called, the Germans were willing to sign, but John came up with a new tactic.

"They want too much," he said.

"They don't want anything," I said. "They are not even asking to be part of the company we may create. They only want to sell us components and give us technical assistance. Without them we have no bus, and without a bus, there is no demonstration. It's a fair deal. We should sign it."

"I'll think about it," John said. "You just stay out of it. Let Tom handle the details. I want you back in Belfast. We have trouble there."

"I'm in Belfast more than I am in New York," I said. "But unless someone keeps up the pressure in Washington, the demonstration you created will fall through the cracks."

"Don't worry about it."

I was angry, but now, in early 1981, I was beginning to have other arguments with John about the company.

The head-to-head bus demonstration never came off, but DeLorean paved the way for several foreign bus companies to build factories in the United States. None of them are building low-floor buses, and the Reagan administration decided not to fight for accessibility for the handicapped on the grounds that it costs too much money and that other local initiatives can solve the problem. APTA applauded the decision. Grumman sold Flxible after their buses cracked and collapsed around the country. GM's buses still burn twice as much fuel as the proposed DMC 80, their air conditioners don't work well and the ADB is in the repair shop as often as it is on the road. They blame local maintenance. Bus operators say they prefer the "new look" bus that predated the ADB.

DeLorean could have changed all that and become a national hero: a six-foot-four Iacocca.

I never understood why John changed his mind. Later I came to believe we had structured a deal too tight for him to squeeze. Or John's goals were not ours. We wanted to build a bus. He had something else in mind.

Chapter Seven

Partners . . . and Friends?

We were running into engineering problems in Belfast, and the date for moving the first car down the production line was delayed from March to October 1980. It was the first of several serious delays. We had enough money in the bank for about thirty months from ground-breaking until launch; after that the money to run the company must come from car sales in the States. Delay meant we would run out of money before the car was built. We had already raised $150 million, but many predicted that we would need twice that much to be successful. Our own calculations indicated that we could make it if we kept to schedule, but in early 1980, John began to look for another $20 million to complete production.

From the beginning we knew we were in a race with time. No car company had ever built a sophisticated plant in eighteen months is peacetime, or engineered a car in two years, or trained a new work force in working with new tooling in six months, let alone all three simultaneously. Porsche had predicted that it would take four years to engineer the DMC-12 into a car that could be mass produced.

What made it possible for us to move quickly was a research and development contract we signed with Lotus Cars, the British automotive company run by Colin Chapman, a world-famous race-team owner. Lotus was noted for its innovative engineering, and the company attracted the best automotive engineers in the United Kingdom. With Lotus as part of the DeLorean team, I thought, we had a fighting chance of meeting the deadlines.

Chapman was a British national hero. Earlier in his life he had borrowed £25 from his wife in order to build racing cars in his garage. Before long he was winning international races and establishing Lotus as both a manufacturer of upscale sports cars and as a center for creative engineering. By 1978, Chapman's Team Lotus had won 66 Formula One Grand Prix races. Stirling Moss won the first Grand Prix for Chapman. Mario Andretti also raced in a Lotus.

John admired Chapman greatly, and whenever someone questioned him about Chapman, John would use a stock answer: "He's the best engineer in the world. We're lucky to have him with us." And we were.

I never really got to know Chapman; he was a private person with a race driver's outward calm, but he possessed a quick temper and had little patience for views that conflicted with his own. He was short and wiry, with a pencil-thin mustache and gimlet eyes. John told me that his greatest ambition was to be knighted.

Lotus was located in Hethel, near Norwich, about eighty miles north of London, among flat farmlands. The bucolic atmosphere at Hethel contrasted sharply with the frenetic activity at the DeLorean Motors plant in Belfast. The Lotus assembly plant was located in the hangars at an abandoned airfield nearby, from which Flying Fortresses had bombed Germany during the war. The airstrip was now a test track. My first test drive in a DeLorean was around that track. It was one of the most exciting moments of my life.

As I began to spend time in Belfast and to win the confidence of our engineers, I began to realize that the Lotus connection was not what it seemed from the outside.

The day I started at DMC was also the day that Bill Collins left the company. He had been DMC's chief engineer, the man who had taken John's ideas and turned them into an exciting car. I was there when he stiffly shook hands with John, said a few meaningless words, and left. Puzzled by the stiffness between two old friends, I asked John for an explanation.

"His wife didn't want to live in Belfast," John said. "She couldn't take it." It was an easy answer to accept. I later learned, however, that it wasn't true.

Collins was replaced as chief engineer by Mike Loasby. Loasby had been the chief engineer of Aston-Martin, and had designed the new engine for their spectacular $150,000 sports car. He was considered one of the best engineers in the U.K. The trade press considered him a fine replacement for Collins.

Loasby and the Belfast engineers wondered why Chapman would share his secrets with a competitor who would surely undercut his market for luxury sports cars. Chapman had successfully argued for several major changes in the DeLorean. ERM (the next generation of plastics, which helped to distinguish our car from the pack) was replaced by a Lotus plastic process, VIRM, which was less flexible and more expensive. Only two small parts of the DeLorean were to be made from the ERM process. The weight problem had serious implications for us. The more weight, the less mileage. We had promised that the DeLorean would do 29 miles per gallon in the city and 40 on the highway. The heavy steel backbone needed to sustain the Lotus plastic process, when added to the other changes the car was undergoing at Lotus, brought us dangerously close to the EPA mileage limits. Exceeding the limits would undermine our sales pitch, which was that we were building a safe, fuel-efficient and ethical sports car.

When I asked John why we were dropping ERM, he was blunt. "We're not dropping ERM."

"Yes, we are. We're using Chapman's process."

"There are ERM parts."

"Two."

"That's enough to say we're still using ERM."

"John, this is me, not some klutz down the street."

"We have enough problems without trying something new."

"What about our commitments?"

"Say we're still using ERM. You don't have to tell them how much."

"You're not going to fool the automotive press."

"We're not trying to fool anyone."

And that was it. John was convinced that using the two small parts meant we were using ERM. Originally, the entire car body was to be molded from ERM. Adopting that revolutionary process was supposed to convince investors, the British government and customers that DMC was a worthwhile investment. The trade press quickly learned of the change, but that didn't prevent John from telling reporters that we were manufacturing the car from ERM, a material that is "lighter than aluminum and stronger than steel" —the phrase I had developed earlier to describe the process. The discrepancy never troubled John. It was his way of telling the truth.

As changes to the original design continued to be made, Loasby became alarmed. One day he told me that our statements to the press were "not the truth." "We're not a stainless steel car — we have a stainless steel skin. We're not going to make the EPA standards in either emissions or mileage. We're not going to be fuel efficient, and we're going to pollute the air. And we need to change the suspension. It's dangerous."*

These were serious charges. The suspension complaint particularly troubled me. The last thing we needed was to have the first cars break down on the road. Other car companies can survive recalls; we could not. We were too heavily publicized, and fine engineering was to be our calling card.

---

* DeLorean cars were later recalled from customers three times for work on the suspension.

Loasby's team complained that the Lotus engineers assigned to DMC were splitting their time between our project and other work at Lotus. They were required by the agreement with Lotus to work full time for us. It didn't take me long to verify this. In government, I had learned to be wary of work subcontracted to others, and when I reported my conclusions to John, he quickly understood what was happening.

"That goes on every day in Detroit," he said. But when I pressed him, he wasn't willing to tackle the problem.

"They have us by the short hairs," he said. "We need Lotus to get the job done. We can't afford to antagonize them now."

I urged him to place a full-time controller at Lotus to report directly to Belfast or New York, but again John refused.

"In short," I said, "we're going to pay their price."

"You got it right," he said, almost cheerfully.

I didn't give up this argument. Later I learned that De-Lorean prototypes, which had been removed from the work area, were returned to it for a tour John made, and the Lotus vehicles that the engineers had actually been working on were set aside. I used this information to reopen my discussion on the subject with John. Instead of agreeing that he had been set up, he exploded.

"I told you the subject is a closed book," he said. "We're going with Chapman and not those kids in Belfast. They couldn't carry Chapman's jockstrap."

John walked away from me.

I was steaming, and when I returned to Belfast I decided to find out if there was more to the dispute than a turf battle between engineers.

Loasby was too close to the battle to be of help now, but one of the men I respected and trusted in Belfast, George Broomfield, would know the answer. George was our unflappable director of manufacturing, a man who had a quiet way of getting people to carry out his orders. He knew all there was to know about manufacturing, and knew the people who had the knowledge we required. When I talked to Broomfield he was uncharacteristically blunt with me.

"They make eight cars a day at Lotus," he said. "When there is trouble on the line, they go out and kick a tire or file down a corner. When you're building eighty cars a day, you can't do that. We need a mass-production precision that Lotus doesn't understand. You can't go out and kick a production line."

When I returned to Loasby, I pressured him for an opinion. He was reluctant to give it. He told me I was regarded as John's eyes and ears, which was a nice way of telling me I was regarded as John's spy. But he was willing to trust me.

"They're making political decisions down there," he said, "not engineering decisions." When I probed, he wouldn't or couldn't explain.

Loasby's use of the phrase "political decisions" triggered something in my mind. Although we were using Lotus to reengineer the car, our payments were being made to GPD Services, Inc., a company in Geneva with a post-office box number for an address. GPD had come up several times, but no one seemed to know much about the company. I was curious, but not curious enough to be suspicious.

When I went to look for the GPD contract, I couldn't find it. There was an early reference in a report, but then nothing. Later, in New York, I found a relaxed social moment to ask John about the contract.

"Why was GPD used?" I asked.

"I don't know," he said. "Chapman wanted it that way. The auditors and the Bank of England approved it, so we went along. I'm sure it has something to do with keeping money offshore to finance Team Lotus."

I accepted John's answer, but I later learned that John had told me only a partial truth. The auditors and the Bank of England had, indeed, approved the transfer of British funds to GPD, but only as a routine technical banking matter. They had not reviewed the underlying agreement nor studied its legality. They regarded the transaction as a business matter between private contractors.

I dropped my inquiries into GPD. I later came to regret having done so.

While this was happening in Belfast, back in New York, John maintained his interest in Chrysler. One day he asked me, "How well do you know Dan Dorfman?" Dan was a respected financial columnist and a friend.

"Fairly well. Why?"

"I think I have a hot Chrysler story for him."

At the time, Chrysler was fighting for its survival. The company was selling off assets and trying to convince Congress to guarantee its debt in order to keep the company from going under.

The next day a handwritten note arrived from John. It read: "T.K. [Tom Kimmerly] spoke to the head of the Chrysler Realty Company on a confidential basis. The word around Detroit is that there was a $60 million profit off the top — without any doubt it is a scam. Does Dorfman want to talk to President of Realty? I'm not certain but I may be able to arrange. JZD." Tom and John were alleging that an illegal kickback had influenced the decision to sell Chrysler Realty.

I arranged for John to meet with Dorfman, who later wrote a story about Chrysler's real estate interests:

"Now, I didn't find any smoking guns," Dorfman wrote, ". . . nor am I suggesting they exist. But when you consider the unanswered questions about what's regarded as a 'giveaway' deal — a controversial transaction that baffles even the pros — it's no easy matter to blithely ignore a nationally known auto executive when he tells me with strong conviction: 'The whole situation stinks.' "

John also had me track Chrysler's progress in Congress and arrange meetings with senators studying the Chrysler bail-out loan.

"I have the solution to Chrysler's problems," he told me without explanation.

I did arrange for John to talk privately with senators interested in the Chrysler loan. It was not a difficult task. They welcomed the opportunity to talk to an "insider" who could cut through Detroit's "bullshit." They felt they could trust John's unbiased views. On a number of occasions Senate staffers called John for confidential opinions on Chrysler's comments.

Curiosity finally got the better of me and I asked Gene Cafiero, our new president (Gene had been vice chairman of Chrysler when Iacocca took over), about John's sudden interest in Chrysler's problems.

"We're negotiating to buy the company," he said.

"Buy the company!" I said, astonished. "Where the hell are we going to get the money to buy Chrysler?"

Gene smiled and told me a mind-boggling story about a billion-dollar tax shelter, involving investment banks, brokerage houses and Saudi Arabians. Halfway through the tale, I realized that my black book on the Bahamas might not have been prepared to help Henry Ford or to get back at Roy Cohn, but for possible use as part of the Chrysler negotiations. At a critical point in the discussions John could put my report and the pictures on the table and leave the room. Perhaps that was why John had kept me out of the Chrysler negotiations.

"Don't worry about it," said Gene. "It's just another one of John's pipe dreams. It's not going anywhere." But Gene didn't know about the black book.

I went back to John to ask him directly if the black book was intended to be part of the negotiations.

"Hell, no," he said. "Whatever gave you that idea?"

"I didn't know you were thinking about buying Chrysler."

"How the hell are we going to buy Chrysler?" he said, laughing. "We may put together the right people and they may come up with a deal and we would get a commission." He used the apparent absurdity of the concept to destroy the thrust of my questioning.

When I came to research this book, I learned that soon after I had given John the Bahamas report, he held a secret meeting with Chrysler executives in Suite 36F at the Waldorf Towers, across the street from our offices. John reported on the meeting in a memo dated January 17, 1980.

As I understood the deal that was discussed at that meeting, John would use a research and development tax shelter to raise money to help bail out Chrysler. Investors would share in Chrysler's multibillion-dollar tax loss, making their investment virtually risk free. Chrysler would reward De-Lorean with a multimillion-dollar finder's fee, stock in Chrysler, and an R and D operation for DMC.

A team of lawyers at Paul, Weiss and at DMC worked for several months, and spent several hundred thousand dollars, attempting to put together a plan for DMC to buy Chrysler. Documents were prepared and circulated to the small group working on the proposal. As I read these documents, it became clear that John planned to manage Chrysler, with DeLorean Motors as a subsidiary. He wanted to undermine Iacocca, to weaken him for the DeLorean negotiations. I have no proof that John actually showed the black book to Iacocca. From all I can determine, Iacocca is a tough negotiator himself, and any attempt to blackmail him might have backfired. After the Waldorf meeting, DeLorean and Iacocca never met again.*

The Chrysler incident served to reinforce my growing concern that there was a second DeLorean, one I had not known before, a DeLorean who was a hard negotiator who played backroom business. I never did another black book for John, although I did continue to develop the case against General

---

* Iacocca not only received congressional backing, but paid back the debt before it was due. He saved Chrysler from bankruptcy. He replaced John as the country's best-known automobile executive. He is sometimes mentioned as a candidate for President, to do for America what he did for Chrysler. Perhaps the same would have been said about John if he had succeeded.

Motors. That, I thought, was in the public interest, and it was fun. And I still believed in the DeLorean car.

Unable to raise the $20 million he said the Belfast delay was costing us, John decided on a campaign to force the British to give us another $28 million, which, he claimed, was actually owed to us.

Earlier, in late 1979, John had asked the British for a loan to begin work with GPD on a four-door sedan that was to follow our two-door gull-winged DeLorean. He estimated it would cost us $25 million to develop the prototypes. He told the British he would need four years to bring the new car to Belfast, but he pointed out that the factory was already designed to accommodate another production line and that the new project would increase our work force. The British politely told him it was not possible to talk about more money before we had delivered on our first series of promises.

Now, however, John believed he had a legal basis for his request for more money. An obscure paragraph in the Master Agreement with the British government protected us against currency changes and inflation. The dollar had been falling against the British pound, and John calculated that the changes had diminished our buying power by £15 million, or approximately $28 million at the then current exchange rate.

John sent Cafiero to England to demand the money. The British listened politely but said that they did not interpret the paragraph as John had done. John kept sending Gene back to ask the same question, but no matter how many times he contacted them, the answer was always the same: no more money until the first car comes off the production line. Any other decision would create an uproar in the already skeptical British Parliament.

John would not accept their answer. On July 15, 1980, in what I was beginning to understand was typical hardball DeLorean style, he asked me to plant stories in the media blaming the delays in our program on the British, for their slowness in funding the adjustment allowance. "If it were said enough times," John wrote, "we would be absolved from the lateness charge and the government would be pressured to respond quickly."

I reminded John that Lotus was our problem. When I added that I didn't think the plan would work — and that both Cafiero and the Belfast directors would agree with me — he smiled. "The British only understand one thing. Who has the larger cock. We have the larger cock on this one," he said.

I found Gene in Belfast. When I read him the memo, he shook his head. He was certain that if I pursued John's suggestion, we would lose any chance of getting the $28 million. "The last thing I want now is a public confrontation with Thatcher," he said. "Nothing is a secret. You plant that story and the government will find out it was you."

That was my conclusion. When I returned to Belfast, I did not stop off in London to plant the story.

Cafiero was already growing disillusioned with DeLorean. Unlike John, he was reasonable in his methods and skilled at bringing together executives with differing viewpoints and then hammering out a pragmatic program. John was often aloof, authoritarian and impulsive.

In early August 1980, John flew to Belfast to meet with Humphrey Atkins, the Secretary of State for Northern Ireland. He had decided that Cafiero didn't know how to argue the case and that he would do the job himself.

No one is quite sure what happened behind the closed doors of their meeting. The NIDA representative, Dennis Faulkner, accompanied John to the meeting but was asked to wait outside. The necessity for the secret meeting was later questioned in both Parliament and the media. Was John showing Atkins his battle plan? Was he letting him know what would happen if DeLorean Motors didn't get its money? At any rate, on Wednesday, August 6, 1980, the British unexpectedly agreed to a $28 million loan. Instead of being triumphant, John was furious.

"It should have been a grant, not a loan," John said.

The British, their patience with John's techniques wearing thin, now demanded as a condition of the loan that the inflation clause be removed from the contract. DeLorean must also acknowledge in writing that this was the last money he would receive from the British until the car was rolling down American highways. John accepted these conditions.

When Atkins announced the DeLorean "loan" there was a rebellion within the Conservative Party. The Belfast *Telegraph* reported that "the Government was strongly attacked in Commons . . . by Tory as well as Labour backbenchers. A Tory MP, Mr. Alan Clark, was cheered on all sides as he told Ministers they were the 'laughing stock' of the motor industry and maybe the criminal fraternity . . . Labour Leftwinger Mr. Bob Cryer condemned the loan as the 'biggest rip-off since the South Sea Bubble' . . . Clark said the Government were the prisoners of small print of an agreement negotiated by the last Government."

Even the Socialists joined in. Gerry Fitt, an Ulster MP, who admitted he had once been enthusiastic about DeLorean and his company, now said he was beginning to have deep reservations about the project.

The infusion of the $28 million, according to our projections, solved our problems. But John was not satisfied. In his mind the British had won the closed-door confrontation. We weren't tough enough, he told us.

"The loan on the books will make it more difficult for us to raise money," John said.

"Let's cool it for a while," I said. "Parliament is in an uproar."

But John stewed about it all summer.

Chapter Eight

John's "Suez" Crisis

Most of the DMC executives turned to me for help when John presented what they believed to be outrageous or dangerous ideas. I knew that side of John. He was apt to react impulsively to unevaluated information. My trick was to allow some time to pass before following through on orders that I believed John had not properly considered. Our long relationship allowed me that freedom. I thought of myself as a sounding board for John's creative ideas and future ambitions, the ones that went beyond the narrow confines of building a car in Belfast.

One battle I lost was over the air bag we had promised to install in the DeLorean. No other company was willing to be the first with the air bag, and our plan was widely publicized, helping John to advance his concept of a safe, ethical car. In Detroit, John had become one of the nation's most respected advocates of air bags. I knew John was bucking GM corporate policy when in the late sixties he openly recommended their use. He told me then that GM had a flat rule against talking in advertising about safety in cars. "It frightens customers," he explained. After he left GM, John had conducted a survey for the Allstate Insurance Company that concluded that air bags not only would save lives, but were practicable to produce.

We had also promised that the DeLorean would use "passive restraints," seat belts that automatically buckle you up. We also promised a design that would permit a driver to "walk away from an 80-mile-an-hour crash." (This was somewhat deceptive. The 80-mile head-on was determined by two cars hitting each other at 40 miles per hour. But even a 30-mile standard is impressive.)

In early 1980, John was forced to explain his decision to abandon air bags to federal transportation executives, who had counted on him to undermine the arguments in Congress of GM's powerful Washington lobby. John said that our steering column was being made by GM, and that when they abandoned the air bag we were forced to go along. To design our own system would be prohibitively expensive. John told Joan Claybrook, the head of the Federal Highway Traffic Safety Administration, and an outspoken advocate of air bags, that it would take $100 million for us to tool it on our own. The transportation executives reluctantly conceded that he was right. But John told me to leave a door open. If someone else came along with an air-bag system, we would use it. Our policy change went virtually unnoticed. Now, when John was asked by the insurance industry to defend air bags before a Congressional committee, he stalled.

"Bill," he wrote me, "I think we should stay out of this at this time unless the Department of Transportation asks us."

When I told him that both DOT and the insurance people had requested his testimony, he wrote back: "Bill H-I think we will get ourselves in a crack doing this — there is a reasonable argument that we could provide air bags."

Later, Claybrook called to tell me that Mercedes-Benz was moving ahead on air bags. I told John. He was skeptical about whether they would or indeed could do it.

"We can't base a production decision on their plans," he

said. He was right, of course, but I urged letting Gene or me find out what Mercedes was doing. John ducked the issue by not replying to either my memos or my requests. Later, when the insurance people again pressed us for a Congressional appearance, John refused to testify. Nor would he allow me to enter a statement on his behalf.

When John entered a fight, he would use every tactic and weapon available to him. Religion was no exception. In 1980, John told me he was a Catholic. It was a revelation. All the résumés he had prepared for GM indicated he was an Episcopalian. I never thought of John as a religious man. In all the years I had known him we had never discussed religion. One day when a writer asked me about John's religion, I routinely asked him about it, showing him the corporate résumé he had prepared for Chevrolet. He looked at it and crossed out "Episcopalian."

"I'm a Catholic," he said.

"When did that happen?" I asked. But he didn't answer.

Later he came into my office to ask me why I was surprised. "I don't give a damn about a person's religion," I replied. "But I never thought you were religious or Catholic. It just caught me off guard, that's all. No one in Belfast knows you are a Catholic. Everyone assumes you are a high Protestant."

"I know," he said. "I want you to change that. I want you to let your Catholic friends in Belfast know."

I was at first unresponsive to this idea. Religion is an explosive subject in Belfast. Whenever anyone in the company wanted to speak to Catholics in Belfast, they turned to me. The directors knew I had made Catholic friends in Twinbrook, the Catholic community at our rear gate, and at the university. John now set out to convince me that he was a devout Catholic and to urge me to spread the word in Belfast. We walked to work together occasionally, and whenever we passed St. Patrick's Cathedral, John would stop at the church and try to lure me inside with him.

"That's not my style, John," I said. "You know that."

"I do this every day I can," he explained to me. "It gives me a chance to say thanks for all the good things in life that have happened to me."

I never questioned his sincerity. I assumed he had kept his religion and his visits to St. Patrick's very private, and that when we passed the church on the way to work on previous mornings he had not stopped there because I was along.

In Belfast I began to drop the information in just the right places, careful not to discuss it in the wrong places, aware that John was using his Catholicism — and me — as a shield against his growing fear of the IRA.

"Is John in any danger from the IRA?" Cristina once asked me.

"They'll never touch an American," I said. "The IRA survives on contributions from Irish-Americans, and half our workers are Catholic. He's safe."

John's fear of the IRA continued to grow, however. One day he came into my office and asked me to find an armed chauffeur to drive him in New York. I found a retired detective licensed to carry a pistol. John told me to hire him, but before he joined us John changed his mind. Then he wanted a personal bodyguard who would travel and work with him as an assistant. I located a White House Secret Service agent who would take the job. John interviewed him and told me to negotiate a contract. With the previous experience still fresh in mind, I hesitated. I would wait John out on this one. As I had expected, he dropped the idea. Next he asked me if it were true that Henry Kissinger had a bulletproof raincoat. I didn't know, but I said I would ask Bill Barry, a former FBI agent and former chairman of the New York Racing and Wagering Board, who was helping me design the security for the Belfast plant, our New York office and John's home. Barry, who ran his own security agency, called me back to say that if John was considering wearing one, it was a "lousy idea."

"Why?"

"It would make him look like a Nazi storm trooper. It's black and it would come down to his ankles. It was so heavy that Kissinger never wore it. If John wants, we can get him a nice lightweight bulletproof vest."

John would not take no for an answer, and I decided to get out of the middle and let him negotiate directly. I know he was eventually measured for the raincoat, but I believe he never had it made.

One recurring theme in my discussions with John at the company was his love-hate relationship with the Arab world. He first revealed the depth of his feelings in a letter to me dated December 20, 1978, several months before I joined the company. John was scheduled to appear on NBC's *Today* show and he wanted to use his appearance to attack the Arabs. He wrote that the Arabs were not content just to quadruple the price of oil. In the process, he said, they had knocked the Western world out of one of our "strongest and longest periods of prosperity." They got away with it, he wrote, because President Nixon was in trouble. He went on:

"Today the Arabs are putting on a display of gluttony unmatched in modern times. They own every mansion in Paris, London, New York and Beverly Hills. They have untold secret bank accounts and they only survive because of America's protection [from the Russians]."

Then he proposed a quick-fix solution: "Let's take back our OPEC wells retroactively — let's nationalize all Arab investments and property in the Western world — in one fell swoop the world's problems would end . . ."

He wanted my advice on how to proceed: "Bill, shall I pursue this?" he asked. "Am I getting into trouble? As an American, it grinds me to have a few hundred Saudis destroy our world."

This was typical of DeLorean. His analysis of the problem was right on target, succinctly summarized and probably in tune with American frustrations. But his solution was off-the-wall. And now he had an opportunity to use television to promote the idea and trigger news stories and editorials throughout America. I convinced him, however, that this was not a subject he should discuss publicly.

In spite of these professed feelings, when he was building DMC, John sought Arab monies to finance his company and was, in 1980, seeking their help to raise another $20 million. John received a steady stream of agents purportedly representing Arab wealth. (I had a unique vantage point from which to check John's Arabs. My father was a French-speaking Jewish Arab who had been raised in Cairo, and I could understand some Arabic. I had come to understand the Middle East politically through Kefauver and Kennedy, and I had met and become acquainted with some Arab leaders.)

John continued to be concerned about the economic and political consequences of our dependence on Arab oil. He believed in both President Nixon's and President Carter's plans to make the nation self-sufficient through the development of alternative energy sources, but every time a report on the subject was issued, John was disappointed.

"They don't know what the hell they're doing," he said. "A bunch of academics with their heads up their assholes are trying to solve a problem they don't understand."

John's answer was to have me prepare a report for the President on his view of alternative energy sources and their development. He used every contact in industry he knew, and I followed through with a team of my own. When the report was completed, I sent it to President Carter, to key members of Congress and to other influential Americans. The White House and others praised it and began to cite it in reports. Editorials soon appeared, and Jack Anderson wrote a column on John's view that hydrogen was the fuel of the future. This was the John I had known in General Motors days.

John never forgot my advice not to talk about forceful takeover of Arab oil fields. Nevertheless, he often reacted strongly to articles about Arab wealth, and would send them to me as if to say: "You were wrong in 1978 and you are wrong now."

One day John decided he wanted to spy on the Arabs for the Israelis. Tom Kimmerly and John had been meeting secretly in Munich with a representative of the Saudi royal family who, they said, was thinking of investing in DMC. After one of these secret trips John called me into his office to talk about the "rising tide of anti-Semitism" in Germany, and the anti-Israeli statements of the Saudis, "who are supposed to be our friends."

"Can you put me in contact with Israeli intelligence?" he then asked.

"Why?"

"I think I can be of great help to them," he said. "The Germans and the Arabs trust me. I have direct contact with the Saudi-Arabian royal family. The Germans see me as a businessman and say things they wouldn't say to others."

"That's a very risky business, John. They play for high stakes. If anyone found out, the next time you're in Munich you might not come home."

"I'm not worried."

"The PLO and the Libyans train the IRA," I said. But John insisted. I said I would look into it, convinced that this idea would soon be forgotten. I was wrong.

A week later John called me into his office and asked, "Have you been able to contact Israeli intelligence?"

"Not yet," I said. But he knew that I was stalling.

"Isn't Howard Squadron a good friend of yours?" he asked.

Howard was president of the coalition of the presidents of Jewish organizations, and maintained close relationships with Israelis.

"He's my lawyer," I answered.

"Ask him to find out."

I alerted Howard, fearing that John would try an end run. I never asked for his help, however, but instead wrote John a note stalling and asking him for more details:

Regarding the Israelis . . . [there are] . . . three questions:
1. Is your information of a "specific" or a general nature?
2. Are you in a position to detail the various conversations?

3. Are you in a position to provide a continuous flow of information as you learn of it . . .?

John responded in a handwritten note: "Bill: I am very concerned. I have an idea that could solve the problem and I am prepared to participate in its implementation."

John would not say what the problem was or how he would solve it. I continued to stall. Two weeks later, he put his head into my office and said, "Forget about the Israeli thing. I made the contact myself."

Later that day, I asked him to tell me more about the Israeli contact. "How can you negotiate with the Arabs and be an Israeli informer at the same time?" I asked. "It could blow up in your face, and you could take the company down with you."

John did not reply. His eyes glazed. He seemed lost in his own thoughts. We never discussed the subject again.

In the middle of the Iranian hostage crisis John revived his idea of gaining control of the Saudi oil fields. He tried out the idea on me one morning over our cup of coffee. Converting America to alternative fuels, he began, was too long a process. More drastic action was needed.

"We have to do it militarily," he said. "We have to take over the Saudi oil fields and make their oil available to the free world. That would restore equilibrium in the world. We would be back to square one."

"That would be nice, John," I said, "but it ain't going to happen."

"We can make it happen."

"How?"

"We need to create an international incident so we can move in the way the British, French and Israelis did in Suez in 1956."

"When Eisenhower found out about that, he made them pull out," I said.

"But they had the right idea. They created the opportunity. We can do the same thing."

John began to outline his idea. He seemed calm and logical and precise. I watched his eyes and his face to see whether he would come to see the absurdity of it, or whether he was already convinced of it.

"The CIA arranges for the theft of a plane and a nuclear warhead," he said. "Then the CIA gets the plane and the warhead into the hands of Arab radicals, who are always trying to buy a nuclear device. When the Arabs are flying over North Africa, we force the plane down and 'find' the nuclear warhead. We blame the Saudis. Then we have our incident and the reason to parachute Marines into the Saudi oil fields."

John's plan was clean and simple. It was also crazy. It reminded me of the plot for his "novel" almost ten years earlier, and the Libyan plan we had advanced to the Israeli ambassador.

"What about the Russians?" I asked, trying to introduce some reality into the conversation. "They'd never allow Americans into those oil fields."

"Don't worry about them," he said. "I have some very good contacts with the Politburo, and they would welcome something like this. It would stabilize the price of oil around the world. The Russians are hurting like everyone else."

I tried to change the subject, but John wouldn't let go.

"What do you think?" he pressed.

"John, there are two documents that specifically prevent the CIA from undertaking covert operations to overthrow a foreign government — a National Security Council memo and a ruling of Congress."

"This will work," he said. "It's the only way."

I shrugged my shoulders and John left the room.

Two days later he mentioned the idea again. Only this time he wanted action on it. "I want to see the President," John told me.

"About what?" I asked.

"To tell him how we can get back our oil and how he can win the election."

"John, you can get to see the President, but not with an idea like that."

"Why not?"

"It's Buck Rogers."

"It'll work."

"The CIA can't do it and the Russians won't stand for it."

"You're wrong," John said. And he kept after me for weeks to set up a meeting with President Carter.

Later that month, when John and I were in Washington, he suggested we meet with Greg Schneiders, a talented former White House aide whom I was trying to persuade to work for us. I called Greg and he suggested that Jerry Rafshoon, another top Carter assistant and principle campaign adviser, might like to join us for lunch. Jerry was at home in Georgetown and, as luck would have it, he was free for lunch.

As we made our round of meetings that morning, I became increasingly apprehensive about what John might say at lunch, and I began to wish I hadn't arranged it.

"One thing you must promise me, John," I said, "is that you won't discuss the Arab oil thing."

"No, not with them. I want to talk to Carter."

At lunch the conversation drifted into politics. John said he was surprised that there were so few great leaders in politics. Rafshoon took up the challenge and asked John to name someone in business qualified to be President.

"You're right," John conceded, "I can't name a single person."

Then suddenly he said to Rafshoon, "There is only one way to win the election, and that's to settle the oil problem."

"How do you do that?" Rafshoon asked, intrigued to find out what a tough and successful businessman would advise. As John began to outline the plan he had earlier described to me, I could see Rafshoon's eyes widen and Schneider's brow furrow.

"You'd not only solve the oil problem," John concluded, "but win this election hands-down for Carter."

"Government doesn't work that way," Rafshoon said, and he attempted to change the conversation. But John was determined.

"I bet I could sell it to the President," he said.

"Maybe you could," Jerry said, looking down at the menu. I moved in to divert John to another subject, pointing out that people could overhear our conversation. Later, Rafshoon told me that it was several minutes before he realized that John was dead serious.

For weeks John kept at me to arrange an appointment with the President. When he finally realized that I wasn't going to move, he sent me a long, detailed memo entitled "Ted Kennedy Is in Serious Trouble," and went on to suggest how his CIA plan, if advocated by Kennedy, would win the election for him. He wanted the senator to take half an hour on prime time television and advocate the "rightful return" of the oil fields to the United States, the United Kingdom and the Netherlands.

Kennedy, John wrote, could not be nominated or elected because he had lost his credibility and was not trusted by the public. He had used up his due bills with the liberals and his solutions to the energy crisis and inflation were weak. But there was one way he could regain all he needed to win: by advocating a war with the Arabs, who, according to John, had virtually destroyed the economy of the free world.

John's proposal for Kennedy was the one he had made to Rafshoon: we should take over the oil fields and sell oil to all nations at past contract prices. All Arab investments in Western banks would be sequestered and divided among nations. Any nation that refused to go along with the recapture of Arab wealth would lose its entitlement to oil. As a result of all this, every Western nation would be put back on its feet economically. And, most important, the United States would regain its prestige and world leadership, taxes would be cut and inflation lowered to 5 percent. And finally, Teddy Kennedy would become a hero.

His argument, for all its absurdity, would have made one hell of a political speech. I suspect it might have rallied a great many frustrated Americans. But I refused to send the memo to Senator Kennedy or to discuss it with him. He would have laughed me out of his office.

As I look back on John's "Suez" plan, I am thankful that he was in business and not in politics. Men like DeLorean have seduced nations with their simplistic solutions to national and international problems. And his was a potent idea.

Actually, we may have come quite close to having John in politics. He once talked to me about running for governor of New York. And in 1980 that did not seem so farfetched. John might have been either a Republican or Democratic gubernatorial candidate. Both parties are partial to successful businessmen with social consciences. If his car had succeeded, DeLorean's name would have been a household word, equated with integrity and honesty. He was handsome, charismatic, wealthy, and had a beautiful wife and a lovely family. He would have been "willing" to give up the comfort he had earned and the happiness he had found to enter the dirty world of politics, once again as an honest man in a den of thieves.

Chapter Nine

Rattling The Saber

In the fall of 1980, John decided to intimidate the British into giving us another $30 million by using his "black book" technique. He had stewed all summer over the $28 million loan that the British government had made in exchange for a pledge not to seek additional financing elsewhere. John believed that this money should have been a grant, not a loan. Now we were in trouble again, and his agreement stipulated that we could not go back to the British for funds.

The Lotus delays were eroding our cash reserves, and John stubbornly refused to cut costs elsewhere. McKinsey & Company, which was advising the British government, estimated that we would need an additional $24 to $28 million to complete our first shipment of cars. And John was beginning to understand that new investors were not going to buy into the company until we had manufactured our first salable cars.

We now had almost 900 workers at the Dunmurry plant, and we were hiring more every week. The first pre-production car was due off the line in early December. We were going to make 500 pre-production cars for testing — which would not be sold — and then begin manufacturing cars for sale. There was genuine excitement, an excitement the British government shared, now that we were in sight of our goal. For John, this was the right time to strike. They weren't going to abandon us now.

On September 20, 1980, John called me into his office for a meeting with Cafiero, Jim Stark (who had recently replaced Strycker as our chief financial officer) and Tom Kimmerly, our counsel. I was surprised to find Bob Dewey in the room. He had had trouble finding a job in Detroit and now rejoined the company as a consultant. (He later told me that he had no alternative but to come back to work for John.)

John seldom held staff meetings, so we guessed that this was something important. John coolly presented his scheme to intimidate the British into providing the money we needed. He got right to the point. "The British screwed us last summer," he said. "The twenty-eight million-dollar loan should have been a grant or, at worst, half loan, half grant. They violated our agreement."

He said the British had agreed to "see us through" our difficulties and provide us all the capital we needed. Now they were reneging on that promise. This was not a new argument; we had a similar discussion the previous summer. When we had asked John to point to this pledge in the Master Agreement, he had become angry and defensive.

"It was an unspoken understanding," he had said. "It wasn't in writing, it was in their eyes."

No one in the room — with the possible exception of Tom — was prepared for this new attack on the British. We knew we would never get another dime until we sold some cars. Finally I said it. John didn't seem to hear me.

"The British also owe us another eight million pounds in adjustments," he said. "They can make the twenty-eight-million-dollar loan a grant, and loan us another eight million pounds. If they do that, we're even."

"There's no way that's going to happen," someone said.

"Then they can give us back their equity," retorted John.

As part of their original agreement, the British had purchased $45 million worth of stock in DeLorean Motors, Ltd., the Belfast company. John was now proposing that they simply give it back.

"No one knows about the equity," he said. "All the British public has heard about are the royalties we are going to pay them." (The British were to receive a $370 royalty on each of the first 90,000 cars we produced.)

"Parliament won't hold still for that," I said. "They nearly hung us when we got the last money."

Cafiero and Dewey quietly argued the same points, but John persisted.

When the meeting was over I looked into Gene's office. "It's not going to work," I told him.

"I know," he said.

"What do we do?"

"Wait."

We didn't have to wait long. The next day John sent Tom his "strategy memo," with copies to Gene and me. It was a plan to force the British into accepting John's demands. There were to be statements from everyone on our side who had participated in negotiating the agreement confirming that the British owed us another £8 million. Outside counsel was to prepare an opinion that "should include the statement that, to minimize personal and corporate liability, the company and its officers and directors are obligated to take all necessary legal remedies, including litigation, to enforce this agreement. Otherwise dealers and investors can demand their money back and money damages — potentially devastating to DMC."

Our lawyers in the U.K. were to prepare this case but not file it. We were to tell the British government that we were forced into making this new demand to protect ourselves from stockholder lawsuits. We would say that we were very reluctant to sue, because such a lawsuit would "destroy the credibility of NIDA," but that nevertheless we were bound to sue, because "our lawyers tell us we must." John called the process "rattling the saber."

"Obviously," he concluded, "this is an idealized scenario fraught with potential pitfalls and problems, but we must pursue it aggressively. We should be ready to spring this in January 1981, about the time they are ready to take the bows for the success of the project."

I was convinced that this plan would fail. The British government was not General Motors. There was Parliament to consider, if nothing else. By December nothing had happened, and I was sure that John had abandoned the plan. But I was wrong.

On December 17, John and I traveled to Belfast for a meeting of the DMCL board of directors. John was in one of his dark moods. On our way from Heathrow Airport to the Ritz Hotel in London, John was looking out the window at a row of tenement houses.

"You know," he said, "the greatest revenge is to live in luxury."

We were riding in a chauffeured Daimler sedan, headed for one of the finest hotels in the world. John was accomplishing what almost all his peers in the automobile industry said was impossible. He had a palatial office in New York and a duplex home on Fifth Avenue worth almost $5 million. He had a ranch in California, farms in Montana, and a multimillion-dollar personally owned company in Utah. He was married to one of the most beautiful women in America, and they had two lovely children (John having discovered that his earlier fears about not being able to have children were unfounded).

"You have everything, John," I said. "You're on top of the world. Who are you angry at?" But he wasn't listening. He was withdrawn, absorbed in his own thoughts.

In Belfast, John presided at the December 19, 1980, meeting of our board. As usual, the meeting was divided between reports on the progress of the car and discussion of our need for more money. Before the meeting was over, John and Jim Stark ducked out to drive across town to meet with the NIDA board.

Tensions were mounting in Belfast. They always did at Christmas, when the IRA increased its terrorist activities. Military helicopters hovered over the factory, monitoring the movements of people in nearby Twinbrook. British troops were on special alert in armored vehicles. Soldiers in flak jackets rode through the streets carrying automatic rifles. Street patrols crept along the walls of buildings, scouts running ahead and signaling them to move forward. Sometimes a shot rang out.

When John returned later that day, I asked him how the NIDA meeting had gone. "I let them know we meant business," he said. "I told them we were legally required to ask for the money or the equity. I told them we had all the statements backing up our position."

Unless the British came up with the money, John said, we would close down the plant and blame the Thatcher government for not living up to the promises of the Labour government. John was confident that he had raised the stakes so high that the British would be forced to back down. The Labour government, in John's reckoning, had promised Catholics jobs, and now the Conservative government was taking them away. The Catholics would not take that quietly: riots would erupt, and the IRA would have a new cause.

There was nothing to say. John had, indeed, "rattled his saber." He headed for London, leaving behind a note for NIDA's director, Tony Hopkins. In it, he warned that counsel had advised that our directors on both sides of the Atlantic would be subject to charges of fraud if we placed orders without having the money to pay for them.

The British government owed DMC £20 million, he wrote. If the British did not come up with the money, he would be forced to shut down all operations immediately.

I felt it was pure blackmail, but John felt he was totally

justified. I sensed then that John had set in motion a train of events he could not control. I couldn't get John's plan out of my mind. His actions were bizarre. He was treating the British government just as he had treated General Motors.

I spent Christmas Eve at my home in East Hampton preparing a tree for my children, who joined me the next day. We had a late Christmas dinner and sat around the tree opening presents; we went to sleep after midnight. I awoke at six the next morning, lit a fire, made myself a cup of coffee, and disappeared into the den.

I began to write a confidential memo to John. I had no idea then that ten months later this memo would cause Prime Minister Thatcher to order Scotland Yard to investigate my charges.

This is what I wrote:

Date: December 26, 1980
To: John DeLorean
From: Bill Haddad

I continue to be concerned about our efforts to set up a scenario under which the British relinquish their share of equity in the program. I just don't think it will work. And, if it does work, it will only follow a storm of public protest which will reach from London to Detroit to Washington.

Perhaps I don't understand the reason for the push at this time. I don't see how it can help our cash flow problem. So I assume the action is taken in conjunction with our plans for a public offering. If that is the case, while it may enhance the DMC equity position and, consequently, what people are willing to pay for the stock, the public outcry may reduce the attractiveness of the offering and even require the postponement of the offering. However, as you will see below, that is not my only concern.

I wasn't there at the time, but for the purpose of this memo, let's assume our position is legally correct.

I know you believe the power of the logic and the facts, presented to the British in a closed room, will create the conditions for them to relinquish their equity position. However, I don't believe that any action of this magnitude can be decided below the ministerial level, the Whitehall level, and that, of necessity, given the British system, will produce, I am convinced, a violent Parliamentary outcry and a mandatory Parliamentary inquiry. Given the Fleet Street nature of the British media, and the cynical attitude toward private enterprise (and DeLorean in particular) exhibited by the BBC, I think you and the company will be painted in the blackest of terms.

I am also worried about what a Parliamentary inquiry will uncover about our expenditures on both sides of the ocean. There are the "official"* complaints which can be sensationalized even though Arthur Andersen, SEC, et al, will give a clean bill of health. The Strycker picture is a highly personal one of John Z. DeLorean milking the company for his private profit. Some of the discredited† Strycker charges can be succulent journalistic morsels for the Fleet Street crowd never overly concerned about separating accusation from fact.

As you know, I am also troubled by some of the Bennington actions regarding the house and some of the expenditures which appear to have been "fuzzed" (like a 10,000 pound expenditure at Harrods for gold faucets, etc.).‡ I recently learned, for example, that we may have hidden some of the capital expenses of the house in

* By "official" complaints, I meant complaints made in the British Parliament by MPs.

† John told me that Arthur Andersen had "discredited" the charges that Walt Strycker made regarding using certain DMC employees to perform tasks unrelated to DMC business.

‡ Our Belfast managing director, Chuck Bennington, lived in a remodeled company house just outside the plant's gates. The radical Catholic press had reported an expenditure of £14,000 for gold faucets when the house was remodeled. When I investigated I learned that we had spent £10,000 at Harrods, a bill that included gold-plated or gold faucets.

expenses for the project. In short, the books were altered. Silly, because the house can be justified.

The Lotus situation troubles me, too. I know everyone approved it, but, no matter the hero status of Colin Chapman, hidden Swiss accounts to avoid British taxes may be viewed differently in the media than in the courts or in the higher circles of sophisticated government bent on getting something done quickly and efficiently.*

There is also the problem of moving so quickly. I understand from my University contacts that it is fairly well known that the architects made a small fortune on us (so did Lotus!). They may have deserved it, but what are the small items which made up this fortune? Did we monitor closely enough? Why wasn't JZD there to oversee everything? Was he, as Strycker charges, pursuing other interests?

If we were in production, and the British could taste the recovery of their money, the contrast between these items and the general state of their economy would not be so dramatic. After all, any of the higher expenses will cost us as well as them, and we, in the end, are not only repaying their investment, but with a dividend in people off the dole and 2,000 new jobs in one of the most unpopular areas of the world (their goal in providing us the money). Perhaps, due to the offering,† we were legally *required* to take this unpleasant action. I know the counter-arguments.

The story which could emerge, however, is that De-Lorean (it is your name on the door), who got £60,000,000 of British taxpayers money is so greedy that he wants to take more and deprive British of their rightful equity.

No matter your legal briefs, the accurate comments of those present at the time, that is the story which *could*

---

*We had paid over $17 million into a Swiss account in connection with our work with Lotus.

†John was constantly preparing plans for raising money.

emerge: The 1890 American robber baron image, enhanced by Fleet Street's love of the spectacular. And the British are on record, as you know from the recent Belfast interviews, as stating they owe us no more money.

That's not what really worries me down deep.

We are *not* now a target of the IRA because we have "good will" on our side. On my last trip to England I met with one of the producers of the BBC show where you were surprised with questions which they had promised not to ask. The producer said he tried to halt this line of questioning during the show, but the presenter kept pushing. However, he did say that *never* in his experience did any show produce such a negative response from the audience. He was literally flooded with angry letters complaining that the presenter was harassing a man who only wanted to do good for Ulster. You are a hero in Ulster, untouchable by the IRA or any of the more loosely organized terrorist groups.

If that attitude changes, and they paint you black, and it sticks for even a short period of time, and evokes a local response, the IRA could put us on the list. They won't go for the factory, they will go for you. In Belfast or, just as easily and more dramatically, here in New York.

Those are the stakes. That is what worries me.

I just want these views factored into any decision you make.

As I said, I don't know the rationale or the urgency, but I do worry about the potential consequences if we continue down this road.

And don't shoot the messenger, just review, carefully, the message.

I had written John the memo to convince him to slow down and look around. His actions seemed to me to be self-destructive. You don't blackmail the British government.

There was still time to introduce reason into his relations with the British.

Cafiero was convinced, as I was, that we could not afford to constantly play a confrontation game with the British. They were our partners. They were our only hope for the money we needed to stay afloat. I believed that my long-standing friendship with John would compel him to consider my fears carefully. I was his friend, not his enemy.

I gave the package to the driver of the East Hampton Jitney, and Ellen Kugler, my assistant, picked it up in New York. She returned to the DMC head office at 280 Park Avenue and retyped it, giving Dee Fensterer a copy. Ellen remembers the memo because of the last line. She was going to be the messenger. My instructions to her were to hand-deliver the memo to John. In the event that he wasn't there, she was to place the sealed envelope on his desk. This in fact is what she did.

When I returned to work I expected a reply from John, but I encountered only silence. I could feel the chill in our relations. But he soon let me know that he had not abandoned the confrontation game. One day he stormed into my office and asked me to draft a press release saying we were closing down all operations.

"What the hell are you talking about?" I asked.

"The British are screwing us and I want to shut down the plant. Let them see what happens in Belfast when we start laying off Catholic workers and start blaming Thatcher for not living up to the government's commitments."

"No one will believe you, John. They gave us one hundred and fifty million dollars."

There was no arguing with him, and it was very hard for me to delay the press release with John only a few doors away. I put in an urgent call to Cafiero and to Shaun Harte. I prepared a press release from John's notes. He read it over my typewriter and took it back to his office to edit. He was pleased.

"If that doesn't get them off their asses, nothing will," he said.

"If you close the plant, there will be riots," I said. "You're going to open up a Pandora's box that you won't be able to close. The IRA has left us alone, but they're looking for something dramatic. And Gene insists this is not the way to deal with the British."

"What the hell does Gene know? He's giving in to them. We're getting screwed."

"Do you want to start a riot that could burn down our factory?"

"I don't give a shit. They're screwing us. It's their fault."

I had seen John when he was flying like this, and had learned that it was better to let him come down on his own. The more pressure, the more resistance.

I returned to my office and looked at the edited press release. It read:

> The DeLorean Motor Company announced today it was suspending its worldwide operations, including its factory in Belfast, Northern Ireland, in a dispute with the British government over the financing of its sports car program.
>
> John Z. DeLorean, Chairman of the DeLorean Motor Company, said the action was "mandated by the refusal of the government to fulfill its obligations under the existing contract.
>
> "Under the circumstances we were left with no other alternatives... We will not commit funds we don't have... It's tragic that, as we reach the end of such a long, difficult struggle, we must take this action..."

When Gene called, I told him what was happening. I sought out Tom, but he just shrugged his shoulders. "John's made up his mind," he said.

In Belfast, Shaun Harte confirmed that John's threat could

set off a chain reaction. The city was already tense. There was a determined hunger strike by IRA prisoners in the H Block at the Maze prison.

John's press release was designed to frighten the British into giving us £20 million he said "they owed us." If they didn't do that, he had a fallback strategy that he had developed over the holidays. He wanted the British to guarantee two bank loans for £10 million. John was planning to mortgage our inventory to the Northern Bank in Belfast and Citibank in New York. He told the British that the banks had agreed to the loans on the condition that the British government guarantee them. "No big deal," he said. "This way the British don't have to give us any more money. They just have to sign the guarantee. No one will know about it."

Gene and I finally convinced John not to release the announcement. But it was a struggle. For one thing, Tom Kimmerly had undermined John's confidence in Gene. One day John asked me why Gene didn't want to be in Belfast. I didn't understand what he meant, for Gene and I were the only ones among the New York executives then spending any time at all in Belfast.

"I think he's frightened to go there," John said.

"I doubt it."

"Tom tells me he's even afraid to lift the tops off his garbage cans because he thinks they might trigger a bomb."

"That's pure bullshit!" I retorted. "I'm in Belfast with Gene every month and that's simply not true."

I returned to Belfast in January to learn that John had devised yet another way to confront the British. This time it was over the Chairman's Report to the DMCL board, which was meeting in Belfast on January 21, 1981. Copies of the report were sent to Dennis Faulkner, the NIDA chairman; Tony Hopkins, NIDA's executive officer; and Frank Mc-Cann, the Northern Ireland Secretary of Commerce.

John read the report to the Belfast directors, including the two representatives of the British government. We were gathered in the windowless board room at the plant. John sat at the head of the table, jacket removed, his half-glasses perched on the end of his nose. He read slowly and carefully, filling the room with a sense of impending disaster. He fixed the blame for the delays on the British, the "Irish troubles" and Lotus. Pre-production cars were moving down the production line. Serial number 501 would be the first car shipped to the States. We would build 210 cars in February and 300 in March, John said. By June we should be on schedule.

John talked at length about how General Motors had been eight months late on the Vega program, fourteen months late on the Lordstown van, eleven months late on the last A car, and eight months late on the new X car. He added that the Kama River truck plant in Russia was four years behind schedule. Then he made the point that none of these programs included the degree of new technology that DMC's did. Our major problems were "delays at Lotus caused by manpower shortages, technical errors and inadequate facilities . . . delays at Lotus caused by their lack of experience in transmitting technical information to another enterprise . . . DMCL's lack of experience with the European Economic Community and U.K. suppliers, who have a very different pace and priorities from those in the U.S. . . . [and] obviously, we made a certain number of mistakes and judgmental errors which have also caused delays."

"You will recall," John continued, "that when we received our Inflation Allowance from the government in July of last year, we had indicated that the company's funding requirement was £20 to £22 million. Giles Shaw [a government official] had indicated his understanding that £14 million was all that was required to complete the budget. I indicated to both Mr. Shaw and Mr. Atkins that this was not the case, but they were firm that this £14 million was the total monies on offer in accordance with the department's Letter of Offer, and we had no alternative but to accept it."

John complained that he was hindered in raising money in

the States because of the "adverse factors of the high political profile from the Northern Ireland problems, highlighted by the H-Block hunger strike, which made daily headlines in the U.S. during our fund raising."

That wasn't totally true. The underwriters were in fact waiting for us to show that we were more than talk. They wanted a car they could drive.

John predicted that "the American market should be stronger in May and June. Nineteen eighty-two and 1983 are universally forecast to be America's largest automotive years ever."

Then John reached the heart of his message. He would shut down the plant unless he received the money from the British. It was the threat contained in the press release.

"In the event we do have to suspend our worldwide operations until additional funding is secured, it is mandatory that this be done in such a manner that all of our bills are paid and enough cash is retained to pay rents, utilities, telephones and a few secretaries to answer phones and correspondence. If we leave unpaid bills and are forced by creditors into bankruptcy, it is unlikely we will ever reopen. The ensuing legal battle and injunctions among the various legal entities would, no doubt, tie up the plant, equipment and tooling for many years.

"Obviously, if we close, it would take much more than £18 million to reopen. Let's hope it does not come to that.

"I am asking Joe Daly [DMCL's chief financial officer] to keep our outside directors posted in relation to our finances on a daily basis. In addition, we ask that in the event you are out of town, we have your phone number so that we may call you in an emergency that warrants unusual action by the board."

Then, having finished his report, John said solemnly, "That should do it." After a moment he pushed his chair back from the table, removed his glasses and smiled. "The fat's in the fire," he said. "It's up to them." There was no reaction from those seated around the table.

The directors had known about the proposed press release, and they remembered the December threat to NIDA. Now John had spelled out in public what he had been saying for weeks in private. When a British director asked about the status of his report, John confirmed that the government already had it in its possession. It had been delivered while he was speaking.

John got his answer, but not in the form he expected. A week after the meeting, his December and January threats to the British were leaked to the Belfast *Telegraph,* which reported them in a front-page headline that ran across the top of the paper: DELOREAN—NEW CLASH ON CASH.

The newspaper added some fresh details. The British, it seems, had compiled a black book of their own:

"The Northern Ireland Development Agency has reached the conclusion that some of the DeLorean executives have been less than frank with their Board, the Agency and the Department of Commerce about cash flow projections. This is apparently based on DeLorean having estimated on December 16 last, that the shortfall next April would be £700,000 — an estimate which was increased to £4.0m on January 5 and £8.1m on January 15."

Then the still secret results of a survey of the company's prospects, completed in December 1980 by McKinsey & Company, were described. The consultants had concluded that the prospects for 1981 could be grim. In making the £14 million claim, the newspaper reported, DeLorean had argued that "the company was only performing its legal duty in demanding that NIDA honour its contractual commitments . . ." The story then proceeded to recount how John had wanted the government to secretly relinquish its $54 million in equity: "Mr. DeLorean said that there was no public knowledge of the existence of these shares in the U.K. Thus, their redemption would go unnoticed — a painless solution for NIDA.

"His London solicitors had assured him the company would win . . . and the entire £14 million would be granted instead of the 50 percent which the DeLorean Company was requesting.

"Mr. Hopkins warned that if these attempts proved unsuccessful, the Government was faced with providing cash or guarantees or see the project fail."

John was surprised that the British had fired back. It was a possibility he hadn't considered. In retrospect, we realized that there had been a flurry of embarrassing stories earlier that month that should have been a warning to John. The wire services and the *Wall Street Journal* had reported that unless DeLorean received the money he was seeking, he could not meet the payroll. This had been one of John's little threats, and it had backfired. Closing down for lack of money was not the story John had wanted to read in the papers, and so he had wired me in Belfast (sending a copy to the British government) that the financing he had in the works had been canceled and that the British were to blame.

"The Department of Commerce and the Northern Ireland Development Agency," John said, "must clearly understand that this 'leak' of theirs had clearly cost us our public financing. It is unconscionable that such confidential information be leaked to the press. In addition, this leak has seriously injured our dealer credibility and perhaps our bank lines."

NIDA's chief executive, Tony Hopkins, denied that there had been a leak. The story had originated when the question of a loan had been raised in Parliament, he said. "This Agency made no comment and was not responsible for the press speculation which occurred."

Frank McCann, the Northern Ireland Secretary of Commerce, was even harder on John. He publicly asked John to "substantiate" his charge that "a tentative commitment" for the money had been made. None had been made.

Adam Butler, the British Minister of State for Commerce, also warned John that the British weren't going to submit to intimidation:

". . . As I told you when we met on 11 February, my view is that Government has provided a most generous measure of special industrial support for your enterprise, and I underlined the fact that there was no obligation to provide the guarantees which will enable you to obtain the bank loans up to £10,000,000 that are needed to bring the car to market launch. I reminded you that you had agreed in July 1980 to accept a loan of £14,000,000 as the Government's final measure of assistance to the project and at that time you expressed confidence that you would raise any additional funds required for it from the private sector without recourse to Government. Against this background, I consider that Government has not only fulfilled its obligations to your Company, but has exceeded them... I now regard the question of further special assistance as closed."

John wasn't listening to this, however. He ordered me to begin a lawsuit against the Belfast *Telegraph* for libel and slander. The idea was so outrageous that I simply ignored John, but he kept pushing. "Take it from a newspaperman," I said. "If you sue, they'll go right for the jugular." In the end, he did not sue.

In late February, John responded to Butler with a proposition "the British could not turn down." He would give up all his profits for four years to create new jobs in West Belfast. John wrote: "As events progressed we both became trapped by the unfortunate and incomplete news leak which escalated an everyday commercial event into a public confrontation. For DMC erroneous news stories about our company needing $1.3 million to survive have all but ruined the ongoing efforts to substitute private capital for Government monies and at the same time destroyed our production schedule by stopping our suppliers in their tracks. The cost to us of this news leak is in the millions of pounds."

John said that in order to avoid the personal liability of the directors he was forced to report all this to the U.S. Securities and Exchange Commission. (He never actually reported the incident.) This was why he had raised his questions about the nature of the loan and additional monies the British owed the company, he said. "In this action, we were not a free agent, but pressed into resolutions by the complications of U.S. laws . . . and by doing so would avoid future unpleasant consequences for both you and ourselves."

Changing his tone, John became the concerned businessman: "Although I am not politically inclined and prefer the safe shelter of a businessman's world, I do understand and appreciate the enormous courage it took to join forces with us. Rest assured we will reward that courage with success. We intend to make the program succeed not only for us, but for the people of West Belfast, who definitely need a helping hand."

Then John applied the "sting." He would operate DMCL *in Belfast* on a nonprofit basis for four years if the British would forgo interest payments on his loans and royalties. That would lower the price of the car — now more than double its original estimated price of $11,000 — increase sales, and result in 400 new jobs for West Belfast.

How could the British turn down such a deal? Four hundred new jobs? And no profit for DeLorean?

What many people did not understand was that John had restructured the two companies — DMCL in Belfast and DMC in New York — so that all the expenses incurred in building the car were charged to DMC, the company in which the British held their equity. By arranging the "transfer price" — the price at which DMCL sold the car to DMC — as John wished, most of the profits would accrue to the American company. This was legally possible, since John had total control of both boards.

The "new deal" that the British could not turn down cost John nothing, since it applied only to Belfast. It did, however, clean up his balance sheet. With no debt service and no royalty payments, DMC became more attractive to investors.

For a time it seemed that the British government had called John's bluff. Eventually, however, the British quietly guaranteed the £10 million sterling that John had requested. In the final analysis, they couldn't afford the consequences of having

the DeLorean plant close in the midst of a hunger strike.
Those of us who had urged restraint were proven wrong. The
British, John had said, understood only one thing. Power. We
had it and they lacked it.

Chapter Ten

The Golden Ring

In early 1981, as the first salable DeLoreans were coming off the assembly line, John seemed to lose interest in Belfast, and his focus shifted from building the car to creating a conglomerate to rival General Motors.

We formed the DeLorean Maritime Company, hiring a shipping executive to manage it. At first John only wanted to lease ships, but later he began to talk about building his own fleet, probably in Mexico, and shipping Mexican oil around the world. We sent lawyers to meet with Mexican officials, and elaborate schemes were prepared; but after six months John lost interest in the project.

John sent Gene Cafiero to Poland and other countries in Eastern Europe to obtain the rights to an off-road vehicle that could be used in rough terrain. We developed a prototype, the DMC-44, which John believed he could market in this country. But Cafiero was convinced it was a wild-goose chase, and he was right. Nothing ever came of the project.

John planned to manufacture replicas of famous old cars in Italy. Underwritings were planned for the production of an engine, the Sterling. For reasons John never explained, certain South Americans were using our credit cards and phones, and oil shipments were being moved by our Telex. John asked me to develop a privately operated intelligence service to accept "assignments" too embarrassing for governments to undertake. We would recruit mercenaries and plant spies in other businesses. When John first raised the idea, I didn't respond. Later he wrote me spelling out in detail what he wanted.

The British government was aware of some of these activities, and reminded John of his commitment to devote all his energies and finances to building the car in Belfast. John's response was to criticize them for not giving him more money. When John was challenged by his own executives he became furious and accused them of disloyalty or of "working for the British."

John also came to believe that the British were going to kill him. Nothing I could do or say would convince him that the British didn't employ hit squads to take out businessmen they disliked. I became so concerned that on March 18, 1981, I sent John a private note saying:

"I've continued to think about the concept that the government is out to put you away, which you say comes from an 'incredibly' reliable, firsthand source. As I said yesterday, I could give the police ten names of people who might want to put you away, but the U.K. government would not be one of them. First, there is no point in it . . . They could embarrass us to the point that someone would destroy the business. They could investigate the hell out of us and delay us long enough for us to go broke . . . The type of activity you describe is no longer possible because there is no one to give either the formal or informal orders.

"If I were out to destroy you, it would not be physically. I would destroy your carefully carved reputation; I would penetrate your secrets . . . I would examine court cases for negative testimony . . . I would examine your financial affairs and, with hints, I would turn loose great reporters to do the story. All of that is feasible and possible under their system without any great overwhelming decision . . .

"Where I come out, John, is this question: Why is your source telling you this?"

But John continued to believe that a British "hit squad" would get him at the right time.

By now my own relationship with John was mercurial. Sometimes he would ignore me, and at other times he would seem to forget our differences. For myself, I had grave doubts about John and about the entire enterprise. Like the others at DMC I was also swept up by the excitement of it all. Cars were by now moved from the back lot at Dunmurry and down the streets of Belfast to the docks, where they were being stored for the first shipment, now due in mid-April. To escape John, I found myself spending most of my time in Belfast, away from what I called the "palace intrigues" of New York.

The atmosphere at the New York office was often poisonous. I remember one occasion when John stormed into my office in a rage, shouting at me before he was even inside the door. "I want you to fire that bitch," he said. "I want her out of here today."

For a moment I thought he might be high on something. He had once told me that he took forty vitamin pills a day, and his moods swung from euphoria to despair.

"What bitch?" I said.

"That no-good bitch, that whore, that cunt that works for you."

"John, you're incoherent."

"The receptionist."

"Debbie? Christ, John, she's one of our best workers."

Debbie had been a receptionist before becoming my secretary. She was one of the most attractive people at DMC, with an outgoing personality that put everyone at ease. She was also a beautiful, tanned blonde with deep-blue eyes and a stunning figure.

"I want her out today," John shouted. "Today."

With that he turned and left, leaving me to carry out his order. When Debbie arrived a few minutes later, I called her into my office.

"Jesus Christ, Debbie, what the hell did you do to John?" I said, and related the incident to her. She was at a loss to explain it. She had no contact with John, who never acknowledged the presence of the secretaries, anyway, or spoke to them unless it was absolutely necessary.

It turned out that Debbie had been dating a young aspiring actor who worked as John's butler and lived in his apartment. He was also Maur Dubin's "gofer." They had announced that they were planning to get engaged, an announcement that had thrown Maur into a petulant rage. John's outburst was to me yet another indication of the strange influence that Maur Dubin had over him.

In Belfast, we had a new managing director, Don Lander, who had once run Chrysler's operation in the United Kingdom. He was a competent and well-organized executive. He sorted out some of the chaos in the Belfast operation and served as a buffer between John and the other directors. Like Cafiero, he had endured the brutal corporate in-fighting at Chrysler, and he tended to ignore John's paranoia.

In March 1981, Loasby and his engineers warned me that the car we had qualified under EPA regulations in the States was not the car we were preparing to ship. There had been many changes made to the model that Lotus had originally tested, and the EPA emissions and mileage tests were no longer valid. Given DeLorean's high visibility and our criticisms of Detroit, the discrepancy could potentially destroy the company.

I was so troubled by this revelation that I flew home to discuss it with John. He assured me that it wasn't true and demanded to know the name of the "disloyal" person who had given me the information. I refused to tell him. He grew agitated and then angry.

"I'm ordering you to tell me," he said.

"And I'm telling you I am not going to break a confidence. It's irrelevant who told me. It's true or it isn't true. I flew home because I wanted to tell you in person and not put it on paper. It's that serious."

"Put it on paper," he said.

I did.

I later learned that Lotus became so concerned about my inquiry into this that the original test car was recalled from the States and dismantled. Cafiero got involved personally in the problem, and after much effort he succeeded in building a car that met all applicable standards for both air pollution and fuel economy. We had announced that the car would get 29 miles per gallon in traffic, but when we came to test the car, we found that the gas mileage had slipped considerably. In the final event, the aggregate mpg of the standard and automatic was 22.5, a bare .5 above requirements.

This experience continued to trouble me, and I wrote John to underline our boast that we stood apart from the crowd because we were doing what they said could not be done. We were going to be judged not by normal standards, but by these standards we had set for ourselves. I pointed out that the car-enthusiast press was highly critical. John's reply was typical DeLorean.

"They're all whores," he said. "They're all on the payroll . . . The Detroit auto press lives off General Motors. They roll over when GM tells them to roll over, and they'll sit up when GM tells them to sit up. And they'll shit when GM tells them to shit. They're paid for it, too."

By April 1981, however, I began to believe that my criticisms were beginning to have some effect. John asked me how he could clean up his image in the United Kingdom.

I described to him the image I believed he had acquired, "the promoter image, somewhat the hustler, posing as the ethical person, but using that image to push the unreasonable bargain. Much of this stems from the confrontations with the

British and is reinforced by the Parliamentary debates which are picked up in the mass media.

"I'm not as much worried about the flamboyant personal image . . . as I am worried about the flamboyant business image . . . In short, we have to go back to basics: an ethical car, a creative engineer, a man who can move an idea into reality, and someone who is not afraid of the challenge or the confrontation . . ."

"You're right," John told me. "Let's work on it when you get back to Belfast. Spend time in London. I'll move around with you."

A week later the Associated Press reported that John had purchased a 430-acre estate in Bedminster, New Jersey, for $3.5 million, a transaction that the New York *Times* characterized as the "most expensive residential real estate deal ever made in New Jersey." John's new neighbors included Jackie Onassis and Malcolm Forbes. This purchase led to a violent attack on John in the British press and in Parliament, which contrasted his lavish lifestyle with his pleas for more money from the British. If he wanted to save the company, editorial writers suggested, he should invest his own money. The London tabloid newspapers ran aerial photographs of the twenty-five-room estate and reminded readers (and Parliament) that John had a $5-million apartment in New York, an avocado ranch in California, and ranches in Montana. The stories counterpointed the poverty and unemployment of West Belfast with John's statement that "God has placed me here to solve the problem."

The attack was devastating. No one except Tom Kimmerly had known of the Bedminster transaction. Tom had quietly formed a new corporation, TK International, for the purchase. But then John had permitted the real estate agent to publicize the purchase. It was self-destructive madness.

John could not understand the press reaction. He must have known about the Bedminster estate when we discussed my plan for changing his image in the U.K. Nevertheless he was adamant that what he did with his money was of no concern to the British. Legally, of course, he was right. But with Members of Parliament accusing him of using British money to sustain a lavish personal lifestyle, the purchase at Bedminster was the worst thing he could have done. Remarkably, John never saw it that way.

My most serious confrontations with John were over his efforts to make what I called "a quick buck" by taking various DeLorean companies public and translating his stock into cash. Going public was fine with me: I had $1 million in stock options. The other executives, all of whom had options, would also welcome the opportunity to capitalize on their hard work. But John's idea of going public was to place a value on his stock and ignore everyone else's interests.

In the summer of 1979, shortly after John had completed the original Belfast agreement, he personally purchased a manufacturer of snow-grooming vehicles for ski slopes based in Logan, Utah, which he renamed the DeLorean Manufacturing Company. John eventually paid for the company with a $9.5 million Swiss bank loan and the ingenious swap of land he owned in California for the land on which the Logan plant stood.

In 1980, when we had all but completed financing negotiations for the eventually aborted bus project, John told me that he wanted to merge our bus operation with Logan. John would pay DMC in New York $165,000 for the bus project, an amount equal to our out-of-pocket expenses. Then the merged company would seek a $30 million public financing from Wall Street. We would use the money for our bus company, John said. But the financing would also place a cash value on his Logan stock.

The plan had a major flaw: DeLorean would be taking advantage of a corporate opportunity for his personal profit. He would also be using his high visibility, sustained by British money, to sell stock in his personal company. None of the funds raised would be used for the car company, which, at the time, was seeking new financing from the British government. As much as I wanted money for the bus company, I thought this was not the way to get it.

When I expressed my concern, John said that the two companies — Logan and DMC in New York — would eventually be merged. "It's six of one, half a dozen of another," he said. But my doubts remained. I finally expressed my fears in a confidential memo. I wrote:

"Shortly [after we file our registration statement with the SEC] . . . I believe this item will appear: DELOREAN TO GO PUBLIC. That headline, I think will be interpreted by dealers as meaning that the DeLorean Motor Company will go public and only after that initial excitement will they learn that it is the DeLorean *Manufacturing* Company that is going public and that the value of their stock will not be a matter of daily public record for purposes of sale or borrowing . . ."

I asked John to decide whether we should inform our dealers and other investors of our actions so that they would be aware of what was happening. I also asked him what provisions we had made for the future merging of the two companies, and whether such a merger was mentioned in the prospectus. I said I didn't know the legal ramifications of such notice, so I was sending a copy of my memo to Tom.

"As you know," I went on, "I continue to worry that we could have a revolt on our hands if this is not handled well. And given the nature of some of the recent Parliamentary debates, I think we can expect a Parliamentary blast at this effort . . . they will view it as bypassing the British interest . . . followed by Fleet Street headline copy. One member [of Parliament] is particularly focused on DeLorean's personal investment, stock, etc. . . ."

At any rate, eventually reason prevailed and the Logan stock offering was killed.

In the late spring of 1981, Buck Penrose, vice-president for corporate affairs, and a real straight arrow, placed a weighty draft of a prospectus on my desk, explaining that John had a new plan for taking DMC public. He said I would be "interested in it." He was right. The plan called for the creation of a new company, the Delorean Motors Holding Company. John would transfer all his DMC stock to the new company. Holding would go public at a share value of between $12 and $14, making it potentially worth $250 million, of which John's shares would be worth $120 million.

As a corporate officer, and as someone the company said it depended upon for management, I would be required to sign the prospectus. I took the inch-thick document home to read. It was five o'clock the next morning before I finished it. If the law firm of Paul, Weiss, and the broker, Bache Halsey Stuart, were not named on the front cover, I would have considered the prospectus another one of John's wild schemes that would eventually fall through. But it was clear that hundreds of hours of lawyers' time had gone into preparing the document. John was serious. If Bache successfully sold this underwriting, John would be one of the wealthiest men in America.

John's plan was to create a new corporation, Holding, without the liabilities created by our debt to the British. Profits would flow "up" to Holding from DMC in New York and DMCL in Belfast, but the debts and liabilities, now in DMCL, would *not* be a responsibility of the new corporation. John would also evade British oversight by denying the British government seats on the board of Holding. (Under the Master Agreement, the British were entitled to two seats on the DMC/New York board of directors.)

As subsequent drafts of the prospectus arrived at my desk, I noticed that the participating car dealers would not be able to convert their DMC stock into Holding stock as John himself was doing. Their stock would remain in DMC and would not be publicly traded. For all practical purposes, their stock would have little or no commercial value. Later I noticed that the management options — which had attracted many executives to DeLorean — would also remain in DMC, thereby effectively losing their value. Clearly, John was isolating Holding and himself from past commitments. He was creating a new corporation without obligations. He was leaving his partners and his executives behind.

If the car company became profitable, its success would increase the value of Holding and of John's personal stock. If DMC failed, however, Holding would not incur any of its liabilities. By then it would be a free-floating company with diverse investments and not dependent on DMC. Under John's plan, he could not lose. And it was all legal. The involvement of a prominent law firm and a famous brokerage house placed the offering above suspicion. But from my point of view it was highly unethical.

I called Dick Brown in California. He had already complained to John about the prospectus, but John wouldn't listen to him. At the time I called, he had not realized that the executive stock options would not be converted. Brown had been concerned about the reaction of the dealers. We would be undermining them just as the first cars arrived, at the precise time we needed their commitment.

"John's not only greedy," Brown said, "but suicidal. He can't get away with it."

When a draft of the prospectus arrived in Belfast, angry executives there questioned me about their options, which they had correctly concluded would be virtually worthless. They asked me to confront John and I agreed.

"You can't cut them out," I told John in New York. "They threw in with you. They took their risks. They're entitled to their reward. And we need them."

"We don't need anybody," John said. "Everyone is screwed up. We're late on production. Cafiero is no good. No one is any good. Why should they have options?"

"Because we promised them."

I switched my argument to the dealers.

"It's insane to leave the dealers downstairs," I argued. "Now is the time we need their support."

"I can't do anything else," he explained. "If we take every-one upstairs to Holding, we can't do a tax-free deal. We'll handle all of that after we go public. They'll understand."

"John, they won't understand. You'll have a revolution on your hands."

I confronted Tom with the same problem, but he said it was John's idea, not his. I doubted that. I went to see Jim Stark, who was clearly angry about the whole business.

"John tells me that if he moves the dealers and executives upstairs, he won't be able to do a tax-free transfer," I said.

"Bache's lawyers raised the same question," he said. "They couldn't understand why John wanted to deprive his execu-tives of their equity. There's no legal reason to do it John's way. But I'm powerless to intervene. John wants it that way, and it's his name on the door."

I realized that Stark had come to the end of the road with John, just as Cafiero had. Solid businessmen both, they were planning to back away from the company after the first cars began to arrive in the States. They would fulfill their commit-ments and then leave quietly. I remembered something Stark had told me when he first came to DeLorean. "I've always worked for an institution," he said. "Over time the institution develops checks and balances, restraints, so everyone is pro-tected. With an entrepreneur, with a one-man show, every-thing depends on the integrity of the top man. Generally, I trust an institution."

"But you came with us."

He smiled. "I thought I would like to see how it was done on the other side," he said. "I decided to take the risk."

I could see that he now regretted that decision.

John knew me well enough to realize I had dug in my heels. I believed he was jeopardizing the success of the company in order to make a quick killing. The British government, the executives and the dealers would all be furious. John did make a concession, however: he would allow the dealers to convert their DMC stock into Holding shares.

In order to bring me into line, John began to use some techniques he had learned, and later developed, at GM. First he restricted my travel style. A memo from him ordered that only officers of the company who were also directors could travel first class or business class; I was an officer but not a director. DeLorean, Cafiero, Kimmerly and Stark were both officers and directors. I generally traveled business class to Europe and California, and from then on I upgraded the tourist class accommodations provided by the company to business class and paid the difference myself. John never mentioned the memo. Neither did I.

Later the DMC office manager told me that my offices in New York would be moved from the penthouse level of senior executive offices to the thirty-fifth floor, where we accommodated the accounting division and second-rung attorneys. The order was so petty that I just didn't respond. One morning John came into my office to tell me that I could stay on the penthouse floor but my staff would have to move downstairs.

"I need to be with my staff," I said. "Running back and forth between the two floors would not be productive." That was not the answer he wanted.

When he could not provoke a response on the relocation of my office, John went after my staff. Dee Fensterer was my most important associate, and the only woman executive at DeLorean Motors. I had hired a new assistant, Mike Knepper, who was to handle the press, and John now authorized a salary for Mike higher than Dee's, even though I had argued for equal pay.

As public affairs director, Dee had been responsible for the extraordinary publicity we had received during our search for an ad agency, and had arranged for "cooperative" advertising in which other companies featured DeLorean in their own ad campaigns at no cost to us. One of the most exciting of these campaigns was developed by Cutty Sark. John was concerned about an ad that related drinking and driving, and Dee had carefully written an appropriate text. Cutty Sark wanted to

feature John and budgeted $2 million for the print campaign.
But when the final release was sent to John, he balked.
Unknown to Dee, he demanded $10,000 "in free Scotch and
wine" as a fee. Cutty Sark agreed, but the anecdote made the
rounds of Madison Avenue and left behind a residue of doubt
about John. For a mere $10,000 he jeopardized $2 million in
free advertising and made doubters out of believers. He had
undermined all the good will that Dee created. It was, I was
beginning to understand, classic DeLorean. He focused narrowly on a target and disregarded all consequences.

One day John sent me a note to fire Dee. There was no
explanation.

"What the hell is that all about?" I asked him.

"The British want us to cut back on expenses."

"Is anyone else going?"

"Not at this time," he said.

The British had just completed an audit of DMC, and their
most positive statement was that my office had generated an
estimated $40 million in free publicity. I reminded John of the
audit and of Dee's contribution.

"If you want to get at me, go at *me*. Not Dee. That's a cheap
shot."

"I'm not going at you. Gene says she has to go."

When I saw Cafiero, he said that Dee was one of the finest
executives in the company and that he had recommended a
salary increase for her. But despite all this, Dee shortly
received a notice from accounting that she would be receiving
her last check. Fortunately, Dee immediately found not only a
new job, but a job with more authority and a higher salary.

As the summer of 1981 approached, John almost pushed
me out of the New York office. He insisted that I spend full
time in Belfast. Buck Penrose was ordered to stop sending me
the drafts of the prospectus, but somehow he always managed
to get a copy to me. It would be in my in-box, or waiting for
me in Belfast, or I would find one in my briefcase, which was
always open somewhere in my office. Whenever I wrote John

a note about some new detail in the prospectus, he would tear around the office trying to find the leak. Copies of the prospectus were numbered, and he recalled all previous copies to determine how I was receiving my information. My copy was clearly outside the system, however.

I had planned to spend at least five years with DeLorean, helping to build the new company and then, financially secure, getting back to my writing or journalism. Now I realized that this wasn't going to be possible. My days with DeLorean were numbered. But I felt I had made a real contribution to the creation of DMC, and I didn't want to admit that I had been mesmerized. My wife recalls that I had to be hit on the head with a baseball bat before I would change my views about John.

Belfast and its problems became a welcome relief from my self-doubts. We had a well-defined job to do there, and I could help get it done. When the first cars were zooming across American highways, then I could tip my hat to John and pick up my career elsewhere. In that sense, I was a little like Cafiero and Stark. But unlike them I was by now also John's target.

In Belfast, Don Lander told me that in business, if you can't go along with the boss, you get out, *quietly.* It was the unwritten code. It was also the way for men like Cafiero, Stark and Lander to survive. That's why there are so few whistle-blowers in the business world. I likened this attitude to organized crime's code of silence.

Belfast, for me, was not the wasteland it was for John. For a journalist, living in the eye of a storm is nourishing. I liked Belfast and I was stimulated by the atmosphere of danger created by the prisoners' hunger strike.

In Belfast, I now learned that we were having troubles on the production line. The machine to punch the several hundred holes in the DeLorean underbody had not arrived, and the permanent tooling for the VIRM (Lotus) process, used to make the car's inner plastic shell, was not completed.

Production-line progress was slowed as the new and inexperienced workers tried to align the holes to attach the body to the frame. Also, as some had predicted, the gull-wing doors didn't fit. The last gull-winged sports car, the Bricklin, had failed in part because rain seeped into the car from the poorly fitted doors. We had engaged Arthur August, the research director of Grumman Aircraft, to produce a unique torsion bar of remarkable strength and flexibility that allowed the door to move up and down and seal with ease. This bar was one of the small miracles of the DeLorean. Nevertheless, we continued to have problems with the doors.

Relations with Lotus remained strained. John, under pressure from Cafiero and his engineers, sent Shaun Harte to "double-check" the billings. His findings left no doubt that the Lotus managers were stretching out the DeLorean work. They only solution — one that Bill Collins had argued for at the beginning and that Loasby was arguing for now — was to move the engineers at Lotus who were on the DeLorean payroll up to Belfast, where we could manage their work at close range.

Within weeks, fifty talented young engineers were moved to Dunmurry. Some came reluctantly, others enjoyed the prospect of moving from the narrow confines of Norwich to metropolitan Belfast. Unlike the others at DeLorean, these engineers moved around Belfast as if they were in their hometowns. They stayed at the Europa, probably one of the most-bombed hotels in the world until the British agreed to make it "off limits" to their officers. When they moved in to complete the work on the DeLorean, we realized that Collins had been right to demand that we have our own engineering center. Without intermediaries who might misinterpret or distort instructions and stifle innovation, the engineers could work out solutions to our problems. That team might have made the difference in getting the DeLorean to market earlier and, I believe, would have ensured that the car we built had the ethical design standards set by Collins and originally articulated by DeLorean. We simply had lost control, for reasons that in mid-1981 remained a mystery, but a mystery I was determined to solve. Down deep my journalistic instincts told me it had something to do with GPD, the mysterious company in Switzerland that served as the conduit for funds to Lotus.

In the late spring of 1981, as Bobby Sands, the first of the hunger strikers at the Maze prison, slipped closer to death, the city filled with reporters, photographers and camera crews from all over the world. I knew many of them from my reporting and political days, and DeLorean was a good story for the reporters as they waited for Sands to die.

Sands died in the early morning hours of May 5. Now the IRA had a famous martyr. Soon the women of Twinbrook, reenacting an ancient ritual, were on the streets banging the covers of garbage cans against the road, signaling the news. The sound rose and echoed through the streets of Belfast. Before dawn, violence swept the city. Cars and buses, which had been stolen and stockpiled, were turned into fiery barricades. Teenagers and hooded men ran into the streets throughout Ulster to challenge the British. Smoke clouds hung over Belfast.

I was on my way back to Belfast from New York on the night Sands died. When I arrived on the morning of May 6, the Quonset hut that we used for a computerized control center had been burned to the ground. When the riots had begun during the night, the British had isolated the Twinbrook Estate, keeping its residents inside. (Bobby Sands had spent his youth in Twinbrook. His mother's home was a hundred yards from my office.) The men and teenagers of Twinbrook retaliated by building barricades to keep the British at bay. Molotov cocktails sailed over the barricades and landed alongside British armored cars, occasionally setting a soldier on fire. As the rain of bombs increased and the residents attempted to break out of the blockade, British soldiers charged, forcing people down Twinbrook's winding streets toward the DeLorean factory's back gate. Behind the factory's ring of two barbed-wire fences the Royal Ulster Constabulary (RUC) and the army waited for the crowd. Realizing that they were trapped between the two forces, the crowd hurled Molotov cocktails over the fences. The RUC and the British troops, out in the open without cover, held their ground and fired back with tear gas and plastic bullets. The Quonset hut, containing the offices of sixty-five DeLorean employees, was hard against the gate, and a firebomb landed on its roof, starting a blaze that could not be controlled. The crowd cheered as the building burned to the ground. Fortunately, no one was hurt.

The next day, as I made my way out the gate and up the winding road to Twinbrook, I found a deserted battlefield. I passed burned-out cars, broken glass, plastic bullets, a shoe, a bloody shirt. Slowly, some of the teenagers who had led the rioters emerged from the houses and we walked together toward the Catholic church while the helicopters overhead monitored us.

I knew many Twinbrook residents. I had been to dinner in their homes. I knew their children and we were constantly exchanging stories. They knew I had worked for the Kennedys, who represented ultimate success to Twinbrook's poor Catholics. I had distributed over a hundred pictures of Robert Kennedy and his children, and recently I had shown the teenagers pictures of my new baby, Amanda Lee Haddad. My second wife, Noreen Walsh, was Catholic-Irish. When I said that Noreen was coming to Belfast, they urged me to bring the baby. I shouldn't live in a hotel — they would find me a house and they would baby sit for me. I liked the idea, and said I might bring over the older children as well. They assured me that everyone would be safer than in New York.

The young men apologized for the firebombing, claiming that it had been an accident. They weren't foolish enough to burn up their own jobs. Yet, as I walked back to the factory, children were filling bottles with gasoline and stuffing in the wicks, preparing for that night's confrontation. They were embarrassed, and some tried to hide their handiwork in the bushes.

"We're not after the factory," they insisted. "Only the RUC."

The Royal Welsh Battalion, special troops kept in reserve in the U.K. in case of trouble in Northern Ireland, had been rushed to Belfast. They made our factory their headquarters. I explained what I had been told about the bombing to Don Lander and to Myron Stylianides, who was in charge of personnel and factory security. They agreed that the army should be kept out of sight. We housed the troops in our new cafeteria and braced ourselves for the riots we knew would erupt as each hunger striker died.

One day I saw ladders being pushed up against our barbed wire and watched as young men built catapults, using old tires that would be used to hurl firebombs farther into the factory grounds. Christ, I thought, we're back to medieval times; next the RUC will be pouring boiling water down the ladders.

The army, which used the picture window in Stylianides' office to watch Twinbrook for snipers at night, advised us to leave the administration building every day at dusk. Nevertheless, Lander, among others, would wait until the firebombs popped on the test track before moving into one of the other factory buildings. No executive ever stopped working, and many slept on cots at the factory. A report accidentally left on Stylianides' desk by the army's night duty officer reported that sniper fire was occurring, a fact we had publicly denied. On one occasion snipers put holes in our water tanks, which we feared was a prelude to a firebombing of our main buildings not too far from the gate.

The military blockades kept the media away from Twinbrook. A camera crew and a stills photographer did film our burning building, however, and the picture appeared throughout the world, but without identification, a break for us. The last thing you want when you're trying to sell cars is a picture of your plant in flames.

On May 14, 1981, I wrote John and Gene indicating that Sinn Fein, the legal political wing of the provisional IRA (Provos), of which Bobby Sands was a member, had singled us out for criticism. It was an ominous development.

"At two separate specific Sinn Fein press conferences called for the world press in Andersontown, the DeLorean Motor Company was negatively mentioned," I wrote. "The first came in response to a reporter's question about the U.K. government providing jobs in Northern Ireland at great expense. The second followed the fire-bombing of the records building.

"In effect, the Sinn Fein, speaking for the IRA, said we were *not* hiring Catholics. When challenged they said we were hiring Catholics only in menial positions. As you recall, this was the substance of two previous communications to us, charges that we effectively dispelled.

"Statistics shown to me at the plant indicate that the Sinn Fein claim is inaccurate."

I asked reporters to tell the Sinn Fein and the IRA that we did have a fifty-fifty Catholic-Protestant hiring policy and that the IRA knew it from previous communications.

"Tell them their communication system stinks."

At six o'clock one night, as soldiers in battle gear urged us to leave the building, the phone rang. It was for me.

"I understand you think our communications system stinks," said the voice at the other end.

I hesitated for a moment, looking at the troops, and signaled to Don Lander, who was standing beside me, to listen.

"Yes," I replied. "You've got your facts wrong. If you check, you'll see I'm right. It doesn't help for you to pick on us at press conferences. We're doing a job here."

"That's not what we hear."

I hastily wrote a note to Lander and asked if his phone had a recording device. He shook his head.

"I can prove it to you," I said. And we arranged a meeting.

I really had no idea who had called. I thought it might be someone from the Sinn Fein. I checked with the switchboard operator, who lived in Twinbrook and knew everything that was going on. She confirmed that the call had come from outside the plant.

I believed that my Twinbrook friends had set up a protective shield for me and that I would not be taking an undue risk. I followed the directions I had been given, got into a car, and was driven toward Andersontown, outside Belfast. There I climbed a flight of stairs and entered an apartment that had been converted into an office. None of the men in the room introduced themselves. Although I felt uncomfortable, I repeated what I had said before. We had fifty-fifty hiring, and when we had been asked before, we had confirmed this. I named the two intermediaries. Once, I said, an intermediary had produced a list of DMC employees with checks next to the names of the Catholics. That list was proven to be outdated.

"I'm no damn anti-Catholic," I said. "In fact, I'm considered too pro-Catholic by some people here. You can check that out."

It was over quickly and I was driven back to the Europa. I wasn't even sure whom I had seen. Was I being set up to prove that DMC was in contact with the IRA?

Whatever the reason, the Sinn Fein stopped attacking us at their press conferences.* But now John had an incident with which to try to discredit me in the months ahead. As it turned out, he did more damage to me than the IRA did.

At the height of the troubles, John grew impatient with the production delays. They were beginning to hinder his plans to go public. To justify the $12 to $14-a-share offering price, Belfast was required to manufacture eighty cars a day. One

---

* It is not correct, as some British writers have said, that DeLorean was not of interest to the IRA. Security forces and my own contacts convinced me that they watched us carefully, but could not interfere because much of their support came from the U.S. Nevertheless, the IRA had a penchant for dramatic events and we were always potentially a target if we lost our favorable image in Ulster.

day a Telex arrived from John. It said in part: "What the hell are you guys doing over there? Get off your asses and get to work and earn your money."

When the riots finally subsided in June, John returned to Belfast for a board meeting. We proudly reported that on the day following the firebombing of the Quonset hut all sixty-five persons had been relocated in new offices and that a large replacement Xerox machine had been loaned to us and installed. None of our computerized data had been damaged and, on the next day, new computer terminals were installed and working. Within a week, the functions of the Quonset hut were distributed elsewhere, something we had planned for later that year. We had saved a number of the engineering drawings that had been stored in the hut, which were being cleaned and dried. Fortunately, another complete set had been stored outside Northern Ireland.

There had been production stoppages following the deaths of hunger strikers. But despite the fact that Bobby Sand's body lay in wake in Twinbrook, there had been no further damage to the plant. In fact, we urged Catholics to obey any IRA requests so they would not be put in any danger. Bomb threats forced us to evacuate the factory several times, but as the workers lingered outside the gates, there was almost a picnic atmosphere, with Catholics and Protestants sitting together to wait out the search for bombs. We later found the person making these threats, and they stopped. He had been using a pay phone inside the plant.

Production returned to normal, and the plant seemed to exude a new spirit, having come through the worst without scars or dissent among the workers. What went on inside the DeLorean gates did not seem to have any relation to the continuing violence outside — or to the intrigues in New York.

John listened to the report of the troubles and asked for an estimate of what the delay and the damage had cost us. It was less than £700,000.

"It sounds more like £8 million to me," John said. After a moment of silence, he ordered the accountants to draw up an estimate of damages for that amount. The Belfast executives were clearly appalled. John had not recognized their achievement. All he seemed to want was an excuse to get more money from the British. No one said a word.

Never was the rift between DeLorean and the company greater than at that moment. I left the board meeting finding it difficult to believe that all John saw was money, not the courage and the success of his team. Now, as I moved through the plant and saw the excitement of the workers, the contrast was striking. Workers stood around each car as it moved off the line to be washed and tested and they walked through the stockpile of "approved" cars on our lots at lunchtime. They felt pride in their work. We were two worlds. In one was John, Tom, the lawyers and the brokers. In the other were the executives, the engineers and the workers. Cars were rolling down a state-of-the-art assembly line, built by workers who, outside the gates, might be members of opposing armed camps. As I walked down the lines, the workers asked me what the directors were saying about the quality of their workmanship and how I thought the car would be received in America.

It was during the hunger strikes that our first cars moved from the factory to the docks for shipment to the States. There was the stink and irritation of tear gas in the air as the trailer trucks drove through town. People stopped in the streets to look. As I followed one of the trailers to the docks in a DeLorean, there was the constant sound of applause behind me. Despite all the hardships, John had achieved his miracle. Belfast was about to ship DeLoreans to America. People said it made the entire city feel a sense of accomplishment. The DeLorean seemed the only light in a dark sky.

Chapter Eleven

Confrontation

When I arrived back in New York from Belfast in May 1981, there was a note from John on my desk. It ordered me to turn around and go back to Belfast — permanently. He phrased the order in terms of corporate patriotism:

"Today DMC is faced with the greatest opportunity of your corporate lifetime," he wrote. "With the troubles in Twin-brook/Belfast, for the first time in our tenure there, *no single person in the U.K. begrudges us the $160,000,000 we got from the government!* Most today think we've earned it! We were the only substantial business hurt in the whole country. We lost 60 percent of our offices, our vital engineering records, our production control records and our employment records. Enough to put any business on its knees. We lost the equivalent of two or three weeks' production, with more losses to come, as a result of the violence and unrest. The government, who dealt with us in bad faith, and in effect made us borrow $50,000,000 that they owed us and should have given us, is in a position where they must become responsive to our needs.*

---

* Most of this is untrue.

Our public offering is, for all intents and purposes, dead if the unrest continues (as it probably will) . . ."

John said that we should be the "industrial heroes of the U.K.," bringing jobs and prestige to an area all Britons now agree is uninhabitable , . ." The government should "throw money at us," not only to continue our operations but to expand. Our failure, he predicted, would doom Northern Ireland industrially "forever," and cost the government another billion or two a year.

Then he got to the point:

"Upon due consideration you should plan on moving to Belfast for at least six months. Take your wife and child with you. Plan to stay there and help get this job done.

"You are assigned to Don Lander until further notice. Mike and Ellen will handle your duties here — and you're only a phone call away."

I walked down the hall to his office, the memo in my hand. "John, this is a piece of shit," I said.

"I want you in Belfast to tell our story," he said.

John didn't wait long to turn up the heat. His next memo accused me of corporate treason. I was "anticompany, divisive and disloyal."

When all else failed, John decided to use his black-book technique on me.

In London I had resumed friendship with a high-school classmate, Victor Lownes, whom I hadn't seen in twenty years. In the interim, Victor had teamed up with Hugh Hefner in starting *Playboy* magazine and now ran the Playboy gambling casinos in London. When I came to the U.K., Victor invited me to spend occasional weekends at Stores, his country house outside London. A car buff, Victor had promised to hold a "special" reception for the first DeLorean equipped with British right-hand drive and to invite some of the U.K.'s leading opinion-makers to race it around his estate. John had accepted this invitation.

Now, in the summer of 1981, Lownes was in trouble for

providing casino credit to Arab sheiks, and Playboy, in order to save its license, had fired him. This was the background for John's next memo to me.

"I have been told," John wrote, with copies to Gene Cafiero and others, "that you spent several weekends at the U.K. Playboy mansion of the now-fired and discredited head of British Playboy. I understand there were a number of 'party girls' there and that narcotics were used freely and extensively. I have been told that your relation to DMC will become a featured part of the soon-to-erupt scandal. If this happens, both our future government financings and public offerings are in jeopardy.

"We need a positive and constructive program to limit the damage to DMC."

I gave my wife Noreen a copy of this note and sent John this reply:

"I'm returning the attached predated memo for your file. The three or four times I was at the Lownes estate for dinner, the other dinner guests included members of the aristocracy, the media, political leaders (including two former Prime Ministers) and people from business and the arts. There was a separate table for the children, whom the parents brought for the riding. The evening began with cocktails and ended with a movie. The most-used game was Asteriods. I saw no call girls at dinner or afterward, and my sensitive nose smelled no narcotics. It was all very quiet and ranged from relaxed to stiff. I rather think your source for this is inaccurate. On two of the occasions I was invited out to discuss *Playboy* coverage of DeLorean."

But John had achieved his purpose. He let me know that he was prepared to raise the stakes of our confrontation to include my reputation.

In New York, Tom Kimmerly took me to lunch to tell me the facts of life. I didn't really want to get into a fight with John, did I? I should just go and live in Belfast until the underwriting was over. We needed to keep a lid on the British until the money was in the bank. John was worried that they could blow the stock offering. He said that if I would help John now, he would help me later.

I listened, and then, on instinct, decided to fire a salvo of my own.

"I'm troubled about GPD," I said. "The *Financial Times* reviewed the Lotus annual report and couldn't find any money from Switzerland. John Griffiths [their writer] told me that the *Financial Times* will go back for a second look when the new annual report is released this month. If they don't find the GPD money, then you'll have a real story on your hands. What do I tell Griffiths then?"

"There's nothing to worry about," Tom assured me. But his head was down, his fork picking at his food, his eyes refusing to catch mine. He was suddenly agitated and nervous. "Chapman is going to end all those rumors himself. There was a delay in moving the money into Lotus. It's there. Anyway, it's Chapman's problem, not ours." He repeated what John had told me: that GPD was an offshore tax shelter and that both the Bank of England and the auditors had approved the transfer. I knew there was something wrong in John and Tom's GPD story, but I couldn't put my finger on it.

I returned to Belfast. One morning, as I walked around the plant, I passed a gathering of workers, one of whom called me over. He told me that they were discussing a strike.

"What's the problem?" I said.

"We want another five pounds a week in body press."

"I'm the wrong one to talk to. Use the grievance procedure."

"We've tried the grievance procedure and it didn't work."

"Why do you want an extra five pounds?"

"Because we do the dirty jobs."

The body-press process required the workers to wear masks to protect them from the fibers used in the production of the plastic body. The plant was neat, precise and clean, but the jobs were dirty. In the next building the assembly line functioned in an entirely different work environment. They were the "clean jobs." The substance of the Sinn Fein's complaint had been that these "dirty jobs" were done by Catholics, while the "clean jobs" were done by Protestants.

In the office there were charts indicating which workers had left their jobs after the hunger-strike deaths. Statistics were kept by trade and by building. It was the Catholics, of course, who left for the strikes. I could tell from the charts whether the body-press plant was a predominantly Catholic building. And so it was. The body-press plant had been out on hunger-strike days, while the assembly plant had been in. One was Protestant and the other Catholic. It was precisely as the Sinn Fein had claimed. And it was a deadly serious matter.

I took the charts to Shaun Harte. "The Catholics are doing the fucking dirty jobs," I said.

Shaun called John Gardner, who handled assignments. He admitted that the Catholics, "being less skilled," were in the body-press plant.

"If anyone finds that out, we'll be blown out of the water," I said.

I arranged with Shaun to make sure that we would have an equal number of Catholics in both buildings. All the newly hired Catholics, he said, would go into the assembly plant. I left a note for Lander, who was out of town, and sent off a strong memo to John.

Earlier, John and I had clashed over his policy of hiring only skilled people for the factory. "We have enough problems without training everyone for this factory," John had said.

I had explained that "skilled" was a code name for Protestant, just as "experienced" kept blacks out of jobs at home. Unless we hired from right outside our gates, we would have trouble. The Catholics in Twinbrook were expecting to work for us. We had already been warned by a radical labor union leader that we were roaming too far for new recruits. Roaming too far meant we were seeking Protestants. John believed that for every skilled person we hired, a job would open elsewhere, and that in consequence overall unemployment would drop. Whatever the merits of this argument, in practice John's ideas had relegated Catholics to the dirty jobs.

All I could think of now was that we had lied on three occasions to people who we believed had given us a communication channel to Catholic militants. And if we lost our credibility, we lost our margin of safety and our access in a crisis.

Back at the hotel that night, I could not sleep. If something this basic was wrong, what else was wrong? The engineers had told me that the information we had given the government on emissions and testing standards was misleading. There was GPD. And then there was the share offering that potentially would make John a multimillionaire, leaving his executives — who were busting their asses for him — out in the cold.

The next morning I decided I wouldn't go to the factory, and instead drove my DeLorean out into the countryside, up along a rocky coast, and tried to think things through. I didn't like the answers I was getting.

What should I do?

If I were a reporter, I would write the story. If I were in government, I would step in and take over the plant. But in my position, what could I do? Go to the media? Tell the British? Complain to the SEC that the prospectus was untrue? Could I make that charge stick? John was being advised by reputable experts, by Arthur Andersen, our blue-chip auditors; by Bache and Oppenheimer on Wall Street; and by Paul, Weiss and other prestigious law firms.

I had to accept that there was some truth in John's view that one more scandal would scuttle the factory. The workers I had come to know and trust would go down with the plant. The executives would have to fend for themselves in a highly competitive automotive world. Did I want to be responsible for this by blowing the whistle on DeLorean?

Whom could I talk to about this?

I returned to New York and went to see Howard Squadron, my New York attorney, who had taken a small law firm and molded it into one of the finest in the city. When I called, I said I had a serious problem and needed his advice. We met for lunch at the Century Club.

I wasn't sure how to explain my problem, so I described a hypothetical situation.

"This is not a hypothetical luncheon," Howard said with his usual bluntness.

"No, it's not. I'm talking about John DeLorean."

So I laid out what I knew, what I had seen, what I suspected, and what my dilemma was. If I remained silent, I said, I wouldn't be able to live with myself. If I blew the whistle, the factory would go down, which was the last thing I wanted. And I wasn't sure what was accepted in the upper echelons of business. How different was John from the norm?

"I need to know, Howard, has John stepped over the line?"

"That's not the question. The question is, 'What is best for you?' "

In addition to representing corporate interests, Howard was also a libel lawyer for magazines and newspapers. He took my evidence apart. What could I prove about GPD? Would the engineers testify about the safety and emissions problems? Would the British tell the world they had been taken in by a "con man"? He suspected that John wanted to clean house, find a new crew to work with, wipe out the past.

Then he advised me:

"I think you can only do one thing. Get out before the bricks fall on you. You can only do so much to save the project. If you want, I can try to work out a settlement between you and the company. And don't let it rip you apart. You should be in the hospital."

I had an operation planned, but had postponed it because of the need to be in Belfast. I told Howard I would think about his advice.

I soon learned that John had ordered our internal auditor to go through my expense accounts. He also decided (without telling me) to deduct my salary for every day since May that I had not been in Belfast. The charge came to $7,700. Until I "accepted" the debt, John ordered that my salary (over $10,000 a month) be stopped.

I told Dennis Patouhas, a young executive who had moved into the controller's slot, that he could deduct the $7,700 from my pay, but there was no way I would concede it was a debt. John continued to withhold my salary. Later that week, Dennis asked to see me in Jim Stark's office. Before I could leave my own office, Stark appeared and motioned me into the hallway. He was clearly afraid that both his office and mine were bugged.

"Whatever you do," he said, "don't sign anything Dennis hands you. Be very, very careful."

Before I could ask him for an explanation, he was gone. I waited a few minutes and entered his office. He was standing behind his desk. Dennis was in the easy chair alongside.

When Dennis joined DMC, he had seemed a bright young executive on the way up. He was a cheerful man whose family was the most important thing in his life; the new job meant that he could add a room to his house in Connecticut. But since then I had watched his face become drawn and haggard, his open style change to one of secrecy. He remained loyal to John, but I could see that he was having a hard time. Now, I sensed, Dennis was about to carry out one of John's nasty little tasks to prove his loyalty and to keep his job. I felt genuinely sorry for him.

"Forget it," I said. "You're here to do John's dirty work for him. I understand. Get to the point. What is it?"

He handed me a two-page document, neatly typed, with a place for my signature and one for John's. It contained the terms of my permanent transfer to Belfast. It began with the statement that despite my disloyalty to the company, the fact that I had unauthorized contact with the IRA, and the British government's displeasure with my work, the company was transferring me to Belfast, effective immediately. I would get the money due me, minus what I owed the company "by

Stark's calculations." I would not, however, receive salary for any time I had spent in New York after May 22. When the numbers balanced out, I owed the company $7,500. And my future salary was cut in half. Furthermore, while all our executives were provided housing in Belfast, I would have to pay for my own accommodations.

I smiled. John was obviously making me an offer I could not accept. The document could also later be used with the British if I got out of hand. Unauthorized contact with the IRA sounded ominous.

"Let me think it over," I said, folding the paper and getting up.

"No, no, no," Dennis said. "You can't have the paper. John says you have to read it and sign it immediately."

"Dennis, I understand the bind you're in, but this is absurd."

"I know," Dennis replied quietly. "I know."

But it was clear that I would soon have to make a decision.

When Dennis left the office, Stark motioned for me to stay. He slipped across the desk his calculations and his memo to John concerning my expenses and withheld salary. His estimate matched mine. Using hand signals because he feared his office was bugged, Stark asked if I would like copies. I nodded yes, and he prepared them for me. The entire episode seemed bizarre. Here was a respected executive earning several hundred thousand dollars a year who was afraid to talk in his own office.

In the late summer of 1981, John began pressuring me for a copy of what we both believed was a file of background information that General Motors had collected on him before he left the company. Some months earlier I had learned that the report might be available to us at a price. A.J. Woolston-Smith (not to be confused with C.W. Smith of Detroit) had stopped by my office "for a chat." "Smitty," as he was known, was a private investigator who had undertaken some confidential assignments for John and me. I had first met Smitty when I was a witness before a Senate committee investigating the pharmaceutical industry, and some concern had been voiced for my safety. When, later, I was working for the State of New York, Smitty had helped me on major investigations, especially those related to organized crime. He had a network of friends and undercover agents around the country that was a newspaperman's dream. One of his specialties was to search for wiretaps, a task he routinely performed for major newspapers worried about people listening in on their calls.

In June 1981, Smitty had come into my DeLorean office, closed the door and lit up his pipe. I knew that he must have serious business.

"How did John come to leave General Motors?" he asked me.

"He quit."

"I don't think that is quite the full story, lad," he said. "Was there some flap over a leak or something like that?"

"There was, Smitty, there was."

"Did General Motors hire any detectives to find out what happened?"

"Not that I know of."

"Well, there is a source in Detroit who has been in touch with someone who obviously wants me to get in touch with you. He has a file on DeLorean. The General Motors file."

I had no doubt that General Motors kept a file on DeLorean. It was probably the source of John's fears that one day GM would swoop down and destroy us.

"Can we get it?" I asked.

"I'm not sure."

"How much?"

"I'm not sure."

"Smitty, if it's authentic, I want it. Bad. But don't let them know how bad."

Within a week Smitty was back. He had made contact with the private detective who had conducted the DeLorean investigation, a C.J. Pickrel of Detroit. He wanted to make a deal.

"First, I need to know if it's authentic," I told Smitty. "I need four points in the report that I can run past John. If they ring true, and the money is right, Pickrel has his deal."

"Fair enough," Smitty said.

Over the next several weeks we negotiated. Finally I had my information. I went to see John.

"John," I asked, "was there ever an investigation of the Greenbrier leak?"

He confirmed that there had been.

"Did you ever have a fight with Dollie Cole?" (Dollie Cole was the wife of a former GM president.)

"She hates my guts. I used to tease her husband about dating Monique van Vooren, and she didn't like it."

"Did you ever ask Noonan [the lawyer who put me together with John] to hire a private detective to help you track down the Greenbrier leak?"

"What's this — twenty questions?"

"Just this last. What about Noonan? Did he hire a private detective?"

"Yes."

Then I told him the story and he filled in the missing links. When the Greenbrier speech was leaked, John maintained he had been set up by his enemies on the fourteenth floor, and to prove his innocence he asked Noonan to help. Noonan had hired Pickrel. But before long, Pickrel was asked by GM to continue the investigation for the corporation, rather than for John.

"John, should I go after the report?"

"I want it," John said.

"Any limits on the money?"

"None."

I told Smitty I would not continue the discussions unless I had a face-to-face meeting with Pickrel. Pickrel flew to New York to meet me.

Pickrel was a wisp of a man. He was there, and then he was gone. Nice enough, liked to drink, talked in circles, and was full of anecdotes. He had the slightly washed-out look of a man on the way down, giving off the aura of a big spender. He wanted to meet at a bar at the Waldorf and I agreed. He told me his report had traced the leak. It also revealed, he claimed, unflattering aspects of John's personal life.

"It was too hot for GM to handle," he said. "They wanted the information, but not the report."

He insisted he was never paid for the report.

"After Nader, they didn't want to leave the report in their files," he explained.

We negotiated like two horse traders, and arrived at a fee of several thousand dollars to be paid in installments.

"The report must hold up to independent verification," I said.

"I understand."

"And no one else *ever* gets a copy."*

"Agreed."

We added one person to the loop, my assistant, Ellen.

The report was nineteen pages long and was written in "cops" language. Like a dectective, he eliminated one suspect after another. And then he raised the possibility that John himself was the leak.

Potentially more damaging were certain allegations about John's personal life. I realized I could discredit each of the sources if it came to that. Two were angry women. That might be what GM had on John. It would not be the first time personal information had been used to win a battle in corporate America.

Pickrel hinted he had a second report prepared, following through on the personal allegations. By this time I had what we wanted from Pickrel, however, and I ignored his bait.

---

* After DeLorean was arrested, Pickrel offered to sell the report to several journalists. Unfortunately for him, he had misplaced his completed copy and, using several ruses, attempted to obtain another copy from me. Later I saw a letter Pickrel had written to John offering to conduct an investigation of me and saying I had come to him to obtain the GM report on John.

The final report sat on my desk for hours on the day it arrived. How could I hand the report to John, I wondered. I decided to let it simmer for a while. That night I stuffed it into my briefcase and took it home.

Every few days I would get a handwritten note from John asking me if the report was ready. Finally I told him I had it. When I arrived to deliver it, John was standing by his window, next to a telescope, looking down at the city. I had the report in a folder marked "confidential," and as I took it out for him, I explained what I had written in the covering note. I was embarrassed to have read Pickrel's report about his personal life. But all that made no difference to me.

He looked at me, took the report and casually tossed it on his desk. For weeks he had been pressing for the report, but now, in one of the coolest moves I have ever witnessed, he showed no interest in it.

We stood there in silence for a few moments and I turned to leave. Outside the door I could not resist the urge to glance back into the office to see if he had reached for the report. He hadn't. He just stood very still, gazing out of the window.

That summer, John set in motion a plan that eventually helped to destroy the company. He ordered that a thousand new workers be added to the Belfast production line. I learned of the orders in a phone call from Peter Moore, a talented young Irishman who was our public affairs officer at the plant. He had developed the training program for new employees that was so thorough the workers jokingly complained they could take the DeLorean automobile apart blindfolded. Peter's program was an essential part of our quality assurance program and had been cited by the automotive media as proof of John's interest in building an ethical car.

At the time, we were experiencing our first field problems with the car, particularly with the suspension system, and the engineers had recommended that changes be made. The engineers and the managers were agreed that we needed to control production to ensure quality. Throwing a thousand untrained workers on the line would not only destroy those plans but create chaos. Cafiero, Brown and Lander argued with John. I sent a strong memo to him. But he would not listen. We knew why.

The prospectus was geared to making eighty cars a day. If we made fewer, the price of the original stock would drop and John's $120 million could become $60 million. So we began making cars we could not sell, and we used up our cash reserves and the bank's underwriting to buy them. It was madness, but John was in a race with time.

Also that summer of 1981 another incident occurred that set in motion a train of events that proved to have disastrous consequences for DeLorean. It all began very innocently. Marian Gibson, who was John's executive secretary and protectress, decided to hire Alnora Shari, a young black woman, to help clean the office. Soon, Tom and I were paying her to take care of our apartments.

Marian was British, a matronly blonde who had been hired by John for $30,000 a year, as much for her accent and her contacts among Arab investors as for her skills. Her closest friend at DMC was Jacquie Feddock, Tom Kimmerly's secretary and now his paralegal assistant. Jacquie was pretentious and arrogant, ordering other secretaries to do her work, and when that failed, or they resisted, seeking to have them fired. Often she would become enraged, and her shouts could be heard throughout the office. "I know too much," she once shouted. "I know too much about how this place works."

Most evenings, Jacquie, Marian and Tom would end the day at the bar downstairs or across the street at Harry's in the Waldorf. Sometimes I joined them, and I was frequently surprised by the candor with which Tom spoke of our problems. These three knew everything that happened, or was about to happen, at DeLorean. At any rate, this relationship ended when Marian was summarily demoted, for reasons that were not clear, to office manager, and then assigned to my office. John told my deputy, Mike Knepper, to keep Marian for thirty days and then to fire her.

"If John wants her fired," I told Mike from Belfast, "let him do it himself. This office intrigue is silly."

Marian was now excluded from the gathering at the bar. Then one day Jacquie, in one of her rages, stormed into my office area and confronted Marian.

"You're responsible for Alnora's leaving Tom," Jacquie shouted. "Now I have to clean up his apartment. You did it out of spite. You made her quit Tom."

Marian, and everyone within hearing distance, was stunned by this attack.

"It's all your fault," Jacquie shouted again, and then, before anyone could respond, she turned and left. I asked Ellen Kugler to find out what had happened.

"Alnora quit working for Tom because she didn't like cleaning up after his cats," Ellen reported. "The place was always a mess when he was away on trips."

Alnora later told Ellen and me that Jacquie went to see her after she had cooled down. Jacquie asked Alnora if she would like a full-time job with DeLorean. She would have medical insurance and all the other benefits. Alnora was delighted. There was a catch, however. Alnora would have to sign a piece of paper containing allegations intended to discredit Marian.

This was Alnora's chance to move up the ladder, with a predictable salary, medical insurance and all the benefits that are so vital when you have nothing. All she had to do was to betray a friend. She refused to sign, and told Marian what had happened. Marian now became convinced that John wanted to blackmail her to keep her from telling the truth about him.

Later that month, Clarence Jones, a Manhattan attorney, came by to see me. Jones had been Martin Luther King's attorney, and we had worked together in the civil rights movement in the early sixties. He had also been publisher of the *Amsterdam News,* the newspaper of black Harlem. He was now a Wall Street securities attorney of substantial reputation. Clarence was tall, articulate, well-dressed and professional.

"Marian is thinking of a lawsuit against John for discriminating against women," he told me.

"So is my former assistant, Dee Fensterer."

"So there's some merit in their claim?"

"We don't have women executives and we don't like women executives."

"Blacks? Puerto Ricans?" he asked.

"One black. Low level."

"I see."

"They claim that women, blacks and Hispanics have not moved into the auto industry, and that we are really only a small corporate headquarters requiring high-level, experienced, professional staff."

"What do you think?"

"They were schooled in Detroit and they feel uncomfortable with women executives. They are insensitive to blacks and Hispanics."

Clarence reviewed some of Marian's complaints: that John was taking money from the company for his own use; that problems with the car were being covered up; that John was feuding with all of his executives. Then Clarence changed the tone of the conversation.

"Is John crazy?" he asked.

"I don't know."

He went on to spell out the full story. Marian was convinced that John was ripping off the British and using the money for his own benefit. What did I think?

"Howard Squadron told me I don't have the evidence to prove my case. Maybe Marian does. She sat outside John's office, taking his calls, reading his letters, writing his memos, paying his bills. She might know."

"What do you think? Is he a crook?"

"As Howard Squadron told me, that is not the question. If

Marian sues John, he'll put her through a meat grinder. All the executives who have challenged him have failed."

"Bill, I've known you for twenty years . . . why are you here?"

"I'm leaving. It was different in the beginning. We were going to break new ground then, do great things."

Then I let it all out. I told him about my suspicions, my fears, what my investigations were turning up, and how John was reacting. I would stay until I found some of the missing links. I pointed out the problems I saw in the draft of the prospectus, saying I felt that the draft failed to touch on my real concerns about the safety of the car. I talked about GPD. Then I showed him my December 26 memo.

Clarence listened patiently. When I had finished he said, "You don't know how these people play the game. Bill, get out before you get hurt."

Marian Gibson called me at my home in East Hampton on a Saturday night in September 1981.

"Bill, I would like to take a week off," she said, in a tense voice. She had been under visible strain since John had escalated his efforts to force her out of the company. That wasn't going to happen while I was there, but Marian sensed that I was about to leave or be forced out myself.

"You need a rest," I told her. "The time off will be just fine."

What I did not know was that earlier that day Marian had returned to the office with an empty shopping bag, which she proceeded to fill with company records. She removed two large black books from the top of her file cabinet. They contained much of John's correspondence and memos for the thirteen months she had worked for him, and copies of the confidential memos I had written to John, which, she later told me, she carefully collected and saved.

That Saturday morning, after a troubled night, she decided what must be done. John must be stopped. The prospectus for the DeLorean Motors Holding Company must never clear the

SEC. John should not be permitted to rob the British of their investment. John was destroying *her* country's efforts to bring peace to Northern Ireland. She would take her shopping bag of documents to Parliament. That would stop John.

Clarence Jones urged restraint. If Marian and John were to fight, Clarence favored the rules of the courtroom. From what he was learning, he feared that John might destroy Marian. But Clarence could no longer control her.

Marian turned for help to a wealthy British antiques dealer named Eddie Koopman, who happened to be in town. She called him and told him her story, but he didn't want any part of a struggle with DeLorean or anything to do with stolen records. Marian grew angry, and as he listened to the frustration and fear in her voice, he began to weaken. He agreed to meet with Marian but insisted that Clarence attend.

They met in a restaurant near the United Nations, and Marian outlined her plan. She would take the incriminating files to Jock Bruce-Gardyne, the Tory MP who was close to Prime Minister Thatcher and who continued to criticize John. It would be a cold call, but she was convinced her position as John's confidential secretary and the documents themselves would carry the day.

Koopman had a better plan. His own MP, Nicolas Winterton, like Bruce-Gardyne a back-bench Conservative, was a good friend. Koopman could arrange for a meeting at his home in Macclesfield. Marian jumped at the idea. She used her week off for a trip to England. The following Tuesday, three days after she had called me at home, she boarded a British Airways flight to Heathrow, her suitcase filled with the documents that she was convinced would destroy DeLorean. After a day of rest in London, she traveled up to Macclesfield for her lunch with Winterton and Koopman.

It was difficult for Winterton to follow Marian's story, filled as it was with new characters, unusual situations and a layman's interpretation of complicated legal and financial dealings. She had so much information to convey that it came across as garbled, but he heard enough to interest him. The British would lose their control over John if the company went public. He would be a rich man and the British would be left out in the cold. There were strong allegations of high living and financial irregularities. Marian said she had the documents to substantiate her story. Winterton suspected that this was not merely fantasy. He asked Marian to return ten days later with her documents. She interpreted this delay as lack of interest, and it infuriated her. She was due to leave for home the following Sunday. They would never stop John, she said. She should have gone to Bruce-Gardyne after all. Winterton listened and finally agreed to see her the next Tuesday. She would bring her documents for him to examine.

The day before Marian's appointment, she called me from England and asked for another week off. It was my understanding that she was visiting her family. "No problem," I said. "Get a good rest."

The papers she showed Winterton were confusing. Her four-page handwritten summary wandered through the history of the company and her allegations. John was to have invested $4 million of his own money in DMC, she wrote, but he had only invested $750,000 of Cristina's money. She said that he was using company money for personal expenses and that she had personally written company checks for jewelry, liquor and artwork. She had copies of John's expense accounts, which included lavish bills from the world's finest restaurants and hotels. She said that John had deliberately over-estimated to the British the damage from the firebombing in Belfast. And finally, there was the mysterious Swiss bank account and GPD.

She showed Winterton John's detailed itineraries, his personal phone book and copies of the memos and checks she had written. She warned Winterton that there was a "mole" in the Northern Ireland operation who, she knew, reported back to John.

Many questions were raised by these documents. Did he,

for instance, pay back the amounts of personal expenses at the end of the year? And there was no law against high living, even though it might make the British angry. There was a good case to be made on the firebombing. Regarding GPD, however, we had only suspicions, not hard facts. Someone must investigate these allegations, for they were clearly not proven facts.

One document, however, jumped out of the stack of memos and papers, and that was my December 26 memo to John, which referred to many of the matters that Marian had discussed. I was a company "insider," and this gave Marian's allegations credibility.

Winterton was sufficiently convinced to move ahead, but he needed to bypass the "mole." He told Marian that he would go directly to the Prime Minister. Marian was satisfied. The next day she was on a plane back to New York.

The day after this second meeting, Winterton wrote to his friend Ian Gow, the Parliamentary Secretary to Mrs. Thatcher:

"I am afraid at this stage I cannot be specific," he wrote, "but information has come to me which leads me to believe that the British government is being misled and deceived, and the taxpayer's money misused in a substantial project with which the British government has been involved for some little while."

He added that he had the documentation and asked to see the Prime Minister. The Prime Minister, however, was in Australia, and when she returned she was off to a Conservative Party conference. Winterton's request would be delayed until after the conference.

Meanwhile, Marian, now back in the States, was growing impatient. She was concerned that the British government was not moving quickly enough. Didn't they understand that the moment the SEC cleared the prospectus, John would have his money? That would happen by the New Year at the latest.

At this point, John Lisners, a free-lance journalist, called

Marian from London. He had just returned from Australia, and their mutual friend Koopman had told him about Marian's material. He wanted to write the story. But Marian told him that she would give Winterton more time.

When Marian returned to the office on the Monday following these events, I took her aside to warn her about our phones. I had been told that they were tapped. This only fueled her anger. She immediately called Koopman in England. What was happening? she asked him. Why was everything moving so slowly? Koopman tried to explain, but Marian would not listen. By Thursday she was angry enough to call Lisners in London. He took the first plane to New York, and before midnight he was in Marian's Sutton Place apartment working his way through the story and the documents. He and Marian agreed that Clarence would clear all his copy, and by morning Lisners had enough of a story to cut an attractive deal with Rupert Murdoch's *News of the World,* a flashy, mass-circulation Sunday newspaper published in England.

Lisners stayed at Marian's apartment and wrote his story there. As they talked, Marian told me later, he probed further into her motivations and explored new areas of her allegations. In her mind, she had set limits to what she would do and say. She wanted the factory to survive. This was not a sensational exposé. It was a story with a goal: to get the British to look more closely at John. She was troubled by Lisners' probings, and when he left the apartment she followed him to the phone in the back lobby of her apartment building. There she heard Lisners reading copy to the *News of the World* editors. This violated their understanding that all copy be cleared by Clarence before being submitted to the newspaper. She grabbed the phone from Lisners and shouted at the editor at the other end, saying that there was no story. But her anger did not faze Lisners.

"These things have a life of their own," he said. "You have

what you want. The story will be splashed across Sunday's front page, and by Monday your story will be all over London. The government will have to act."

But Lisners had not counted on Rupert Murdoch's being in London that Saturday. The Australian publisher was having lunch with Lord Goodman, London's foremost libel attorney. Lord Goodman had a reputation as a brazen, no-holds-barred fighter, and his contacts reached into the innermost corners of the British government.

Murdoch kept in close touch with his newspapers on three continents and, as was his practice, he called the editor of the *News of the World,* Barrie Askew, about that week's lead stories. Askew told him about the DeLorean story. Murdoch liked the idea, but warned that the copy would have to stand the test of British libel laws, which are much stricter than those in the States. Murdoch said he would be down to read the copy. Murdoch is one of the few publishers who like to spend time in the newsroom, and it is not unusual for him to edit a story or rewrite a headline.

That Saturday afternoon I got my first clue about what was happening when Clarence called me in East Hampton.

"Bill," he said, "Marian is telling the DeLorean story to a British reporter."

"What does she have?"

"Everything."

The trip to London made sense to me now. I was apprehensive. If I had my choice of how to release information, Marian would be the last person I would use. She was a good source, but she created complications when she was aroused. And when you took on John, you had to be prepared for any contingency. He had great resources, while Marian had none.

When Murdoch looked at Lisners' copy, however, he decided against running the story, because he was concerned about the potentially libelous nature of some of the material. Some people have wondered whether Murdoch killed the story because he and John were neighbors in New York.

Personally I doubt it. There is nothing Murdoch likes better than a good story, and the DeLorean story was certainly that.

On the previous day, Friday, Clarence had called Winterton to warn him that the Lisners story was coming. Winterton immediately understood the message. He informed the Prime Minister's office, and the Prime Minister finally decided to ask the Solicitor General and Scotland Yard to investigate.

Winterton told Askew at the *News of the World* of the impending investigation. Word began to filter through Fleet Street that something was in the wind, and by Sunday small items began to appear in the media about a Whitehall investigation of DeLorean. By evening, radio and television had picked up the story. Winterton was known to be the source.

When Lisners learned that the *News of the World* had spiked his story, he quickly shopped around for another buyer. The *Daily Mirror* was intrigued, and bought Lisners' copy, planning to run the story on the following Tuesday.

That weekend John called me in East Hampton. He wanted to discuss my contract, and asked whether I could come into the city. I told him that I didn't want to leave my children, but I would be back in the office on Monday. He was going to Florida that day.

"Why don't you come along?" he said. "We'll have time to talk on the phone. We're coming right back."

I agreed, and on Monday morning I joined John and Mike Knepper at Kennedy Airport. Until then I had trusted Knepper as a friend. I had shared with him some of my misgivings about the company and had also protected him from the riptide of internal politics. Now he seemed almost afraid to be caught alone with me. Something was in the air — but what? John and Mike huddled over a pay phone until it was time to board the flight to Daytona Beach. The first rumblings about a possible investigation were coming out of the U.K., but details were lacking. That day's New York *Times* carried a one-paragraph story about it on the business page, but I had missed it, and knew nothing then of any official investigation.

John was going to Florida to give a speech in Daytona Beach. Then we were to met with Bunkie Knudsen and Smokey Yunick, a brilliant inventor who was working on a new engine that saved fuel by recycling its own heat. Bunkie and John had formed an engine partnership with Smokey. We were going to ride in a car fitted with the new experimental engine.

Aboard the plane, John sat alone and Mike and I sat together on the other side of the first-class aisle. Once we were airborne, John asked Mike to change seats with him and settled into the seat next to mine, taking care to face me fully. It occurred to me that he might be wearing a microphone. But why? At any rate, I resolved to be very cautious.

"Bill, we've been friends a long time," John said. "Too long to end the relationship in a stupid fight. I will work out a decent, fair settlement with you —"

"Great."

"— but you have to answer some questions that trouble me. I just want to clear the air."

"Sure, John, fire away," I said, now convinced from the way he positioned himself that he was wearing a microphone.

"Did you send Bruce-Gardyne a letter and a marked-up copy of our draft registration statement with a number of allegations of impropriety?" John asked me. His language was stilted lawyer's language, and I thought I recognized Tom's fine hand.

"You mean the prospectus you asked me about in Belfast?"

"Yes."

"Now, John, why would I want to do that?"

John just grumbled.

"I think it is useless to discuss a settlement if you harbor these suspicions," I said. "Clear them up in your mind first and then let's talk again. I'm in no hurry if you're not."

John allowed a deep frown to cross his face and he began to

speak of disloyalty and to ask what he had ever done to me to deserve what I was doing to him and to the workers in Belfast.

"John, I would give my left nut to have this company succeed, not because of you but because of what you are doing in Belfast. I also have a stake in our success. If we shape up and work together, we can still make it. All we are doing now is sowing the seeds of our own failure."

John was in no mood for a lecture. He flipped open a magazine and buried his head in it. I felt no sorrow or sense of rejection. Nothing. Yet here was a man I had respected and trusted for years, and now I was wondering whether he was trying to set me up.

At a stopover in North Carolina, John rushed away to make a call to the U.K. He came back to report that he had talked to Adam Butler, now the Under Secretary of State for Northern Ireland.

"We're in deep shit," he said, "and you're the cause."

"I don't know what the hell you're talking about."

"Have you been working with Marian?" he asked.

"On what?"

"In England."

"No. She's on vacation there. Why?"

"She's trying to destroy us."

In London, Marian had been identified as the source of the information for the Thatcher investigation. The wires were already carrying Marian's story. Later, at a previously scheduled press conference following his speech in Florida, John brushed aside the charges, saying that Marian was a pool typist, and "a frustrated old maid." The local reporters present didn't press the issue. They accepted John's story that it was a "domestic" dispute.

At two-thirty that afternoon, after the press conference, John drew me aside for a talk. He had just spoken to Tom.

"I know you're not involved," he said, "but we have to find out what documents Marian took with her. There is talk of a memo you wrote me."

"I wrote you a lot of memos."

"About gold faucets."

"That was the Bennington trouble."

"That must be it," John said, sounding relieved. "She must have taken the memo off my desk. But you cleaned the matter up?"

"I gave explicit instructions to clean it up."

Driving with Bunkie to Smokey Yunick's, I felt like it was old times again. John was open and friendly. When we huddled around Smokey's new engine, he became the brilliant engineer talking about a historic breakthrough that we would use in our car. Smokey had also worked out a simple solution to a nagging clutch problem that our engineers and consultants had not been able to solve. For a moment I thought it could still be fun to work for DeLorean. This was the ambience that had attracted me to the company in the first place.

My euphoria did not last long. We had a two-hour stopover in Atlanta on our way back to New York. When I called the office, I was told that Chief Inspector John George of Scotland Yard was trying to reach me. He was in New York and wanted to see me immediately. Meanwhile, John was talking to Tom. There was serious trouble, he told me when I joined him, and I was right in the middle of it. He handed me the phone.

"Tom, what's up?" I said.

"Did you write John a memo last Christmas?"

"Yes. A confidential memo. Why?"

"Marian has turned it over to the British and they're investigating."

"Investigating what?"

There was no reply.

I told Tom where he could find a copy of my December 26 memo, and we made arrangements to meet at eight the next morning. When Clarence had told me Saturday that Marian had everything, he meant it. But how had she got hold of that memo?

"Scotland Yard wants to talk to you," John said. "No need to make things worse than they are. Why don't you stay here in Atlanta until this thing blows over? The British detectives will be going home soon."

"I can't do that. My wife knows I have an old girl friend here and if I change my plans, she'll think the worst." That was the best excuse I could offer on short notice, but John wasn't buying.

"I'll call her. This is too important. Stay here. Take a motel room near the airport." Now his voice was demanding. I was at the crossroads. He knew it and I knew it. "We can work out that settlement you want," he said, looking me right in the eye, which is unusual for John.

Without thinking, I said, "John, I can't do that."

John said nothing. He turned and walked over to another part of the lounge. I was left to talk to Mike. I explained the memo to him. He recalled that I had shown it to him. At Kennedy Airport, John's car picked us up. It was a quiet ride into town.

"Think about it," John said as he got out of the car at his Fifth Avenue apartment. I thought about it for the ten minutes it took to get across town to my apartment on the West Side.

Before I left the apartment the next morning, Chief Inspector Hefford, the second man in the Scotland Yard team, called me and we made an appointment to meet at four that afternoon. I kept it tentative, wanting to talk to Howard Squadron first. I went to Dee's new office, for I felt it would be wiser for me to spend the day there than to confront Tom and John. I left the number with Tom's secretary.

Before noon I received a phone call from John and Tom. I asked Dee to listen in. They had been in touch with the British government, they said, and everything was being worked out; they urged me not to heat up the situation. They began to speak of the "alleged memo," which they said no one in the office could find or remember.

"I know you're going to see the Scotland Yard inspectors at

four today," John said. "They're going to ask you about the gold faucets and the IRA. You don't have to tell them anything. You don't have to say you wrote the memo. Just say you don't recall . . . Leave it vague . . . That's all they need to hear to clear up this mess. Then they'll go home and it will be over."

Clearly, John was trying to impress me with his access to the highest levels of government. I had talked to Chief Inspector Hefford only a few hours earlier. Apparently the inspectors had reported to the Yard, the Yard had in turn reported to the politicians, and the information was back to John in less than three hours. Whoever John's mole was, he was good. If John wanted to impress me, he had succeeded.

John kept talking away, throwing in the name of Adam Butler. He wanted me to believe that Butler was his contact. When I didn't respond, John stepped up the pressure. "You could be in serious legal trouble if you are in cahoots with Marian," he said. "I wouldn't want to be in your shoes if we have to close the factory because you helped Marian."

Somehow, I kept my temper under control. I had no sooner hung up the phone when Clarence Jones called. "I'm sitting here with two chief inspectors from Scotland Yard," he said, "and they want to talk to you."

"Can they hear what I am saying?"

"No."

"John knows I talked to them and made a tentative appointment. Ask where I can reach them later today. Don't let on about John."

Later that afternoon I called Chief Inspector George at the FBI headquarters in Manhattan. I told him to find a phone where I could also speak to Hefford. When they were on, I let loose.

"I've been around law enforcement all my life," I said. "I've been an investigative journalist and never in all those years have I known a law enforcement official to break his confidence and jeopardize a witness. Never."

They started to interrupt, and I raised my voice.

"Hear me out — you asked to see me. I said I would see you. One of you called the Yard, which, until this moment, I respected and trusted. One of you called the Yard and the Yard called Whitehall and someone high up called John to tell him we were meeting and what questions you were going to ask me . . ."

They were quick to assure me that they had nothing to do with what had happened. Yes, they had called the Yard and reported. That was routine. Whatever happened after that was political. They apologized.

I told them to call me the next day. I was putting them on notice that whatever information I might give them had to be secure. Chief Inspector George later told me that he called Scotland Yard after our talk and got a senior official out of bed to find out how they had been compromised.

The next day, Friday, I made arrangements to meet George and Hefford in my lawyer's office. I was prepared to tell them everything I knew about the memo. What I didn't realize at the time was that the British government didn't want to know what I had to tell them.

Chapter Twelve

WhiteWash

In the newspaper business you acquire an instinct that tells you when a coverup is under way. My instincts told me that despite the dramatic announcement from Whitehall that the Prime Minister was investigating DeLorean, the government was in fact rapidly distancing itself from the issue.

On Tuesday, October 6, 1981, the Irish *Times* reported DeLorean's claim that the allegations could shut the factory down. He was now saying in public what he had threatened in private. DeLorean said that if the inquiry damaged his banking relations, he would be forced to come back to the British government for more money. By Tuesday, the day after the Whitehall announcement, the Northern Ireland government was already backpedaling. The police inquiry, they said, was "normal . . . routine," and did not imply that the government was giving any credence to Marian's allegations. John's message had gotten through.

On Wednesday, the Solicitor General, Sir Ian Percival, said that the inquiry was not really an investigation. The *Guardian* reported that similar inquiries had been made in 1978 and that "they produced not a single shred of evidence against Mr. DeLorean's probity." A union representative in Belfast accused Winterton of "seeking publicity." John said he was going to sue those who were defaming his company.

On Thursday, Cristina met with the press in New York. She said that John had invested $4 million* of his own money in the company and that 2,500 people had jobs in Belfast because of him; she worried that they might bring John home in a box some day. Marian was a lowly typist who didn't know what was going on. Why were some people trying to destroy an honorable man? She was tearfully beautiful and very effective. After the initial charges, only a few U.S. newspapers carried more than an occasional paragraph on the inquiry, which, meanwhile, was page-one news in Britain.

The Lisners story broke in the *Daily Mirror* of October 9, 1981, and the British got their first look at my December 26 memo. It confirmed Parliament's suspicions about John. The memo was succinct and provided a trail of clues. Suddenly someone other than a "pool typist" was pointing a finger at John. As soon as my name surfaced, John downgraded me in the media from vice president for planning and communications (the spokesman for the company and one of his most visible executives) to a "public relations" director assigned to Belfast. Most newspapers accepted John's version without checking or confirming it. The London *Times*, however, printed a picture of my business card, which showed my correct title.

By Thursday evening, Winterton had come under attack. He truthfully denied that he had given the media the document Marian Gibson had shown him. He sensed that the government was leaving him in the lurch.

---

* No newspaper reported the contradiction between her estimate of $4 million invested and a statement of John's two days earlier that he had invested $25 million. The media was "reporting," not "evaluating." John had learned the political lesson of how to manipulate the media.

John flew to London on Friday. Dressed in slacks, a turtle-neck shirt, expensive sports jacket and dark glasses, he said he was there to clean up the mess, and intimated that he was the victim of a conspiracy by "an organization or a country." He wouldn't identify either, and reporters let this outrageous statement stand. John said he didn't recall seeing my memo of December 26, but "we are not saying that means it is a forgery." Unable to prevent me from meeting with the Scotland Yard investigators, John seemed to be buying time to see if I had any more ammunition. Questioned about my future, he said I was "still officially with the firm."

In London, John called Rupert Murdoch and asked him to recommend a lawyer. Murdoch recommended Lord Goodman, who, surprisingly, took the case.

Lord Goodman was an imposing figure, politically, intellectually and physically. He had been made a life peer by his close friend, former Prime Minister Harold Wilson. With Lord Goodman as John's lawyer, Fleet Street would surely back down, for few editors or publishers wanted to face Goodman in court.

On Friday morning, in New York, I met with Chief Inspectors George and Hefford. I had slipped into Squadron's office at 661 Fifth Avenue through an entrance on the floor below in order to avoid the press and TV crews that had been alerted to this story and were waiting in the foyer.

The detectives came in the front door but had little to say to the reporters. For the interview we were joined by Squadron's partner, Ike Sorkin, a former prosecutor and SEC lawyer who would manage my case, and Ray Beckerman, who was reviewing my files. Earlier, Sorkin asked me to remain non-committal until he had a chance to analyze the extensive files and the detailed chronology of events I had prepared for him.

After the pleasantries, the detectives asked me if I had written and delivered the December 26 memo and if I was prepared to tackle each point listed. I said yes, but Sorkin stopped me. He wanted to set the ground rules. He was troubled by the leak from Scotland Yard that had alerted John to the questions the inspectors would ask me and enabled him to attempt to frighten me away from his meeting.

"At least let me tell them a few things," I said, "so I can rest easy." Sorkin reluctantly agreed.

"First," I said, "the memo is not a fake or a forgery. It is authentic. I wrote it on December 26, and my secretary retyped it and delivered it to John's desk. I am prepared to document that statement with third-party validation. So let's put that thought to rest.

"Second, the gold faucets are not in John's Bedminster estate as some have reported. They are in Warren House, next to the factory, where Chuck Bennington lived.

"Third, to the best of my knowledge we have never made payments to the IRA." (Many establishments buy peace in Belfast with payments to the IRA, and my reference to the IRA in the memo had created speculation that we were doing so.)

"That's it," Sorkin said. He told Inspectors George and Hefford he would read the documents over the weekend and then would be available at their convenience. They suggested Monday, but when Sorkin checked his calendar he discovered that he had an out-of-town deposition to take.

"What about Tuesday morning?" he asked.

They agreed, and I said that after the lawyers had read the files I was prepared to document each item mentioned in the December 26 memo and provide confirmation as required. I was convinced by now that they had no doubt the memo was authentic.

Sorkin remained concerned about the leak at Scotland Yard. He wanted a guarantee that the documents and testimony we provided would not be leaked. George said he could not give that guarantee because the director of public prosecutions was also involved. He did promise that no leaks would originate from the Yard, however, and he apologized for what had happened earlier. "That was something new for me," he said.

We ducked out and left Sorkin to meet with the reporters. He confirmed that I had written the memo and that it had been delivered to John. He said we were prepared to substantiate these statements.

By that Friday afternoon Mike Knepper was stating that "our checks lead us to believe the memo is a fabrication." He said I had stopped working for the company in September.

Meanwhile, John, in his interviews in London, began to call the memo a forgery. On Saturday, Knepper met with the Scotland Yard detectives. Later I discovered a statement he had drafted for John in which Knepper said that he had seen the memo some months earlier, but it was his impression that I had not delivered it. He speculated that I had written it for the media. The memo was too tightly reasoned, he said, and it did not ramble like my other memos.

By Saturday, Whitehall was hinting to reporters that the investigation was winding down and that, from what they could see, their inquiry had not supported the allegations. An official statement would be made on Monday or Tuesday. On Saturday morning, Inspector Hefford called me in East Hampton to say he had been called back to London and could not make the Tuesday meeting. He wasn't sure whether he would return. I reminded him that I could validate the memo whenever he was ready.

I called Sorkin at his home and told him the news. "It's a very strange investigation," he said. "I guess they don't want your proof. They want it left as it is."

On Sunday, October 11, the *Sunday Telegraph* began to probe the GPD connection. Fred Bushell, Lotus' financial director and Colin Chapman's right-hand man, was quoted as follows:

"It goes without saying that all monies collected by GPD for our work on the contract came back into the United

Kingdom." (This statement was untrue.) Later, Chapman himself told the press that "DeLorean wanted the deal done like that — ask him why GPD got the contract and then subcontracted it to us." No newspaper asked, however, as far as I know.

Bushell went on to say that GPD was "an international design and development concern . . . its personnel travel the world looking for deals . . . they found Mr. DeLorean for us. After all, in 1978, who was DeLorean?"

Another *Sunday Telegraph* story reported that Scotland Yard was charged with determining how much money DeLorean had invested in the company, what had happened to the GPD monies, and whether there had been any misuse of public funds. (The two chief inspectors were by then on their way back to London without having asked me any questions relating to these matters.)

The *Sunday Times* Insight Team, which was one of the best teams of investigative reporters in the world, looked at the proposed underwriting and raised disturbing questions. The "share deal," they said, "gave DeLorean the bargain of a lifetime."

Another *Sunday Telegraph* story predicted that a statement to be made the following day by Sir Michael Havers, the attorney general, would say that "the allegations appear to be unfounded."

On Monday, the *Daily Mail* reported John's accusations that the entire affair was "a plot to ruin us." At his suite at the Savoy, DeLorean said that "somebody is determined to prove Northern Ireland is not economically viable. When we set up in Belfast after turning down the offer of a plant in Limerick,* the IRA made a few angry statements, but they left us alone, presumably thinking we would fail. Well, we didn't fail. Now we're coming good — and it's obvious that someone is trying to ruin us."

* It was, in fact, the Republic of Ireland that turned down John.

DeLorean dismissed Winterton and Gibson as "two people of limited ability," and admitted that the expenditures for the gold faucets in Warren House were "stupid."

The *Times* repeated John's charge that the allegations could "destroy" the company and that "if we cannot overcome the damage done by this scurrilous and scandalous publicity, we shall have to finance externally or ask the government for help, or we shall have to close." John was, as usual, planning ahead. He would make the British pay for this episode. He now had new arguments for his old claims.

An editorial in the London *Times* defended John and attacked the motives of those making the charges, saying: "The nature and circumstances of the allegations raise almost as many questions about those who have made them as they do about Mr. DeLorean." Another *Times* article quoted an unnamed DeLorean source in Belfast who said that I was "regarded as sympathetic to the Irish Republican cause." That "cause" led to exploding bombs in the United Kingdom and the killing of innocent civilians.

I was becoming convinced that someone inside government was working to restore John's reputation and to destroy the credibility of his accusers, Winterton, and — because of the December 26 memo — me.

It was an eerie feeling to have the British government against me. I was trying not to be melodramatic; but how else could Scotland Yard, the attorney general and the director of public prosecutions be manipulated, and through them, the media — first to isolate my criticisms and then in effect to destroy my reputation? Politics were one thing, but how could DeLorean get the *Times*, one of the world's most respected newspapers, to argue his case and attack my credibility? I still don't know.

The furor ended as quickly as it had begun. In a short statement made on October 13, eight days after the authorization for the investigation, the director of public prosecutions announced that John had been cleared of "criminal violations." Scotland Yard and the attorney general quickly issued supporting statements giving the impression that a full-scale investigation had been completed, and that all the charges had been analyzed and discounted. My name was never mentioned. Nor was Marian's. When the press asked for details, there were none. How had they investigated GPD? Did John take money from the company for his own use? The British government wouldn't budge from its original statement that John had been cleared. But the announcement didn't satisfy the press. The *Daily Mail* ran a headline that read: DE-LOREAN IS CLEARED—NOW HE WILL SUE. The story expressed the newspaper's discontent with the government's findings. John DeLorean, it said, was cleared "after one of the fastest Scotland Yard investigations on record."

James Prior, the new Secretary of State for Northern Ireland, was delighted, however. The car, he said, "shows every sign of being a success."

John rushed to Heathrow to catch the first shuttle to Belfast, the DPP statement in his hand, "to share the good news with the workers." At his Belfast press conference, John examined the details of the December 26 memo. He claimed that I had spent too much time in New York and not enough time in Belfast (I had spent four and a half months out of the last seven in 1981 in Belfast) and that Marian Gibson was a troubled, disturbed typist who, with an unemployed writer, attempted to sell a sensational story that could not be supported.

He "answered" the GPD charge by saying, "We contracted with a Swiss-based company called General Product Development as prime contractors . . . GPD retained Lotus cars . . . Some prepayment was demanded, since over two hundred engineers were to be added . . . The contract with GPD was submitted to, approved by and . . . is on file with the Bank of England [Exchange Control], the Department of Commerce and the Northern Ireland Development Agency. Each of the agencies reviewed, approved and consented to the arrangement before any payment was made.* The only benefit I or anyone else in our company has received from the contract is a truly outstanding automotive design delivered in less than half the normal time at a fraction of the normal cost."

On the "fabrication" of the December 26 memo, John said, "I term the widely quoted Haddad memo as 'fabricated,' since he has confessed to Scotland Yard that it was never sent to me and that it may not have been written on the date shown."†

On the salary he drew from the company, John said, "I'm only getting what I am entitled to . . . which is still only half of what GM paid me eight years ago, ignoring inflation.‡ . . . My accountant has said many times that I'd be a wealthy man were it not for this project . . . I should like to make one thing perfectly clear . . . whether this project succeeds or not will not change my lifestyle one iota. The implication that I started this project purely for profit is ludicrous."

"Who organized this conspiracy?" John was asked.

". . . it may be a country."

"What country?"

"I can't say."

The next day John announced that he had authorized Lord Goodman to file $250 million in lawsuits against Winterton, Gibson, Lisners, the British media (including the *Daily Mirror*, the BBC and Independent Television News) and me. (Eventually, the lawsuits against Winterton, the *Daily Mirror*, Lisners, Gibson and me were dismissed for lack of prosecution. Winterton was awarded the bond DeLorean had posted. The other cases were not pursued by DeLorean.)

John was cocky in victory. As if to thumb his nose at

---

* In fact, however, these agencies were only asked to approve the currency transfer, not the substance or terms of the contract.

† This is, of course, untrue. Later the *Times* reported, inaccurately, the same version.

‡ In fact, estimates of what John earned at GM range from $400,000 to $650,000 a year, including bonuses. At DMC he was paid $444,000 a year plus expenses.

Parliament and the press, he held a press conference in the British Airways lounge at Heathrow Airport just before he boarded the Concorde to return to New York. These expensive flights had become for the British Parliament a symbol of his extravagance.

"Some of the media have claimed I have taken too much money from the company," he said. "My hope is that when we've won the libel actions I won't be taking any more money from the company."

The battle of London was behind him. After all that innuendo and speculation, John had a clean bill of health signed by Scotland Yard, the British public prosecutor and the British attorney general. It would be difficult if not impossible to resurrect the old charges now. And GPD seemed to be behind him, too.

John's incredible luck was holding. Winterton, who had set in motion the train of events leading to the government inquiry, had been humiliated and abandoned by his own Conservative Party. His personal fortune was seriously threatened by lawsuits. He would be forced to battle John in court against one of the United Kingdom's most famous and aggressive attorneys. An honest man, Winterton was now the accused.

John's strategy for bringing the British to their knees by threatening to close the factory and blaming it on the Conservatives — the strategy I opposed and that led me to write the December 26 memo — had worked. The British government had backed down and no real investigation had taken place. After Winterton's public humiliation, other Members of Parliament were not likely to step forward to challenge John.

In New York, too, the troublemakers were gone or on their way out: Dewey and Collins, who had made John's dream possible; Strycker, Stark and Cafiero, who had helped to build the company and make it attractive to Wall Street; and me. For John, it was clear sailing ahead. By Thanksgiving the prospectus should clear the SEC and he should have a new company unencumbered by British controls.

Meanwhile, in Belfast, 2,500 people were at work producing twice as many cars as Dick Brown could sell, in the process eating up export credits and forcing the company into a race with time. Would the prospectus clear before the export credits were used up and the plant was forced to close?

Despite this desperate situation, John brazenly reported — and what is more remarkable, the press accepted — that DMC in the third quarter of 1981 turned a $3.7 million profit, no small accomplishment for a start-up company. John later reported that for the year the company cleared $10 million profit. What John was speaking of was profits accumulated by DMC in New York. He omitted to make the distinction between DMC and DMCL in Belfast, where an equally impressive debt was being racked up.

When John returned in triumph from London, I knew I was in for a long siege. John could now use the company's money to come at me with detectives, lawyers and frivolous lawsuits that I would have to defend. I knew he would go after my reputation and, building on the Scotland Yard report, try to discredit me. And I had learned that John's vengeance was powerful. Suddenly I was suspect.

Most disappointing to me was the response of the U.S. media, especially that of American reporters in London. They had accepted Scotland Yard's verdict. When I asked them to look behind the headlines they were polite but cool. For the first time in my life I felt helpless and, frankly, a little frightened for my family. It didn't take me very long to find that my fears were justified. As long as I was around asking questions, I was a danger.

John now began seeking out reporters to tell them that Scotland Yard had cleared him of the charges I had raised in my memo. He claimed, as was inaccurately reported in the London *Times,* that I had admitted to Scotland Yard that I had not sent the December 26 memo and may not have written it on that date. And he reiterated the statement, first released in Belfast, that my memo was a forgery and that the GPD deal had the approval of both the auditors and the Bank of England. He began circulating a four-page, single-spaced document that outlined my career in harsh terms. I was an anti-establishment leftist who had betrayed everyone I had worked for; I was a political assassin who had destroyed the careers of responsible public officials by my news stories. If it had been written in a less emotional tone, it would have been a devastating, if nevertheless untrue, document.

Even though Howard Squadron had urged me to put DeLorean behind me and begin a new life, I knew that I couldn't let well enough alone. I was sure that John was out to find a way to discredit me because he feared that I would somehow block the underwriting of the DeLorean Motors Holding Company. Howard warned me that John would use the company to hire the best lawyers in town. A defense would not only be beyond my means but last for years. Nevertheless, Howard and Washington attorneys David Shapiro and Len Garment said that they would defend me against John if it came to that, and would do it "on the cuff."

The lawyers forced me to ask myself: What did I know, and more important, what could I prove in a courtroom? No one, now, would believe a rehashing of the charges raised in my memo.

My journalistic instincts — and my inquiries at DeLorean — convinced me that if I could unwind the GPD mystery, I would finally know what had happened at the company, and would restore my own reputation. What I knew was that over $7 million earmarked for Lotus through GPD Services in Switzerland had never arrived at Lotus in Helthel. The money had simply disappeared, it seemed, and for the moment no one seemed to care. DeLorean and Chapman were telling different stories, and no one was challenging them. Newspapermen in the U.K. had been blocked by Goodman's law-suits, and the ability of the government to simply refuse to turn over documents (there are no Freedom of Information laws in the U.K.). Even when Members of Parliament sought the GPD contract, they were refused; it was a private business document and not subject to publication, the government said. When John filed the contract as part of his SEC submission, it was still denied to the British media. I could not find the GPD contract at the SEC, even though it had been filed there. Nor could other reporters. It had vanished without explanation.

I knew that when the complete details of the DeLorean agreement with the British government had been made public on November 15, 1978, there was no mention made of the GPD contract, which I discovered had been signed in Geneva two weeks earlier. Again, when the DeLorean-Lotus partnership was announced, there was no mention made of GPD. I knew that $12.5 million had been moved from OPCO (DeLorean Research Limited Partnership) in New York to GPD in Switzerland and that the remaining money had been transferred directly from Belfast. My charges had been raised in Parliament, but the British had refused to investigate. Were they afraid of what they would find?

When my December 26 memo had first surfaced, Colin Chapman was asked why an offshore company had been used to pay Lotus. He said that it was John's idea, and this response was printed in newspapers. When John was asked the same question, he said that it was Chapman's idea, and this response was in turn also printed. Fred Bushell, Chapman's right-hand man, said the GPD "offered" the business to Lotus; but Bill Collins, who seldom cursed, told Ed Lapham of *Automotive News* that Bushell's version was a "bunch of bullshit . . . where were the GPD people? . . . I never met any GPD people." Collins also recalled that Chapman and his Lotus team were in Phoenix testing the DMC-12 prototype in 1978, before GPD was formed.

When John Griffiths of the *Financial Times* combed

through Lotus' annual reports in the early summer of 1981, he could not trace the more than $17 million from Switzerland back to Lotus. He knew that someone must be lying. Was it DeLorean or Chapman? By now I knew better than to believe DeLorean. I also knew that Chapman had control of Lotus through an ingenious series of off-shore corporations from Guernsey to Liechtenstein to the Cayman Islands and down to Panama.

My ability to probe these connections was severly restricted. I didn't have a newspaper to back me up, and I no longer had access to DMC. For all practical purposes, my trip to Florida with John had been my last assignment at De-Lorean. Within a few days a team of private detectives hired by DMC were investigating my personal life and questioning DeLorean employees and others about my habits and what I had done in Belfast. Accountants were combing my expense accounts and my phone index, looking for clues that might embarrass or intimidate me. Certain DeLorean employees were asked to lure me into conversations by pretending that they had information to give me. Arthur Liman of Paul, Weiss, one of New York's top lawyers, began negotiating on behalf of John the severance terms of my employment contract. You don't hire a Liman merely to settle an employment contract, however. John was sending me a message: If I persisted, it would be not only tough but costly.

Although John had announced that he would sue me, as he had Winterton, Gibson and the media, he never served me. Nevertheless I realized that once the Holding Company prospectus had cleared the SEC, and the stock was on sale, he would come at me hard.

My best resource was the investigative reporters I had known for most of my public life. I knew that in order to succeed I would have to call on those who were not skeptical or suspicious of me and see if I could get at the truth through them.

I started with the London *Sunday Times* Insight Team.

Their reporters had asked to see me, and now I said I would talk to them. This team worked independently of the editors and publishers and had broken some of the world's best investigative stories. The thalidomide tragedy was one of their exposés. They had a reputation for integrity, and I had no time to waste.

I met the Insight Team reporters at the Roosevelt Hotel in New York, and I set the ground rules for our investigation. I insisted on remaining anonymous as a source. More important, the reporters had to keep in mind that I didn't want to cause the factory in Belfast to be shut down. They agreed. I gave them all I had on GPD, and agreed to work with them as the story developed. Next I sought out, with Jack Newfield of the *Village Voice*, the best investigative reporters we knew. Jeff Gerth of the New York *Times* and Tim Metz of the *Wall Street Journal* agreed to help, but could not work on the story themselves; Metz did put me in touch with a young reporter on the *Wall Street Journal* who began to cover the story. I spoke with Stella Shamoon on the *Sunday Telegraph* in London, and I shared my information with Ed Lapham, who was already working on the GPD story. I also worked with John Griffiths of the *Financial Times*, Ira Silverman, the top investigative reporter for NBC network news, and Hillel Levin of *Monthly Detroit*.

Even though I knew I was violating Howard Squadron's good advice to get on with my life, I continued to seek out and interview everyone who knew DeLorean and could help fill in the gaps in the GPD story. A. J. Woolston-Smith agreed to check leads in Panama and Switzerland, and the teletypes buzzed as private detectives in these two countries went to work — without payment — to help unravel the mystery. Newfield and I engaged in the dialogue that is so essential to investigative reporting. As each fact was pinned down by a reporter, I circulated it to the others, along with Smitty's information and the details of my interviews.

One day I opened my mail and out fell the first printable

clue. Entitled "Information Document Request," it was addressed to DeLorean Research Limited Partnership (the OPCO partnership) at 100 West Long Lake Road, Bloomfield Hills, Michigan (Tom Kimmerly's office address); it was signed Mathew M. Novak, Engineering Agent, IRS. It was dated January 13, 1981. The IRS wanted to know everything about GPD:

De Lorean Research Ltd., Partnership   Request No. 2E
100 West Long Lake Road
Bloomfield Hills, MI 48013

Subject: GPD Activities

To supplement the one-page explanation of the $8,500,000 expenditure by DeLorean Research Ltd., Partnership to GPD during 1978 the following GPD records are requested:

1. Registration Files recorded with Panama and Switzerland showing:
   a) Name of officers and stockholders of GPD
   b) Purpose of GPD
   c) Financial statement at date of incorporation of Panama
2. History of activities performed by GPD prior to receiving contract for service from DeLorean Research Ltd., Partnership.
3. Copies of all 1978 GPD purchase orders, contracts, correspondence and directives related to the $8,500,000 expenditures sent to:
   a) Lotus Automotive Entities
   b) Lotus stockholders or officers, etc.
   c) All other vendors, suppliers, organizations or individuals
4. Invoices and records of payments for the activities covered in previous paragraph (#3).

5. Copies of all 1978 DeLorean Research Ltd., Partnership purchase orders, contracts, correspondence and directives issued to GPD relative to the $8,500,000.
6. Progress, status reports and correspondence covering completion of activities mentioned in paragraph 3 above.
7. Copies of agreements and documents relative to ownership of any tangible assets generated by GPD from the $8,500,000 expenditures by the taxpayers.

I was never sure who sent me this document, but I believe it was either a former DeLorean executive who knew what I was doing or a reporter in Detroit. I immediately circulated the memo to the reporters investigating the case. Now we finally had something to work with. The IRS had asked our questions. Had they been answered?

When reporters called Mathew Novak at the IRS he seeemed surprised, and was noncommittal, as he was bound to be. The reporters concluded that there had been no inquiry and that none was planned. Had it been killed? And if so, by whom? These were serious questions, especially since approximately a hundred and fifty investors were involved, including such well-known names as country singer Roy Clark, author Ira Levin and singer Sammy Davis, Jr. I called several OPCO partners I knew, but none of them was aware of an IRS investigation.

I remembered once asking Tom Kimmerly if OPCO was being investigated by the IRS. He said that it was routine for tax shelters of this size to be reviewed by the IRS. In my personal files I located my note to him and his handwritten answer. He later personally denied to me that he had anything to do with the contract between GPD and OPCO and DMCL. In the course of my investigations I discovered that he had in fact been in Geneva with DeLorean and Chapman when the GPD contract was signed.

Meanwhile, Hillel Levin tried without success to find the

GPD documents at the SEC. We confirmed that both a two-page version and a longer version of the contract had been filed. Ike Sorkin, Squadron's partner, who had worked with the SEC, told us where to look for the documents, but we were unable to find them. Had they been removed from the file? This seemed highly possible, and, besides, I doubted whether any lawyer would risk trying to remove an SEC file. But where the hell were the contracts?

I knew that early drafts of the Holding Company prospectus contained a footnoted reference to GPD but that later drafts did not. Without a contract it would be difficult to prove what had taken place.

One day I opened my mail to find a copy of the GPD contract. As with the IRS document, there was no indication of who had sent it to me; somewhere I had a friend, it seemed. The contract was ten pages long, and on each page there were two handwritten signatures, "DJ" and "JZD." The contract was between the OPCO Partnership, DMCL (Belfast) and GPD Services Inc., P.O. Box 33, Geneva 21, Switzerland. It was dated November 1, 1978. John signed for both the OPCO partnership and DMC (DMC being General Partner in the partnership), and "Juhan" signed for GPD. Who was Juhan? Nobody had heard his name before.

Woolston-Smith and the Insight Team subsequently learned that "Juhan" was Madame Denise Juhan Perrin, a Swiss woman in the diamond business. Her husband was a former Czechoslovakian who had tried motorcycle racing in South America and now lived in Geneva. The Juhans had worked with Chapman and his racing team. The Insight Team also learned the GPD was not incorporated in Switzerland.

The team published their findings. With John Griffiths' story in the *Financial Times* that the GPD money had not turned up in the Lotus books, and the new Insight revelations, it seemed to me that the British government had enough information to begin an inquiry. But the government ignored these findings. Why? I wondered. Who was pulling the strings?

Just as I was about to run out of leads, I had breakfast with a New York investment banker who had helped John during the early days of DMC. He told me that John still owed him payment for some of that work. To my surprise, the banker said he could fill in the gaps in my GPD investigation. He said that the money had never left Switzerland. Was he sure? I asked. Absolutely. But if the GPD money had not gone to Lotus, where had it gone?

I tried out my theory that some of the money had moved from Switzerland to pay for John's multimillion-dollar purchase of the Logan Division of Thiokol, the manufacturer of snow-grooming vehicles in Logan, Utah, now called the DeLorean Manufacturing Company. Its sole shareholder was the Nevada-based Cristina Corporation. Cristina's sole stockholder was John DeLorean.

What my friend told me next suggested that I might be close. He knew the details of the financial arrangements involved in the purchase of Logan. Part of the money to buy Logan came from a land swap with some Texans and involved four hundred acres of John's avocado farm in California. It was a complicated deal that was closed simultaneously with the Logan purchase. The land swap made the transaction tax exempt and gave John control of the land under the Thiokol factory, enabling him to charge his own company rent.

To make the deal work, he said, John had borrowed $7.5 million from the Continental Illinois Bank and Trust Company. Some $1.5 million of the loan was for working capital, and the remainder was applied to the acquisition cost for Logan. Only a few months after the complicated transaction had been finalized, John suddenly decided that he wanted to repay the loan, and presented the bank with a $7.5 million check to wipe out the debt. Continental was unhappy and suspicious. The bank had invested time and capital in what was to be a long-range transaction, not a short-term payback. They were also curious about the source of John's windfall. His financial statement had not revealed that he had several million dollars in available capital. Where had John found the money? That was my question as well. My friend said he could help me there. One of John's associates had told Continental that the money was a loan from the Rothschild Bank in Zurich.

"But when Continental checked with Rothschild," he said, "they said this wasn't true."

Continental reported the denial to DMC, and was told that it had been an error. It wasn't the Rothschild Bank in Zurich, but a correspondent bank of theirs in Amsterdam. That bank, Pierson, Heldring and Pierson, listed some of the world's richest people among its customers.

"In the end," my friend said, "Continental was disgusted but closed the loan. They never liked the idea of a loan repaid with money they could not trace."

How had the loan worked?

My friend speculated that the GPD money was used as a cash collateral to guarantee and make possible the loan to John. That loan was then used to pay off Logan. He told me that John kept an account in New York, and he suggested that the money might have flowed from Switzerland, through Amsterdam, to John's account in New York and on to Logan. He had given me a road map.

I remembered that on a dozen or more occasions I had heard John ask Tom, "When is the money coming from Switzerland?" Once, when I asked about that, John explained that DMC was going to get a low-interest loan for $20 million from a Swiss bank.

Now it was beginning to fit together. I circulated my new information to several reporters. Ed Lapham was now investigating leads on his own. He had received permission from his publisher (incidentally a close friend of DeLorean's), to travel to Panama, Switzerland, England and Ireland to unravel the GPD story. In Panama, Lapham found his first solid lead.

In August 1977 a corporation called ILC had been formed by Panamanian lawyers, and in Septembers 1978, ILC changed its name to GPD Service, Inc. Under Panamanian law, names of stockholders in a corporation are kept secret, but Lapham was able to establish that Chapman and De-Lorean were somehow involved with GPD and that Panamanian lawyers had confirmed this. He also learned that in October 1978, Madame Denise Juhan Perrin was given authority to act on behalf of GPD.

The timing was significant. In September 1978 the OPCO partnership had been formed in New York. In October 1978, shortly after Madame Juhan emerged as the principal in GPD, the Chemical Bank in New York issued a check from DeLorean Research Limited Partnership to GPD for $12.5 million. Investigators later learned that Harry DeWitt, Walt Strycker's assistant, had personally delivered the check to John, who casually folded it and stuffed it into his wallet.

At about the same time, in Belfast, DMCL wrote a second check to GPD for $4.9 million. Later an additional sum increased this to $5.15 million.

On November 1, 1978, the GPD agreement was signed. Subsequently, investors learned that on November 6, Madame Juhan endorsed the slightly worn check for $12.5 million and deposited it for collection at Geneva's United Overseas Bank. Subsequently, Chemical Bank paid the check from its partnership fund account.

But the trail stopped there, however. Without subpoena power or the cooperation of the Swiss, this circumstantial evidence could not be converted into legal fact. I could speculate that GPD money was used to buy Logan, but I couldn't prove it. For the moment, John was in the clear.

Chapter Thirteen

The End Of The Road

In November 1981, John realized his announcement that he would sue me had not prevented me from continuing to probe GPD or from asking questions about the prospectus. He knew I was working with a team of investigative reporters and that the "fact sheet" on me that he had distributed had not been printed anywhere. That's when he sent word to lawyers that he would like to "discuss my contract." John had stopped my salary in July, but my contract with the company ran until 1985.

Squadron continued to advise me that DeLorean was too much baggage to carry around. I felt differently, and what's more, I knew that time was running out for my investigations. Paul, Weiss had by now completed its work on the Holding underwriting and was waiting to hear from the SEC.

Paul, Weiss filled in another piece of the DeLorean puzzle for me. Like Oppenheimer, they would profit from a successful underwriting. They held warrants in DMC enabling them to purchase up to 100,000 shares of common stock at $10 per share at any time during the following five years. Despite the publicity surrounding my allegations about GPD, the publication of the December 16 memo, and the fact that I knew at least two dozen partners at Paul, Weiss no one from the firm had contacted me.

In his negotiations with my lawyers, John was now using two Paul, Weiss partners, Arthur Liman and Max Gitter. I assumed that John wanted me to think that unless I settled (and as part of that settlement curtailed my investigations) I would face them in a New York courtroom.

John's lawyers and mine eventually drafted an agreement that was reasonable. My hands would not be tied. I would agree only not to "defame" John. To me this meant that I could continue my inquiries. We had all reviewed the final agreement, and now, seated at opposite ends of the long conference table in Squadron's office, we read the final version of the document. As we prepared to sign, John said he had one addition to make. "I want Bill to write a book about the company," he said, as Tom handed the amendment to Squadron. "These payments will be progress payments on the book. To be fair, we can have a third party — you can pick him — evaluate the quality of the work."

It was a classic DeLorean tactic, introducing a new demand at the last second. I said, "John, you don't really want me to write a book about the DeLorean Motor Company."

"It would have to put the company in a favorable light," Tom added.

After a few questions were put to John and his team, Squadron asked me into another room.

"You understand what this is all about?"

"Yes."

"If you don't write the book they want, the payments stop."

"If I make myself a whore, the payments continue. With that book they can mute my criticism."

"You've got it."

"Fuck'em."

"There's a lot of money on the table," Squadron said. "I'm not sure you'll get it all, but you have to consider that."

"I have."

"And I agree," Squadron said.

We returned to the conference room.

"We'll get back to you," Squadron told DeLorean.

We never did.

Shortly after that meeting I had a call from Roy Nesseth.

"How are you doing, ole buddy," he said in his soft Western drawl.

"What do you want, Roy?" I asked.

"You and John shouldn't be fighting. Why don't you let me try to settle your contract?"

I knew John had moved Roy into Cafiero's office (Cafiero was negotiating his separation from DMC, and no longer came to the office). For all practical purposes, he had become the company's president. He was being paid $150,000 a year, twice his previous salary as a DeLorean consultant who reported only to John. His assignment was to settle John's disputes with his executives and to keep the lid on their criticisms until after the SEC approved the prospectus. From what I heard from others, I knew that Nesseth's tactics ranged from charm to rage. I wondered, as he talked, how the law firms and Mache liked having an ex-con running DMC.

"I don't think my contract can be settled," I said. "We tried it with lawyers and it didn't work."

"Lawyers, lawyers," he said. "That was the trouble. I'm going to offer you a deal you can't refuse."

I finally agreed to meet him at seven the next morning at the Waldorf-Astoria. I called Squadron at home and he urged me only to listen and not to sign anything. "And keep your cool," he said. As it turned out, that was good advice.

When Roy arrived in the lobby, the restaurant was still closed, but he knew the staff and they set a corner table and found us coffee and rolls. In that empty room Roy outlined his proposal for terminating my employment with John.

"Look," he said, "I'll give you $40,000 right now, today, and then $5,000 a month until the end of your contract." I was earning over $10,000 a month.

"What about my options?" I asked. I had over $1 million in options, $400,000 of them immediately available to me.

"I can't do anything there. John won't move on that. Just give it up. You don't need it."

"What do I have to do for the money?"

"Not much, just be around, be a consultant, be on call, work with John, and I bet in no time you two will be back together again. He respects you."

This was Roy at his charming best, the mediator, the man who understood both sides and was coming up with an equitable solution.

"What other conditions?"

"Not many . . . not many . . . you and John have to sign an agreement that you won't defame each other . . . routine . . . you can't write a book about him or the company . . . not much."

Roy had the agreement in his jacket. As he handed it to me, he took the top off his pen and laid it on the table. It was a straightforward agreement, but I knew John, and I wanted to make sure Squadron read anything I signed.

"Doesn't look bad to me," I said, "but I want to have my lawyer look at it."

"Hell, you don't need no lawyer," Roy said. "Why spend the money?" His voice was rising, his blue eyes hardening.

"No, he's not going to charge me anything. Let's wait until Monday."

"We can't wait. You sign it now, here . . . and . . . then," he said, his voice softening, "I will add another $5,000 . . . right now . . . right here on this table, if you sign before noon." He reached into his jacket for his wallet: the used-car salesman in Roy at work.

I said I would rather wait until Monday.

Suddenly his face contorted and his voice changed. He just stared at me, not blinking, anger flowing through his entire body. My own adrenaline began to flow, and I had the half-scared feeling you have just before the bell rings for the first round of a fight with someone whose punch you have not experienced.

"Haddad, you have children . . . you love them . . . I know that . . . you should think about them . . . about their safety, what might happen to them."

I knew I had to act quickly. You never give a bully an inch — I had learned that lesson at sea. My jaw was clenched and my head was shaking with anger.

"You fucking bastard. Don't you ever threaten my children again," I said, and left the room.

Breakfast was over.

I called Howard and told him what had happened. He instructed me to write John immediately claiming a "fundamental violation of contract" and demanding full pay and options through October 30, 1984.

Shortly after my meeting with Nesseth, my nephew and ward, Charles Haddad, called. He was at the time an investigative reporter on the Buffalo *Courier Express,* having come north after turning Monroe, Louisiana, upside down.

Charlie put his friend Mimi Hunnicutt on the phone. She received a call from her father, a fire captain in Monroe, who that day had been visited by a private detective named "Johnson" who said he had been hired to investigate me. He was tracing several phone calls made from my home to the fire captain's unlisted number and other calls made to his brother, a former police captain. Johnson had been hired by Southern Research in Shreveport, which, in turn, had been hired by a New York detective agency, John Curran Associates. Johnson wanted to know about me. Why had I called? Angry about the intrusion, Hunnicut had cut short the interview and called Mimi.

Curran's name rang a bell with me. I remembered that

earlier, when I discovered that detectives from his agency were probing into my background, I called the agency to warn them to get off my back. I now quickly understood how the calls from my home phone had led to Monroe. I had allowed Charlie and Mimi to charge their long distance calls to my phone. The fact that someone had a record of my home toll calls was a serious matter. I wondered whether my phone was tapped.

This kind of harassment didn't stop there. On November 9, 1981, a man who worked part time at DMC went to see Alnora Shari at home. Alnora had triggered the confrontation between Marian Gibson and Jacquie Feddock. According to Alnora, the man asked if she would go downtown to the New York office of the *News of the World* and tell them as many bad stories as she knew about Marian. Alnora said that he offered to pay her $1,000 if they ran her story and that the *News of the World* would give her another $1,000. Alnora refused.

On November 13, when Alnora came home from work, the same man was sitting in a car in front of her house waiting for her.

"Do you still work for Haddad?" he asked.

Anora, anticipating what was coming next, said that she didn't any longer.

"Call Haddad and see if you can go up to clean his apartment." He went on to suggest that Alnora get my key and search my apartment. She would be told what to look for. And she would get $2,000. Alnora refused, and went upstairs to call and warn me. She had had the key to my aparment in her handbag all along.

Ellen Kugler, my assistant, had married a reporter and moved to Washington, D.C. During the Marian Gibson crisis, Maur Dubin called her three times to discover what she knew about the memo and to suggest that I had put Marian up to the trip. Now Maur began to refer to the "so-called" and "make-believe" memo. Ellen told Maur that she clearly remembered both typing the memo and hand-delivering it to John's office. Maur wanted to know if I was going to write a book. Ellen told him that she hadn't spoken to me and didn't know my plans. On a later occasion, Ellen was contacted by a private detective, Jim Kehoe, who wanted to talk about the memo and the Gibson incident.

For a while after I left DMC, I kept my personal DeLorean files in my apartment. But after two break-in attempts, I moved them to my office at 600 Third Avenue. Then, after a break-in there, Howard Squadron suggested that the files be stored in his office.

Around that time also, "old friends" called my wife and Dee to ascertain my whereabouts. Several times they left messages to lure me into meetings for "information about DeLorean." They weren't old friends at all, however, and I was not about to be enticed into secret meetings with strangers. I think my caution may have saved me from the fate that Hillel Levin met when he responded to a similar enticement.

Hillel had a contact with Viking Press to write a book about John. On several occasions Roy Nesseth offered to meet with Hillel in various parts of the courtry to share "inside information" on DeLorean. Hillel declined the invitations. Then, on the Saturday before Easter, 1983, Hillel received a phone call at home from a man using a voice distorter who offered specific DeLorean documents that he had been seeking. Hillel went to the Detroit airport and waited at a particular phone booth for a second call. There the phone rang and the voice, still using the distorter, told Hillel to reach under the phone, where he would find a key to a nearby locker. Inside he would find the documents.

Hillel took the bait. He located the locker, opened it and found a large manilla envelope. As he moved toward the lounge to read its contents, however, three detectives stopped him. They had a search warrant. And inside the envelope was an ounce of cocaine. Hillel was arrested for the first time in his life. It was the lead story on the local evening news.

This trap might easily have worked and Hillel's credibility been destroyed. The police had also been tipped to the drop by a person using a phone distorter, however, confirming, in part, Hillel's story. And a similar call had been made to the Associated Press. In order to convince the police, Hillel took a lie detector test, which substantiated what he had said. Within a week, all charges had been dropped.

Hillel had been set up. He had been given a message. Did he understand it? Yes, he did. Would that stop his investigations? No, it would not.

The British government finally found its backbone and objected to the underwriting of the Holding Company. The trouble had begun earlier, in August 1981, when someone in Belfast secretly sent Jock Bruce-Gardyne an early draft of the prospectus, highlighted with succinct comments in the margin. John's intent, the comments warned, was hidden behind lawyers' language and generalized references. Without a road map, the British would not be able to divine John's intent in restructuring the company.

The comments explained how, under John's plan, the British would lose not only their equity but also control over John's future actions; they would lose their representation on the board of directors of Holding, which would be the controlling corporation after the reorganization. The British stock, like that of DMC executives, would be kept "downstairs," and be virtually worthless. After the lawyers and the brokers had been paid their fees, there would be very little left for the design of the DeLorean sedan, or to help John through the cash crisis on the horizon.

The comments explained how the restructuring would establish Holding as a company independent of DMC and DMCL. It would receive their profits, but not be responsible for their debts. Not only would John quickly realize a multimillion-dollar profit from the sale of some of his shares (part of the $120 million value the offering would place on them), but he could use Holding stock to purchase other companies. He would no longer be dependent on the profits from the car company to keep him going. The restructuring would in effect free John to do all those things that the British had tried to prevent him from doing. He could devote time, effort and money to new ideas. The British, in effect, would have financed a conglomerate in which they had little interest and over which they had no control. The comments concluded that now was the time for the British to act, not only in their own interest but in John's. The writer feared that in John's grab for the golden ring he would destroy the company — and himself.

I am so familiar with this document because I myself wrote it during my last visit to Belfast. No one inside the company, I had concluded, could deflect John from what I regarded as a self-destructive course. We needed outside pressure to keep the company alive. For me, it was a desperate move. I was being disloyal.*

The *Sunday Telegraph* had reported the prospectus story before and after the Gibson incident, and other papers had picked it up. Parliament was soon contrasting John's windfall profit with the British government's risk. The *Sunday Times* learned that the facts were worse than they had appeared from the *Sunday Telegraph* report. If the Holding underwriting was successful, John could buy out the British at its initial cost plus a 15 percent interest charge. There was no way the British government could ever participate in the success of the company. They had taken all the risks, and John was about to make all the profit.

---

* Before I left Belfast, John learned about the comments and asked me to investigate them — after first accusing me of writing them. I later learned that after Bruce-Gardyne turned over the comments to the British government for investigation and validation, a "mole" had given John a copy. I was never able to discover who was John's mole inside the government, although I have a strong suspicion. I believe that the same person informed John of the questions Scotland Yard detectives had wanted to ask me earlier in New York.

After the news stories, Dennis Faulkner of the Northern Ireland Development Agency said that British acceptance of the arrangement was contingent on John's retaining his Holding stock for two years. NIDA also demanded the right to convert its equity into tradable stock in Holding. John was outraged. In a blunt Telex he charged that NIDA was "attempting to get by blackmail what it could not get by negotiation." If they persisted, he warned, there would be dire consequences.

Now NIDA called his bluff. In cool language, NIDA reminded DMC that it had disbursed only half of the $14 million that DMC had been awarded for damages incurred during the hunger strike, and given the threats John was now making, it would be difficult to disburse the other half. John got the message. He settled down to negotiations. Some British shares were eventually moved upstairs, but John refused to accept restrictions on the sale of his own stock. "I have a perfect right to sell my shares," he said, "and I am far enough along in negotiations to do just that." The British settled for a promise from John that he would add a government board representative to Holding, "if it were possible." Finally, the British government signed off on the agreement, clearing what John believed was the last obstacle to the underwriting. Now, with the legal problems behind him, John had to contend with the problems of the car itself.

The car-buff magazines had been critical in their technical assessment of the DeLorean, but most balanced their negative comments with raves about the look and feel of the car and John's incredible accomplishment, and they acknowledged that the first cars that came off any new production line always contained problems.

Johnny Carson, who had invested $500,000 in the company and was to serve as its spokesperson, received one of the first cars. On his second drive, the alternator gave up and the car stalled in front of a group of Johnny's admiring fans. At a display of the car in Cleveland, a customer climbed into it, pulled down the gull-winged doors, and then couldn't get out for several hours, since the door stuck and the windows were not designed to open fully.

Early reports from customers indicated that the doors were not properly fitted and that they leaked. The electrical system had gremlins in it. Visibility was limited. And every time the stainless steel was touched, visible fingerprints were left on it. Zora ArkusDuntov, the father of the Corvette and now a consultant to DeLorean, inspected the car and listed several pages of problems. John brushed them aside, however.

During my last days at DeLorean, I made a final attempt to get John to focus on these problems. I wrote him that Mike Knepper, who had once been an editor at *Car and Drive* and could see the car through the eyes of the car press, had spotted several potentially serious and dangerous problems. I recommended that John talk to him, but John refused, and asked Mike to put his observations on paper.

To create the best possible public impression, Dick Brown was spending over $2,000 on each car — half the projected profit — to rebuild the DeLoreans in his Quality Assurance Centers. But in July a serious flaw in the front suspension system was discovered, and 18 DeLorean mechanics flew off around the country to locate the 350 DeLoreans in customer and dealer hands. When another serious suspension problem occurred in November, John was forced to recall 2,200 DeLoreans that had been sold. Meanwhile, in Belfast, engineers urged John to slow down production in order to correct the problems — problems they had spotted earlier — and some urged that we go back to the drawing board to make major revisions. A slowdown in sales would give them time to correct the underlying problems. They were convinced that they could produce the car John was advertising. Since we could break even at 6,000 to 7,000 cars a year, why did we need to produce three times that many? John refused to slow down the process as the engineers requested, however. His objective now was not a well-engineered car but the prospectus, and the $120 million reward.

Despite the flaws, there was an overriding excitement about

the DeLorean and the way it had been born. The DeLorean mystique, even under those circumstances, was still at work. Dealers sold the first cars for up to $10,000 above their $25,000 sticker price. As predicted, both sports-car buffs and former Cadillac owners were buying the car. The DeLorean was a head-turner.

Then, John's fabulous luck began to run out. The winter of 1981-1982 was one of the most severe in modern times. The economy took a nose dive and Detroit faced the worst depression in its history. Auto sales were generally low, and many of the cars that were making it out of the showrooms were manufactured in Japan. All our research had indicated that luxury sports cars were virtually recession-proof. DeLorean was now the exception that proved the rule, however. Sales dropped, inventory accumulated, cash reserves were depleted, and export credits were running out. For John it was a footrace to the end of the year. He could not cut production before the SEC cleared the prospectus and the underwriting was sold to investors, and he could not pay for the cars he was building. So John just stopped paying bills in Belfast. He continued to collect for the cars he sold in the United States, however. He was in control of both companies and there was no one to argue with him.

Almost from the outset, McKinsey & Company, the auditors hired by the British to evaluate and later to monitor our progress, was skeptical about DeLorean's claims for the car. The auditors believed it was unrealistic to project car sales of 20,000 to 30,000 a year. In the early fall of 1981 they reported that DMC was running out of money and would need £10 million to continue operations. Another £17 million in government guarantees was due to run out in December.

Then in December, McKinsey became optimistic. The production and sales figures they had seen made it appear that John could actually make $30–$50 million in profits in 1982. In fact, the numbers given to McKinsey by DMC and DMCL were misleading. John was making twice as many cars as he was selling, but McKinsey didn't know that. Only 745 DeLoreans had been sold in October, and only 123 during the first ten days of December (645 cars were ultimately sold in December). The projection for January 1982 was 600 cars.

Not everyone was fooled, however. On December 8, Bob Cryer, a Labour MP, rose in Parliament to question Adam Butler, the government's spokesman. Did Mr. Butler know that the men on the supposedly "independent" DeLorean audit committee had financial interests in the company? Cryer asked. And he went on to note that production was far exceeding sales. Butler dismissed these statements, and warned that such unwarranted criticism could only hurt Northern Ireland. Sales were in fact exceeding production, he said. Cryer's other criticisms were just as wrong.

James Prior, who had been named Secretary of State for Northern Ireland in Margaret Thatcher's Cabinet reshuffle, arrived in Belfast with a dim view of DeLorean. (The same reshuffle moved Bruce-Gardyne into the Cabinet as a junior minister in the Treasury, where he could now act on his own suspicions and on the questions raised in my memo.)

Prior was convinced that John was using the troubles in Northern Ireland to force the British into unjustified expenditures. When Prior visited the factory, however, he seemed impressed, although he immediately recognized that it was overstaffed. He noted the air of excitement there. The managers seemed extraordinarily competent and professional. Nevertheless, when John arrived (late as usual), Prior greeted him coldly. John told him that there were 5,000 solid orders for the next quarter compared to a maximum production of 3,800 cars, substantiating what Butler had said. He showed Prior the McKinsey report.

Back in London, facing the Cabinet, Prior set aside his earlier suspicions and fought to extend the government's guarantees to DeLorean. After a battle, the Cabinet decided to go along. They would give DeLorean one last chance.

Prior did not know that at almost the same moment he was

arguing DeLorean's poverty before the Cabinet, both De-Lorean boards, on the motion of a British director, voted to award the highly paid DMC executives a total of £406,417 in year-end bonuses in recognition of their achievements. John, who was making around £400,000 a year in salary, would get a £54,010 bonus; Tom, who had received $1 million in legal fees and was earning another $180,000 a year, would get a £40,641 bonus. (This resolution was later canceled, and the bonuses were never paid.) All board members received an increase in directors' fees.

The SEC clearance arrived on January 4, 1982. John's stock would go on sale that week. All that he had worked for now seemed within his grasp. He could convert stock into cash and buy new companies without interference from the British.

But things did not work out as John had planned. A few days later he received a call from the brokers, Bache Securities. Could they see him immediately? they asked. They wanted to discuss some "problems" they were encountering with the offering. When they arrived, Tom Kimmerly, Jim Season (who had helped to prepare John's Bache presentations) and Buck Penrose were there. The Bache people came right to the point. They could not interest enough other brokers in joining their sales syndicate. Institution buyers, who were essential to any quick offering, weren't buying auto stocks. What they didn't say was that a day earlier, Glen King Parker, the respected publisher of New Issues, had warned investors of DMC's "shaky financial condition," which he concluded represented a "classic case of 'go public or go broke.'" The offering price was too high for such a risky venture, he said, pointing out that with John's holdings, the offering assumed an exaggerated company net worth of over $220 million. Finally, it seemed, someone had taken a close look at the prospectus. There would be no sale of the offering the next day, the Bache people said, nor could they say when it might be sold.

I believe that John now knew he had lost the race with time. As Gene Cafiero had predicted, without British help John lacked the resources to continue. When the media had discovered the executive bonus arrangements, the British government was severely embarrassed. Even if they wanted to help John now, public opinion would be against them.

Prior called John to London. Hardened and angered by his embarrassment before the Cabinet for having recommended the financing extensions as necessary even as John was awarding himself a bonus, Prior told John there was no leeway. DMC must go into receivership. Either he would agree to do so voluntarily, or the British would do it for him. Prior listened patiently while John brazenly demanded £47 million he said the British owed him, but Prior was in no mood for threats. He gave John seven days to give him an answer. Prior had asked Sir Kenneth Cork, well-known liquidator, to undertake a study of DeLorean's finances. Meanwhile, John could do business on a cash-only basis.

Sir Kenneth, of Cork Gully, was the personification of the British old guard. He had once been Lord Mayor of London. He was tough but fair, and was known for the financial creativity he had used to keep insolvent companies alive. He had saved Rolls-Royce, which, after having been close to bankruptcy, was once again doing handsomely. If anyone could save DeLorean, it was Sir Kenneth.

John failed to evaluate the potential consequences of Sir Kenneth's involvement. John thought he held the trump cards. The British couldn't sell the cars without the DeLorean organization in the United States, and the OPCO partnership, not DMCL, owned the manufacturing rights. John reckoned that he could get another country to build a factory for him. (Later, in a quirk of coincidence, Dick Brown's phone was accidentally connected into a conversation between Roy Nesseth and John. Brown heard John order Roy to hire ships and move all the equipment and tooling out of Belfast.)

Prior had asked Sir Kenneth to meet DeLorean at eight the

next morning at the Connaught Hotel in London. John was leaving later that day for New York. Sir Kenneth didn't like the idea of rising early and battling the traffic from his country home into London. John was not there at the appointed hour, but fifteen minutes later he arrived with Tom and Don Lander. DeLorean promptly asked what Sir Kenneth thought of his plan to sue the government for $50 million in damages. If John thought he was going to faze Sir Kenneth, he was mistaken. Sir Kenneth advised him not to go ahead unless he was prepared to lose his money. Now, he continued, about the matter at hand.

John had been so brusque and rude that Lander felt the need to apologize for him. But personal feelings would not cloud Sir Kenneth's judgment. His was a financial review.

John returned to New York and called a joint meeting of both boards at the Waldorf-Astoria. He had no choice. Nevertheless, he ordered 1,000 workers laid off immediately to increase the pressure on London.

When the Cork Gully study was completed, it revealed that instead of the profit John had reported, DMCL (Belfast) had lost £26.6 million, that creditors were owed another £20 million, that borrowings had reached their limit, and that DMC (New York) had lost, by November 30, 1981, £10.5 million. DeLorean's U.S. bankers had ceased to provide credit for further car shipments, since they had not been paid for previous shipments. Until that debt was paid, there would be no income from sales for either company.

Sir Kenneth, mindful of his success with Rolls-Royce, offered John an incredible opportunity to save the company. John could lease all the Belfast facilities for a nominal fee and pay back the government $20 million in interest-deferred long-term loans. The cars already built would be sold to pay off suppliers. All John needed to do was raise and invest $10 million. In short, the British investment of over $160 million and the unpaid debt of over $80 million could be wiped off the books with $10 million in cash and a long-term note for $20 million.

John balked. Instead, he preferred to explore a long list of potential buyers, many of them mysterious or nameless. But as one "sure bet" after another failed, Sir Kenneth lost patience. On February 19, 1982, Sir Kenneth reported that "DeLorean is insolvent and cannot continue in business without the injection of further substantial finance." DeLorean Motor Cars Ltd. was now going into voluntary receivership.

John was not daunted. He met reporters at Claridge's, one of London's most exclusive and expensive hotels. At London airport, on his way back to New York, he paused to tell a puzzled Steve Rattner of the New York *Times* that he was "delighted at the outcome." Later that day John told the newspaper: "We came out largely unscathed. The government has the problem and we have the fun end of the business." He boasted that the deal had wiped out $130 million of DeLorean debt; the usually reticent Sir Kenneth called the statement "codswallop." John hinted that he might take the plant to the Mediterranean; Sir Kenneth labeled this threat "a lot of nonsense."

"I may have made a mistake in coming to Belfast," John went on to say, citing the political unrest. He said that the factory had been bombed 140 times, and that his executives had been under constant sniper fire. There had in fact been one major and a number of minor attacks on the plant, but no executive had ever been sniped at. The image John was painting was greatly exaggerated, but he knew precisely what he was doing. If he was going down, Belfast would go with him, and no other business would ever want to move to Belfast.

The spring of 1982 brought several offers for the company, but none went through. Alan Blair, a Californian, put together a consortium, but when he learned that Nesseth was involved he quickly withdrew. Budget Rent-A-Car was interested in purchasing the cars, but John could not give them clear title. He had not paid DMCL for the last cars shipped, the transit-financing credit line from the Bank of America had been overdrawn, and some dealers had been charged twice for cars shipped to them. Peter Kalikow, a wealthy New York realtor, was willing to invest $35 million in the American company, but the British wanted help in Belfast, too.

In New York, the Bank of America was closing in on John. He owed them $18 million, and the cars in his Quality Assurance Centers in New Jersey and California were their collateral. No car could be shipped out to a dealer without the bank's prior approval.

Early in March 1982, Ed Hansen, who was responsible for the Quality Assurance Center in Bridgewater, New Jersey, received a call from Roy Nesseth instructing him to ship out fourteen cars. Without a confirming invoice or a call from the Bank of America, however, Ed refused to release the vehicles.

The next day, Bill Mahr, who managed the DMC head office in New York, arrived at Bridgewater demanding that the fourteen cars be released. Hansen was away, but he had forewarned Fran Clark, his Bridgewater manager, not to release the cars without the bank's approval. Mahr left, only to return later that evening with two armed private security men. He said they were there to secure the premises, although other guards were already there for that purpose.

The next day the Bank of America in effect called its note on DMC. A payment had been missed, the bank claimed, and the cars now belonged to the Bank of America.

That evening Mahr returned to Bridgewater with four other men — they were either "associates" or "armed guards," according to whose interpretation of what happened next you believe. He now demanded that fifteen cars be released, but Hansen again refused. When Hansen lifted the phone to call the police, one of Mahr's men slammed it down. Hansen later called the police from a pay phone nearby. By the time they arrived, Hansen had not yet received the written order from the bank foreclosing on the cars, and Mahr would not allow him to use the telecopier to get a copy of the order. Influenced by the fact that DeLorean owned the property, the police sided with Mahr, and Hansen was asked to leave.

Hansen was determined, however, to discover what would

happen to the cars. Mahr's team drove the cars, one at a time, out of the Quality Assurance Center and into the darkness. Hansen told Fran Clark to follow, and he discovered that the cars were being delivered to DeLorean's estate at Bedminster, just a few miles away.

Dick Brown had been alerted to the Bridgewater escapade, and had called the Quality Assurance Center in Santa Ana, California, ordering them not to release any cars. He called the local police and the QAC staff. Eventually there was a stand-off: armed men hired by DeLorean faced armed police.

Brown arrived at the QAC just as Roy Nesseth and Tom Kimmerly called from the Peacock Alley bar at the Waldorf in New York.

"What the hell are you doing?" Roy wanted to know.

Brown told him. A few minutes later, Nesseth put Tom Kimmerly on the phone.

"You're fired," Tom said.

"You can't fire me," Brown replied.

"You're fired," Tom repeated. His voice sounded slurred to Brown.

The cars, Dick was proud to say, were not moved. He knew that this defiance would cost him his job, but he said he had no choice. He had negotiated the financing arrangements with the Bank of America, and he was determined to keep his word even if John wouldn't. It was sad for him to think that the DeLorean Motor Company had degenerated into a gunfight at the O.K. Corral.

The next day John himself told Brown that he was fired for insubordination. The entire episode had been a mistake, John said, but Dick was no longer a loyal soldier. Ten little Indians. Now only Tom, Roy and John were left. Brown later told me that some of his files were stolen from his office a few days later.

Unable to move a single car without the Bank of America's approval, John agreed to a tightly controlled system for paying off the multimillion-dollar debt through the sale of the cars in the QAC's. The process took months, but the bank was one of the few corporations ever to get complete satisfaction from him.

In March, sales were down to 204 for the month, and on May 31, 1982, after the deal with Kalikow had fallen through, the receivers moved in and closed the plant in Belfast. The workers staged a sit-in, and the unions attacked the Conservative government. There were no riots, however.

When the gates closed, the company owed millions of dollars to suppliers, many of whom were reportedly forced into bankruptcy. Renault, owned by the French government and the source for the car's engine and transmission, was one of the largest commercial creditors. The British government had invested $160 million. In all, by DMC's account, John had raised and spent $217 million. Not bad for a skinny engineer.

Throughout the summer of 1982, Sir Kenneth tried to piece together a deal that would prevent the plant from being dismantled. By late September it began to look as if he would succeed. Sir Kenneth attracted the interest of Minet Financial Management, a subsidiary of Minet Holdings, a major London insurance broker. Minet was a specialist in investing off-shore tax-haven monies in high-risk ventures. The plan was that Minet's clients would invest $100 million in a new DeLorean Co., Inc., of Delaware. John would move his assets into this company. The new company would acquire the Belfast plant and tooling for about $25 million. Another $30 million would settle debts to commercial creditors. The new company would own all the remaining cars and materials in Belfast. John would have the British off his back, the government would have a fraction of its money back, and the jobs would be resurrected. A nice deal. John liked it.

For this part, John would have to come up with $20 million to invest in the company, and he could not get it back once it was invested. John said he could raise only $10 million. Minet and Sir Kenneth could help there, too. They knew a small firm near Washington called FSI Financial Services, which specialized in high-risk investments. They would call the top FSI executive, Jeannie Farnan, and see what she thought of the deal. As luck would have it, she was in London at the time. She went to the plant at Dunmurry, was excited by what she saw, and agreed to try for the $10 million. Back in the States she talked with John, and began to make the necessary arrangements. She had to move quickly, since Sir Kenneth had set October 20, 1982, as the final date before liquidation. By Monday, October 19, she was ready to close the deal.

She worked all the previous weekend, and on Monday she completed the paperwork and sent the documents to New York by courier, where they arrived at the DMC head office by midmorning. She called to verify that John's secretary had received them, and asked her to make sure that John signed immediately, since she needed to take them to England that evening. She called again later, but John had not yet signed the papers. She explained the urgency, and John's secretary said she would talk to John the minute he arrived. John came in shortly afterward, but he did not sign the papers. He was in a hurry. He had to clean off his desk, and he was on his way to Los Angeles. When his secretary asked him to sign he didn't reply, but left for the airport without signing them. By this time Jeannie Farnan was frantic. The future of his company depended on his meeting the deadline. What was wrong?

John called his New York office from the Los Angeles airport. He asked for his messages, but didn't respond to those from Jeannie Farnan. He hung up the phone, strolled over to the Sheraton Plaza Hotel and went up to Room 501. It was three in the afternoon. Inside the room federal agents were waiting for him. By four o'clock John was leaving the hotel in handcuffs, arrested on suspicion of dealing in cocaine. It all seemed inexplicable. With Farnan's money, he might once again have bargained for control of the DeLorean Motor

Company. He could have picked up where he left off and slowly rebuilt his car company and his reputation. It wasn't the golden ring, but it was the way back for him. Instead John chose the long shot. And he lost.

Chapter Fourteen

A Leopard and his Spots

When my wife and I returned home from parents' night at school, her ten-year-old son Steve Walsh was waiting for us in the lobby. "Niles called," he said, "John's been busted for selling twenty million dollars' worth of coke." For a moment we weren't sure if he was putting us on or repeating an actual conversation.

Niles Latham was Rupert Murdoch's bureau chief in Washington. When I returned the call from the pay phone in the lobby, Ellen Kugler, his wife and my former assistant, answered. She confirmed that John had been arrested for conspiracy to sell $24 million worth of cocaine. I returned to the apartment and clicked on the television, and there, in a crawl at the bottom of the screen, was the confirmation of her story.

I called Niles for details. He had the wire-service copy and had talked to the U.S. Attorney's office. John had been caught red-handed in an airport hotel room in Los Angeles. It was an Abscam operation by the FBI and the Drug Enforcement Administration. John had walked into a trap. There were videotapes of meetings in California and Washington.

"What's the reaction?" I asked.

"Total disbelief."

"Nesseth or Dubin show?" I asked.

"No. Why would John do it himself?"

"I don't know. Did they catch him with the coke?"

"They set him up. They delivered it to him. The undercover operation was going on for months."

The eleven o'clock news opened with a film of John in handcuffs, his hands behind his back. He was wearing a sports coat, a shirt open at the neck, and he needed a shave. He seemed calm, almost placid, as the photographers' lights flashed and the reporters crowded around him. It was the end of the dream.

I turned off the set. Tears welled in my eyes. I felt angry and betrayed. John had further cheapened all we had worked to achieve.

The British press wanted details of a story I didn't know. Did I feel vindicated? No. For me, John's crimes were in Belfast, not Los Angeles. He had destroyed a company and wrecked the lives of innocent people. There were two different stories. But I knew they would merge. Editors would want to understand how the moral man who had left his position at General Motors on principle could end up in a holding pen with petty thieves. This was the man who, in an interview with the Detroit *News*, published on August 29, 1982, repeated the story of how he had sold his interest in the San Diego Chargers football team because of a scandal involving the team physician giving drugs to football players. The interview took place during the time the government claims that John was arranging to finance the cocaine deal.

I unplugged the phone at home. I couldn't explain to reporters how I felt. The DeLorean story was not about drugs. This was not a vindication. No matter the outcome, there would be no factory in West Belfast, no jobs for 2,500 families. There would be no "ethical car." John had robbed a community of hope. Even after the British had announced the receivership, the workers had sided with John. Now he had stolen their pride.

As reporters lifted the lid on John's life, they came to see what I had seen. When the bankruptcy lawyers got into DeLorean's books, they found that more than $17 million had just disappeared. Was it diverted to buy Logan? A DeLorean Creditors' Committee was formed to examine the wall of respectability that the lawyers, accountants and financial underwriters had built for John, and raised questions as to whether any of them shared liability. Were they innocent victims or had they failed to protect the public interest?

The inquiries into all of this will not be easy. John will claim that he was doing what he did for the poor Catholics in Northern Ireland who had been betrayed by the Conservative government. Or that he was the victim of a sinister plot, like the one he had attributed to a "country" after the Gibson incident.

John assembled a team of lawyers for the cocaine trial, hiring some, firing others, seeking trial delays, continuing to weave tangled webs as he had always done. There was some confusion over John's bail and his assets, and for a time he remained in jail. Television coverage made certain that the picture of the ethical man of industry dressed in prison garb was imprinted on the minds of the American public. At first the bail was set at $10 million. Prosecutors feared that John had secret bank accounts overseas and would leave the country to avoid trial. Later, bail was reduced to $5 million. John pledged his three homes as security, but they later turned out to be mortgaged elsewhere. In requesting reduced bail, John's lawyers revealed that he needed $130,000 a month to live on.

John's lawyers began a campaign to delay his trial by a series of court actions, many reaching higher courts. When it seemed that they had run out of legal options, John's luck returned. A week before he was scheduled for trial, CBS obtained and showed on television the FBI and the Drug Enforcement Administration's tapes of his arrest in Los

Angeles hotel room. In these tapes, John, with the cocaine on a table in front of him, is heard to say, "This came just in the nick of time. It's better than gold."

CBS said that it had obtained the tapes from Larry Flynt, publisher of the pornographic magazine *Hustler*. Flynt at first claimed that he had obtained the tapes from "a government source" as part of a $25 million package that also included the "Bloomingdale tapes," which others claimed showed members of the Reagan Administration involved in perverse group sexual acts. Flynt said he would release all the tapes. Subsequently, he offered two networks the opportunity to see the Bloomingdale tapes, but they refused.

Along with the DeLorean videotapes, Flynt released an audio cassette of what he said was a conversation between John and a federal agent. In it, John purportedly attempts to get out of the cocaine deal but is forced to remain a partner after the lives of his children are threatened (this supports a claim that John had made after his arrest). The networks and other authorities authenticated DeLorean's voice on the tape but not that of the agent. The judge in the cocaine case ordered Flynt to disclose where he had obtained the tape, and when he refused he was fined $10,000 a day. At one point Flynt arrived in court and paid the fine in dollar bills (he was ordered to count them himself). Later he came to court with an American flag wrapped around him like a diaper, and was jailed for psychiatric observation. Investigators eventually concluded that the tape was a fabrication.

The cocaine trial in Los Angeles raised questions about the ethics of Abscam. John was eventually acquitted, and when the smoke cleared, John and Cristina became "born-again" Christians and were baptized in the swimming pool on their New Jersey estate.

While the Bloomingdale and DeLorean tapes were creating daily news stories, the DeLorean Creditors Committee in Detroit, and the British creditors, were investigating John's management of the company and beginning to search for hidden assets.

Earlier, when Sir Kenneth Cork was evaluating the various plans being floated to save the company, he hired an American law firm, Skadden, Arps, Slate, Meagher & Flom, a firm specializing in corporation merger battles, to help him. A young attorney with the firm, Malcolm Schade, was assigned to the case. At first he was attracted by John's fierce desire to save the company, but he soon learned that many of John's plans were pure fantasy. John and his lawyers might have been able to create confusion and get support at the cocaine case, but if Schade could prove that John had diverted company funds for his own use, it would be a clear case of fraud.

Schade is a hardworking, conscientious lawyer who likes to work in his shirtsleeves. Although Skadden, Arps occupies six high floors with impressive views of New York City, Schade's office was little more than a cubicle piled high with files and records.* He began his search for hidden assets by systematically interviewing everyone associated with DeLorean and carefully assembling all the public records. When DMC refused to provide him with company records, he went to court to get them. And, of course, he had access to all of Sir Kenneth Cork's findings.

Although cautious by nature, Schade became convinced that my hunch about GPD was true, and that the missing $17 million was potentially the major asset of the company. If he could trace that money, then the company would have funds to pay off some of its creditors. I told him what I knew and turned my records over to him.

For me, John's highly publicized trial was a sideshow. I never believed that he entered into the conspiracy with federal agents to save the company. When I heard the tone of John's voice as he opened the briefcase of cocaine in the hotel room and toasted the undercover agents on their accomplishment, it

---

*In 1984, Schade left Skadden, Arps to join another firm in New York City, Alexander & Green, where he continues to represent Sir Kenneth Cork and the British government.

removed any doubt in my mind about what had transpired. I knew that voice. It was John's "pig-in-shit" voice, a tone he used when he was so pleased with himself that he could not restrain his excitement.

From the outset I was worried that the jury would only see one side of DeLorean, the one he wanted them to see. He would hold Cristina's hand in the courtroom and his defenders would cite the pressures on him and his outstanding record at General Motors. The jury would not know him in the wider context in which I had come to understand him. His story was that whatever he did had been the act of a harassed, desperate and susceptible man of good reputation who was trying to save his company and the jobs of poor workers in Belfast. The agents, he said, had understood his passion and lured him past the point of no return. For a time, I confess that I thought John might plead temporary insanity.

I became a "stop" for reporters covering the trial. When I tried to interest reporters in GPD, however, they would shrug their shoulders. What did it matter? John was a dead man. There was no way to escape the hard evidence on videotape. The past remained a concern, however, of the people and companies hurt by DeLorean's decline. Six days after his arrest, the DeLorean Motor Company declared voluntary bankruptcy under Chapter 11, an action that restrains creditors and is intended to give the company a chance to reorganize. Few believed there was even one chance in a million that the company would survive. But Chapter 11 gave John control of the company records. Nevertheless, his total control of DMC was lost with the formation of an unsecured Creditors Committee, made up of those who would be the last to collect any due bills from DMC. Under Chapter 11, the committee could petition the bankruptcy court for information and block any actions that they could convince the court were not in their interest. Bob Dewey, John's first chief financial officer, became a member; Malcolm Schade was elected chairman. Theirs was the first comprehensive inquiry into the complicated legal maze of John's corporations and transactions. By the time it was completed, the Creditors Committee had solved the GPD mystery and located half of the missing $17-plus million.

I turned over my files and summaries to Schade and the committee and spent days talking to him about DMC and its personalities. Schade had a quick, ananlytical mind, and he seemed to store the facts and impressions I conveyed in a computer memory bank. If anyone is going to do it, I thought, it will be Schade.

In early November 1982 — just as reporters and creditors were about to concede that they might never locate the GPD bank accounts, a letter arrived in Belfast that opened the door to discovery of the missing money. The letter, dated November 2 (two weeks after John's arrest), was addressed to the Joint Receivers and signed by a Swiss attorney, Jacques Wittmer. He wanted to know how to dispense $396,453.37 that he was holding for DMCL and GPD. He said he had written Tom Kimmerly for instructions, but received no reply. Would the joint Receivers advise him how to proceed?

The letter identified Wittmer as the lawyer who had arranged the GPD deal and handled the missing money. Sir Kenneth Cork rushed to Geneva to question him, but by the time he arrived Wittmer's attitude had changed. He had spoken to the Swiss government and to the bar association, and they reminded him that he was bound by his lawyer-client relationship and could not discuss the details with the Joint Receivers until he was released from that bond. One of his clients was the OPCO Partnership, and he could not reveal any further information without their consent. DMC was OPCO's general partner. John's consent would be required to release the information.

Schade began a series of court actions designed to gain access to Wittmer's information. But with DeLorean in control of Wittmer's client under the provisions of Chapter 11, it was a difficult case. All that would change, however, if the bankruptcy court decided that there was no hope of a DMC reorganization and appointed a neutral trustee under Chapter 7 to manage DMC's assets. That trustee would then become Wittmer's client and could legally authorize Wittmer to reveal all he knew.

As the court neared a decision on Chapter 7, it was suddenly presented with a plan to reorganize the company. A California attorney, James R. Gorman, representing "undisclosed clients," offered to provide financing to revive DMC, and asked the court to delay action on appointing the neutral trustee. Schade was skeptical of the offer. It sounded too much like the plans John had proposed when the British were attempting to revive DMCL. His suspicion hardened when he learned that one of Gorman's clients was a Panamanian corporation whose owners could not be easily traced. Gorman initially told Schade that neither DeLorean nor Nesseth was involved with the reorganization plan, and he agreed to Schade's request for a $100,000 "good faith" escrow that would be held by the court until his client presented their plan.

Schade's suspicions were confirmed one night as he read pretrial transcripts of John's efforts to lower his bail in the cocaine case. John had claimed that he could not afford the bail, but Scott Fossel, Logan Manufacturing's banker at Continental, had testified that John was making withdrawals from Logan. One was a $100,000 payment to a California attorney, James R. Gorman. What did Gorman do for Logan? the Creditors Committee later asked Fossel.

Fossel said that DeLorean had told him the money had been deposited in "an escrow account . . . at a bank and he did not tell us where. As I recall, there was a reference to a Far Eastern bank, negotiations that had something to do with Hong Kong . . . it was, candidly . . . the explanation was quite confusing." The name of the buyer involved was "Prince Sulamin." It was all fantasy, of course.

Schade obtained a court order to question Gorman, and Gorman then acknowledged that the had been retained by

Nesseth. Logan's banker testified that the $100,000 had been transferred to Gorman by Logan, at the direction of De-Lorean. John's bid to forestall Chapter 7 had failed.

It was once again Schade's instinct and a coincidence that led to the discovery of the records that supplied the missing links in the GPD story. The Creditors Committee had the court's permission for an onsite inspection and evaluation of John's Bedminster estate, and had hired an appraiser and photographer in order to evaluate it. One of John's attorneys accompanied them when they visited the estate on August 31, 1983.

Schade had been told that missing DMC records had been moved to Bedminster, although John said there were no DMC records there. Schade remained skeptical, however, and asked the appraiser and photographer to keep their eyes open for DMC files. And sure enough, while he was wandering around the DeLorean house evaluating the furniture and art, the appraiser noticed file cabinets and cartons of records, some of them bearing the distinctive DMC logo, stacked in the basement, the den and the living room. Opening one carton, he found correspondence on DMC letterhead. Later he noticed indentations in the rug where furniture or possibly other files had been recently removed. There were also indications that ornaments had been removed.

The appraiser was troubled. The court had issued instructions that nothing was to be moved from the estate pending the appraisal. That evening he reported his findings to Schade.

Schade kept these discoveries to himself until the next morning, when a routine matter was due to be heard by the court. Then the Creditors Committee revealed their discovery and reminded the court that John had said there were no company records at Bedminster. The judge listened carefully. This was not his first experience with DeLorean: he had been sitting when the Bank of America reported that fifteen cars had been removed by force from Bridgewater to Bedminster.

The next day sixty-three cartons and nine multi-drawer cabinets of files were moved to the security of the judge's witness room and the U.S. Courthouse in New York City, where Schade and the Creditors Committee could review the company records they contained. After a preliminary inspection, Schade moved thirteen cartons and one cabinet to his office, and he began his search for the missing link between John and GPD.

In one carton were the neatly typed itineraries for John and Tom's trip to Geneva to meet Wittmer. Meetings with Wittmer, according to the records, were set for Saturday, October 28, 1978, and Monday, October 30. Next, Schade found a copy of a letter dated September 1979 from John to Wittmer pinpointing a previously undisclosed escrow account, and a letter directing Wittmer to release the funds in that account to parties to be designated by John. Was that how GPD funds had been diverted? Now more than ever, it seemed that only Wittmer knew the answer.

In September 1983, OPCO's limited partners met in New York and ended DMC's control of OPCO, thus freeing Wittmer from his obligation. On Friday, October 21, a Swiss attorney telephoned Schade to tell him that copies of Wittmer's GPD files were on the way by air courier. Schade spent a restless weekend speculating what the long-sought evidence would reveal.

The Wittmer file contained the original escrow agreement, never disclosed to the SEC, to the British or to DeLorean investors, which established Wittmer as custodian of $8.5 million of GPD monies, authorized to release the fund on John's personal instructions. The documents revealed that Wittmer had in fact subsequently paid out, on John's instructions, the $8.5 million plus $800,000 interest. With this information the Creditors Committee subpoenaed various bank records. After a temporary restraining order was obtained, the results were reported in a quiet, nearly empty Detroit courtroom on November 15, 1983. Schade and Yale Levin of

Price Waterhouse alleged to the court — over the vehement objections of John's lawyers — that John had diverted at least $9.3 million from OPCO. That money, Levin said, had been used to finance the purchase of Logan Manufacturing. The allegations I had heard in early 1982 were now on record. Now, no matter what was decided in Los Angeles, Schade and the Creditors Committee had done what two governments, a dozen newspapers, company executives, auditors, lawyers, brokers and bankers had failed, or refused, to do. Now I knew that a grand jury would in time evaluate the evidence and that the full story of the DeLorean Motor Company and its extraordinary financial transactions would become public knowledge.

Chapter Fifteen

Reflections

For a long time I could not decide whether John had created DeLorean Motors intending to build a dream car, or whether from the very beginning it had all been an elaborate scam. Was his code of ethics a convenient façade erected so as to conceal his unethical practices? Did he begin as an honest man only to be forced by events to chart a new course for survival, or was he simply amoral?

Whatever doubts I harbored were dispelled on the day I read the documents that Schade had received from Wittmer. Most damning to me were the dates on the documents: October and November 1978. John had only just signed with the British government. He had devised his scheme to divert money to Switzerland even before the Belfast contractors had broken ground. That was my answer. John had never intended to build an ethical car company. It was a scam from the beginning.

Those of us who have challenged John always believed that this final judgment would come not in Los Angeles but in Detroit. Schade and the Creditors Committee were able to substantiate many of our suspicions by obtaining the legal authority to look behind the façade John had created. If these proofs hold up in court, John will be stripped of his fortune. Even if the creditors accept a negotiated settlement, what is left will be seized by the IRS. We cannot know for sure, of course, if other monies are hidden in Panama, Switzerland, the Cayman Islands or Bermuda — tax havens of the rich.

Sending John to a gentlemen's prison will not repair the havoc he has created, however. In Belfast, John's conduct has reinforced the collective despair of people who hoped that a successful DeLorean automobile would bring them employment and, as a Twinbrook priest once told me, help restore their manhood.

John disrupted the lives of British, American and Irish executives, many of whom had given up secure careers to join him to prove that the impossible was possible. When John's integrity wore thin, he hid behind ours. In the end he made fools of us all.

Watching John closely was like watching theater. Plot and dialogue were made up on the spot or, at best, the night before. For DeLorean there was no tomorrow. He was interested only in immediate goals. He presented to people the DeLorean he believed they wanted to see. To me he was at bottom a liberal who knew the secret to solving social problems by creating jobs and making the process profitable, a role model for American industry. To the DeLorean investors he was a charismatic leader and financial wizard. To the automobile dealers, who were essential to the sale of his new car, John was the hero of Chevrolet who had walked unannounced into their hometown offices to ask about their problems. To the media, John was the man who had thumbed his nose at $650,000 a year and was out to prove the automotive establishment wrong. To the British government he was the answer to an intractable political problem.

Why did it take a coke bust in California to reveal the other DeLorean? One reason, I believe, is the unwritten corporate code that dictates that you fight your battles inside the corporation, and if you fail, you leave quietly. There is no place for whistle-bloweres in private industry. I also believe there is an unhealthy attitude in many American corporations that the only business of business is making money and that how much you make is often determined by your knowledge of the legal labyrinth.

If John had succeeded — and he came so close — no one would have seriously questioned how he had done it. Business success is determined by the risks you are willing to take. It is not much of a penalty to be fined a nickel on the illegal profit of a dollar, or to have to plead "no contest" before a court, not conceding that you have done anything wrong.

The major corporations of this country have a system of checks and balances, of rewards and punishments, that are used to control executives on the way up. They are shaped by the corporation, but also controlled by it; collective judgments protect the individual. Once you rise above the crowd, however, new rules apply. Within the inner circle, executives become hardened to the reality that they will be inside only as long as their stockholders are making money on a quarterly basis. Hard rules for hard men.

I came to believe that revenge more than greed was the motive that drove John. I remember once asking my good friend Adam Clayton Powell, the black congressman from Harlem, why he was so outrageous in his personal conduct, flouting the system and taking money that wasn't his. "I do it for my people," he said. "It is what they wish they could do. It's revenge. They live vicariously through me."

John wanted revenge against the system that forced him, as a child, into the back streets of Detroit. When he got to Bloomfield Hills, he found that this in itself wasn't enough. He had seen and desired other worlds. Now he wanted not millions of dollars but hundreds of millions of dollars . . . and the power of politics. In 1984, he still said he was thinking of running for President.

In reaching for these fantasy goals, John became everything he despised. Rereading *On A Clear Day You Can See General Motors*, I understood how closely John resembled what he had criticized at G.M. He had condemned GM for hiring private detectives to follow Nader, but he had no qualms about hiring private detectives to investigate his own dissident employees. He said that GM cared little for the quality of their work, and then he turned around and compromised the quality controls of his own car in order to make a greater killing for himself on Wall Street. He said you should not build cars you cannot sell, and he did precisely that. He wrote vividly of how "moral men often make immoral decisions," but at DMC, executives who refused to carry out DeLorean's instructions were intimidated or fired. When it came time for him to share his success with his executives and workers — as he had promised — he cut them out. He condemned GM for considering itself above the law, yet he later became convinced that he himself was above the law.

I will never fully understand how, given my investigative reporter's background and instincts, I was fooled by De-Lorean for so long. Part of the answer was that I wanted to believe in him. I was excited and challenged by his ideas, and drawn into a world that I believed could be a model for American business. Maybe that is why the sight of John in a prison uniform, with his hands cuffed behind his back, was so devastating.

But for me, the greatest hurt comes from the knowledge that the company itself was successful. It was John who failed. *The company was a success.* A team of men built a plant out of a swamp; poor Catholics went to work in West Belfast; engineers produced a car that, given a little time, could have had as much quality as it had style.

We almost succeeded in turning the dream into a reality. I, for one, still believe in that dream.

About the Author

William F. Haddad has had successful careers in business, journalism, education and government. He is currently the chief executive officer of a pharmaceutical company and chairman of the Generic Pharmaceutical Industry Association. In government, he was a founder, Associate Director, and Inspector General of the Peace Corps and the poverty program. In journalism, he won twelve awards as an investigative reporter for the New York *Post* and the New York *Herald Tribune*. In politics, he was special assistant to Senators Estes Kefauver and Robert Kennedy and most recently was the campaign manager for Mario Cuomo. He was a member of the New York City Board of Education and has taught politics at Sarah Lawrence College. He worked for DeLorean Motors from April 1979 until the fall of 1981 as vice president for planning and communications.

Have You Missed These Great Horror Bestsellers

by J. ROBERT JANES?

_____ **THE TOY SHOP (7701-0191-7) / $2.95**
"A stunning blend of terror, sex and innocence."

_____ **THE WATCHER (7701-0223-9) / $3.95**
"An hypnotic tale with the awful terror of _Psycho_ and the intimate secrets of _Peyton Place_."

_____ **THE THIRD STORY (7701-0226-3) / $3.95**
"A chilling tale of danger uncovered."

_____ **THE HIDING PLACE (7701-0291-3) / $3.95**
"Behind the pretty face was a terrified victim desperate for somewhere to hide!"

Prices subject to change without notice.

Fine Fiction By
TOP WOMEN WRITERS

Novels that speak to women's needs, desires, problems.
Novels about women who are sensitive, talented, demanding and ready for anything.
Great new novels by women for women who are not afraid to ask for what they want.

NO ENEMY BUT TIME,
Evelyn Wilde Mayerson

7701-03286/$3.95

A tale of love, family innocence, growing up, sacrifice, tragedy and the bleak realities of life – set in Miami Beach during World War II.

GOOD DEEDS,
Denise Gess   7701-03391/$3.95

"A smart, snappy novel about modern urban life . . . written with style and energy."
– Newsweek

THE NORMANDIE AFFAIR,
Elizabeth Villars   7701-03014/$3.95

Romance and intrigue aboard the opulent ocean liner the Normandie.